FINDING GOD IN THE EVERYDAY

To Amber
Blessings

xoxo
Janet Evans

This was written by
Janet, my dear sister
in Christ. These are her
daily devotionals. She
is the mom of Shay Evans
in Warren III's class at HP.
Enjoy Love in Christ Pressy

FINDING GOD IN THE EVERYDAY

365 DAILY REFLECTIONS

Janet Evans

TATE PUBLISHING
AND ENTERPRISES, LLC

Published by Tate Publishing & Enterprises, LLC
127 E. Trade Center Terrace | Mustang, Oklahoma 73064 USA
1.888.361.9473 | www.tatepublishing.com

Tate Publishing is committed to excellence in the publishing industry. The company reflects the philosophy established by the founders, based on Psalm 68:11,
"The Lord gave the word and great was the company of those who published it."

Book design copyright © 2016 by Tate Publishing, LLC. All rights reserved.
Cover design by 70kft
Interior design by Jake Muelle

Published in the United States of America

ISBN: 978-1-68164-722-7
Religion / Christian Life / Devotional
16.08.03

Dedication

This book is dedicated to the people who have believed in me and have loved me through it all. My husband, whose unfailing support and constant love has carried me along through all of my endeavors; my children, whose unconditional love has shown me what the love of Christ looks like; their spouses, who have been the answers to my prayers for them; my grandchildren, who provide me such great joy in life. I love each of you beyond measure. Gregg, my precious and patient friend from whom I learned how to navigate some very difficult waters; my brother, Paul, whose constant love and unending support reminds me that the love of family is not anything to be taken for granted and for his encouragement to get that CT scan that literally saved my life; my Nuggies, who have been with me through all of my writings, putting up with grammatical errors and sending a stream of support that encouraged me each and every day; my Bible study group, whose sacrificial love is an inspiration for me; my minister and dear friend, Pastor Paul, who cares for our family and whose gifted spiritual teachings give me food for thought and truths for each week. It is my greatest honor to be able to share these thoughts with each of you, praying that we all find God in the everyday.

Hallelujah! For our Lord God Almighty reigns. Let us rejoice and be glad and give him the glory!

—Revelation 19:6, 7

xoxo Janet

A special thanks to Kim Bonfadini and the team at 70kft for their priceless help in proofreading and marketing this book. Our Father has blessed me with their expertise and friendship, and for that I will be eternally grateful. Thank you, sweet friends.

Introduction

"Hello?"

"Janet, this is Dr. Anderson. Get a pen and paper."

And so began my journey through pancreatic cancer fourteen years ago.

My brother, who is an internist in Hilton Head, South Carolina, encourages all of his patients to have a baseline CT scan at the age of fifty to check for any abnormalities or cancers that might be found, even though his patients are free of symptoms. So it was with me. Although I had turned fifty, life had gotten in the way and I was too busy to take a break and follow his recommendation. On top of that, my internist had just passed away, and I needed to select a new physician because Texas had just passed a new law that required a person to have their physician order a CT scan. Getting a new internist wasn't a quick process. After reviewing doctors for several months, I decided on one and my first appointment was scheduled for six months from that time.

I am finally at my new internist's appointment, over a year since my brother had made his recommendation to get a CT scan. I tell her what he had suggested. Thanks be to God that she was fine with the idea. You see, a lot of doctors at that time were adamantly opposed to this idea because CT scans can lead to false positives, which means that one can spend time and money chasing possible problems that are not serious. In fact, my new doctor told me to walk down to her basement right then and get it done. I had a full day of stuff to accomplish, so I put it off.

Meanwhile, I was enjoying walks with my rescue dog, Sister, a black and white Australian shepherd. On one particular July morning it was very hot and humid, and I had my hair pulled back into a ponytail. As I was chatting with the Lord, my rubber band holding my hair back broke. Distracted by my hair hanging down, I said, "Lord, if you would just get me a rubber band for my hair, then we could go on with our conversation." Not two steps later—right in front of me—was a rubber band, the kind used by mailmen to secure customers' mail. Smiling to myself, I thanked him for his ever-present help and continued on. Thus began my "Rubber Band Blessing." I had no idea at that time that these simple objects would provide so much comfort to me in the coming months, a constant reminder that God is always working in our lives.

It is late August, and I popped over to my internist's office to get that CT scan that my brother had recommended way over a year before. Two weeks later I received the phone call. The CT scan showed something alongside my pancreas that was worrisome. My brother Paul graciously took the lead on how to proceed. He found the most amazing doctor named Joe right here in Dallas, and Joe worked me right in.

So now it is early September, and the doctors are not sure what is going on inside of me. Joe orders an endoscopy, where a camera on a long tube is threaded down one's mouth and into the pancreas, to try to visualize the pancreas and determine a treatment plan. This test was unsuccessful, which had never happened in this doctor's thirty years of practice. Joe decides to operate and recommends a Whipple. Also called a pancreatoduodenectomy, this complex procedure removes part of the pancreas, the top third of the small intestine, and the gallbladder. I was scheduled to undergo surgery in two weeks.

It was during this time that I truly came to know what our Lord's words mean, "let go and let God." I realized that I had no power to impact this situation; the power was all his. The words that I had prayed in the Lord's Prayer all of my life became real—very real: "Your will be done." A peace that surpasses all understanding washed over me, and I knew with certainty that my future was in my Father's hands. Walking my dog in the days that followed, waiting on my surgery that was scheduled in two weeks, I found rubber band upon rubber band—hundreds of them—on different routes in my neighborhood. The Lord was speaking to me and reassuring me, "I got this." And he did.

During surgery, Joe found that I had a very rare carcinoid tumor located in the mouth of the duodenum, which is the top third of the small intestine leading into the pancreas. This cancerous tumor was encapsulated, which means it does not cause much harm until it breaks open at an unspecified time— then it's too late. It was then that I came to understand exactly what God's timing meant to me and my situation. An eight-hour surgery and six weeks later I was back walking, slowly down the block, and my life had changed for the better.

I began to see the Lord's glory everywhere—in the landscape, in the clouds, in the birds and squirrels—even in the worms on the sidewalk. He was speaking to me in these ways every day, often many times throughout the day. I wrote down my reflections, emailing them to my friends who knew my story, my Nuggies. Thus, 365 reflections later, this collection became a devotional called *Finding God in the Everyday*. To God goes the glory!

Foreword

I met Janet several years ago through an introduction by a minister at our church. As the counselor in residence at the church, he wanted me to meet "this incredible woman" who had her own way of ministering to people.

Janet told me she had just starting writing her devotional e-mails and was sending them out to her very close friends and family. I think she had written about four when we met, and her distribution list consisted of fewer than ten people. I asked to be put on her list. A few days later, I received my first. It was about two weeks (and a few more e-mails) later that I told Janet she only needed to write 355 more and she could publish a daily devotional!

She laughed, thinking I was kidding. I wasn't. As a pastoral counselor, I am often asked if I could suggest any books or references that would be helpful to my clients. I read a lot of books and devotionals looking for resources for my clients, knowing what many of them need are guidance, faith, and hope. I was totally amazed with Janet's ability to provide these in her e-mails.

I was told a long time ago by a very dear friend, "If you want to get closer to God, you need to spend more time getting to know him." I am reminded by my own experience and reports from clients that the days we spend in the presence of God are much better days, in many ways, than the days we miss that opportunity.

Janet is incredibly devoted to her faith, family, and friends. This characteristic does not only show in her writing, but also in her ability through her writing to inspire, help, and heal us. Each day you spend time reading the daily devotional readings, you will not only be spending time in relationship with God but you will also be opening yourself to receive hope, faith, love, and peace in your life.

I am truly grateful that Janet took on the challenge to keep writing and had the courage to send it to Tate Publishing. I am grateful to Tate Publishing for seeing the same thing in Janet's writing that I saw several years ago!

—Gregg Medlin

January 1. Jesus All Year Long

Thanks be to God for his indescribable gift!

—2 Corinthians 9:15

We have begun packing up all our Christmas decorations. We shake the dust off that has collected over the last month, gently putting them away. Somehow it is a feeling of *starting anew* as we move into the new year. This year, I took photos of where my decorations are to be placed, knowing that I will not remember where to put them when next year comes around. I was thinking about this *forgetting* thing of not remembering where everything goes as I was putting away the nativity. I looked at baby Jesus, and this thought came to mind: *Am I only packing you away physically, or am I also subconsciously tucking you away into the recesses of my mind until next Christmas, as we start again to celebrate your birth? Am I packing away the knowledge that you are the perfect gift, only to remember the manger story next year when I unpack you and the whole nativity?* Although the time has come to put away all the Christmas decorations, let us, each and every day, keep our eyes ever upon him, the perfect gift given at Christmas that will last all year long.

January 2. A Soft Place to Fall

> Great is our Lord and mighty in power;
> his understanding has no limit.
>
> —Psalm 147:5

Not being fond of cold weather, I have relegated my workouts to inside on a treadmill. The other day I was watching one of Oprah's programs, and, during it, she quoted Dr. Phil, a well-known psychiatrist. What she quoted really hit home with me: "Family is a soft place to fall." "Family" in this instance can have many different meanings, because all of us find a soft place to fall in different places; all of us have that somewhere where we can find this place of restoration and comfort. Take some time and reflect on where you always find a soft place to fall. It could be family, a friend, your church, your small group, even a pet that you love. But for all of us as believers, we always have a soft place to fall, into the waiting arms of Jesus. There are days when things get upside down, when the road gets mighty bumpy, when life is difficult, when we take two steps forward and three steps back. Yet throughout it all, we always have that soft place, that place of acceptance, understanding, and love in Jesus, who knows the road that we have traveled and longs to soften the way. When we find ourselves needing a soft place to fall, treasure this knowledge deep within our souls. He is there just waiting to scoop us up and wrap his protective and loving arms around us, the perfect place to lay all our troubles down. Face this New Year with great hope and the expectancy of joy, knowing that, as the days unfold and we are longing for that soft place to fall, we can always fall right into the arms of Jesus, the softest place of all!

January 3. The Heavenly Cafe

> For as high as the heavens are above the earth, so great is
> his love for those who fear him; as far as the east is from
> the west, so far has he removed our transgressions from
> us. As a father has compassion on his children, so the
> Lord has compassion on those who fear him.
>
> —Psalm 103:11–13

Welcome to the Heavenly Cafe.

"I would like to order a *do-over*, please. Actually, make that two."

"I'm sorry. We don't serve any do-overs here. Would you like a *give it up* instead?"

Do-overs—I have been thinking lately about how many do-overs I would need if I were given the chance to use them. After all, lots of situations in life do give people a second chance—a do-over. Golf has a mulligan, teachers let students redo for a better grade or extra credit, and many games in life provide a second chance or another try. But in this game that we call life, there aren't any do-overs. What you do is what you get. And what you do makes up that crazy quilt that we each get to call our past. But praise be to God, we don't need do-overs, for in his mercy and grace, we are given hope and a future. God forgets the times that we would like to do over and fills it with his grace. In order to let go of our goof-ups, he calls us to give it up—give up our trying to change the past, give up carrying around guilt, give up hanging on to the "If onlys" and "Why didn't Is" in our lives. Humans resist giving up. The irony of it all is that in trying to never give up, we must give up—give up the control of our lives to Him. Give up, give up, give up, and let him lead the way. The only do-overs that God loves are the ones going forward, day by day, as he calls us, his saints, to do over and over again the acts of loving his people, feeding his sheep, caring for the poor, and forgiving others. When times get really tough, and they will, giving it all up to the Lord is the only way to make it through these trials. How glorious, indeed, to give up our control to the only one who needs no do-overs. After all, didn't he give it all up for us?

"I will have another *give it up*, please. Delicious! Thank you!"

January 4. Right in Front of Our Eyes

Then you will call, and the Lord will answer;
you will cry for help, and he will say: Here am I.

—Isaiah 58:9

In reading an article in our morning paper about aging and living well, the last sentence caught my eye. It says: "What if there are better approaches, right in front of our eyes, waiting to be recognized?" This sentence is in reference to the subject of the article, but I think that it plays quite well into our faith system for believers and nonbelievers as well. There always is a better approach, right in front of our eyes, waiting to be recognized, and his name is Jesus. When we face trials in life, go through a difficult time, have a decision to make, or even if we are feeling badly about a situation about which we do not know how to handle, the better approach, the best approach, is always right in front of our eyes, and his name is Jesus. He is the answer, the one and only answer to all of our problems that we will ever face. Whether it is about parents or children, friends or foes, call on Jesus, and he will shine his light to show us the way. He is there, right in front of our eyes!

January 5. One Bite at a Time

> When I called, you answered me;
> you made me bold and stouthearted.
>
> —Psalm 138:3

I was having coffee the other day with a friend, and we were talking about the elephant in the room in relation to an experience that my friend had been having. This seems to be something that we all face at one time or another. Who among us has not had that elephant in the room at some time in life? So the thought process here is *how do we get the elephant out of the room?* This looming problem that no one wants to talk about, face, nor deal with. Suddenly that old joke about "how do you eat an elephant?" came rushing into my mind. The answer is one bite at a time. So that's it, then. The answer of how to move that imposing animal out the door and back to the zoo where he belongs lies in Jesus. Jesus was the only way that my friend could begin to eat that elephant one bite at a time, and she will be first to tell you that. Through God's grace, she began to take bites, small yet effective bites, of that elephant until that looming problem was gone, removed by the grace and mercy of our Lord, Jesus Christ. Was it easy? Not at all. Was it quick? Nope. But that is how life is. We give our Lord the lead. Then every so often, we want to take it back, maybe just for a moment. But all the while we are learning and trusting, and he is teaching and loving, until we have eaten every bite of that elephant, down to the last toenail. No matter how many elephants show up this year in our lives, we have the secret to successfully showing them out the door—his name is Jesus, Immanuel. God with us, all the time!

January 6. New Year's Revolution

And the peace of God, which transcends all
understanding, will guard your hearts and
your minds in Christ Jesus.

—Philippians 4:7

I am sure that many of us have made New Year's resolutions and already moved past a few of them. I really don't like making them for that reason. Too much pressure! But I continue to laugh out loud at the ad on television with the five-year-old children sitting around the table who are discussing funny thoughts with a clever guy. The recent one has a boy talking about his New Year's *revolutions*. Often we are actually making New Year's revolutions, for we put them out there, and then they come right back at us, just like a revolving door, already gone before we know it. The one New Year's resolution that we should all undertake is to trust and obey. That's all, just trust and obey the Lord. Then things get hard. Life comes roaring at us like a lion. The pressure builds, and uncertainty rears its ugly head. Are we still trusting and obeying? That's the call of Jesus. That is what we should set out to do every new morning that we step into the light. Give him the lead. Give him our trust. All of a sudden, peace will wash over us that cannot be explained. This is one New Year's resolution that we can keep, not letting it become a revolution revolving back around at us and out the door. The one resolution worth keeping!

January 7. Underpromise and Overdeliver

> You know with all your heart and soul that not one of all
> the good promises the Lord your God gave you has failed.
>
> —Joshua 23:14

Recently, a friend and I were talking about how people end up disappointed in another person's behavior or how a plan ends up not being what we had expected it to be. The word "disappointment" in the dictionary is defined as "the condition of failing to fulfill the expectation, hope, or desire of a person." I heard the following explanation of how to not find ourselves disappointed in anyone or anything. Although so often people overpromise and underdeliver, we need to remember that it is best to underpromise and overdeliver. I wonder if it is human nature to want to overpromise, because we usually want to give the very most to whomever we are delivering something. Yet it is often difficult to make this happen because life gets in the way. You run out of time, one situation supersedes the other, or somehow it just doesn't happen. We have a Savior who can *overpromise* and *overdeliver* each and every time. We can know with all assurance that his promise is exactly what will happen and that we can stand on the absolute knowledge that he will always overdeliver. He has given us more, so very much more than we ever deserved, and that is exactly what overdelivering is! So as we continue to move forward into this New Year, let us constantly remember that often we, or someone we know, will underdeliver, but the Lord will always deliver more than we could ever expect!

January 8. Waiting for Forty

As for God, his way is perfect; the word
of the Lord is flawless.

—Psalm 18:30

Believe it or not, I have finally found the solution to the headaches that I have experienced daily for forty years. Yes, that's right. Forty years! I have been chasing around answers all these years thinking that they were sinus headaches and having all kinds of sinus surgeries and treatments to no avail. Then, a few weeks ago, my new internist suggested that I go see a headache neurologist. He diagnosed me with migraines. So after all these years of treating my migraines as sinus headaches to no avail, I now know the right answer. Better late than never. In applying these thoughts to our faith, our God will always answer our cries for help. Although he may not answer right away, the answer is coming. Some of us have received his answer in forty seconds, some in forty minutes, some in forty days, and some in what seems like forty years, the same as my headaches. And sometimes no answer is the answer. Yet he is faithful. He will send them to us, never late, but right on time—in his perfect timing, always faithful and true—for "his way is perfect; the Lord's word is flawless"!

January 9. A Match Made in Heaven

> Praise be to the God and Father of our Lord Jesus Christ,
> who has blessed us in the heavenly realms with every
> spiritual blessing in Christ. For he chose us in him before
> the creation of the world to be holy and blameless in his
> sight. In love he predestined us to be adopted as his sons
> through Jesus Christ, in accordance with his pleasure and
> will—to the praise of his glorious grace, which he has
> freely given us in the One he loves.
>
> —Ephesians 1:3–6

We are at that time in our lives when we are being included in lots of wonderful weddings with our dear friends and their children. I just love weddings, seeing the precious couple joined together in God's covenant. Each wedding is different, reflecting the personality of the bride and groom. Some are formal, some are casual, some are large, and some small, but all are special. Often this comment can be heard, "It is a match made in heaven." This comment implies that the couple getting married is well suited for each other, bringing just the right mix of personalities to balance each other. The one clear thought that comes to mind with certainty is that we can all claim that the match made in heaven by God is the match of Jesus with each of us. Now there's truly a match brought together freely and through God's grace that was made in heaven. God knew how very much we need Jesus, how desperate our lives would be without him, and gave us the one true match for all eternity that would make our lives better. When we hear someone say at a wedding that this is a match made in heaven, we can think of our perfect match, knowing how deeply God loves us to have matched us up with his son, Jesus, our love.

January 10. Finding That Silver Lining

> The Lord is faithful to all his promises
> and loving towards all he has made.
>
> —Psalm 145:13

There is just nothing quite like the day we had a few days ago: a crisp, sunny, bright blue winter day, then followed by several frigid ones. Today is another rainy, dreary day, but we know deep in our hearts that this day won't last forever. Beautiful, clear days are predicted for next week. As we get out and about in the weather, whatever it may be, we can know for certain that no matter what today looks like, it will soon be different tomorrow or the day after that. This is exactly what our Farther promises us about life. We have days that seem to never warm up, keeping us miserable and chilled to the bone with life's journey. We may find that our days resemble these wintry days of dark clouds and chilling winds where it is very hard to find warmth and resolution. But what great news is given by our Father. He has promised that behind every cloud is his ray of hope. Behind every gray and foreboding day, he has a brighter one in store for tomorrow. His plan for us is to give us hope and a future, and he will restore us to those sunny days in his perfect timing. It's hard to wait on the Lord. It's hard to remember his promises. It's hard to walk through trials. But let us remember that through every trial that we endure, we are being drawn closer and closer to the one who knows us best, and that is where we will always find that silver lining.

January 11. Tell Me More

> This is the confidence we have in approaching God: that
> if we ask anything according to his will, he hears us. And
> if we know that he hears us—whatever we ask—we know
> that we have what we asked of him.
>
> —1 John 5:14–15

My sweet friend was telling me this story about going to a wedding out of town last weekend. The rabbi doing the service was encouraging this precious couple to lift each other up as the years roll by. He said the best advice he could give them was that when one of them came to the other with a problem or needing to talk about something important, the best response the other one could say is three little words: *Tell me more.* Having been married the better part of 45 years and knowing many who have also, I know that all of us will find this suggestion so very helpful. To encourage someone whom we care about to continue on with their thought—showing them that we care enough to listen and listen well to all that they have to say—is quite a gift. This is what our Lord and Savior does for us. He hears our cries for help; he hears our pleas for restoration. And he says, "Tell me more." He longs to hear each and every part of what we need to say to him so that we feel encouraged, so that we feel that he has heard each and every part of our needs, and he understands. We all are so thankful when someone listens and understands what we are going through in life. Jesus understands. He cares, he loves. That is all we need to know.

January 12. Stretching It Out

> And we pray this in order that you may live a life worthy
> of the Lord and may please him in every way; bearing
> fruit in every good work, growing in the knowledge of
> God, being strengthened with all power according to his
> glorious might so that you may have great endurance
> and patience.
>
> —Colossians 1:10–11

I really don't like to stretch. Not before I work out, nor after, really. Even though I know that it is what I should do, somehow my body resists it. Yet when I do stretch my muscles, I can sense how much better that makes me feel. Recently my sciatica has been flaring up, and doing certain stretching exercises is so beneficial for this situation. So it is with Jesus. It makes much more sense for us to stretch our muscles in Jesus when life is going smoothly so that when we pull a muscle in life, we are familiar with his mercy and grace and know exactly what to do to make things better. How do we stretch our muscles in Jesus? By spending more time in his presence; by praying and sharing time with him; by reading the Bible and gleaning his wisdom there; by thoughtfully going over the times that he has been exactly what we needed, guiding us through the rough seas of life or just sharing his joy with us in all the earth. There are countless ways to stretch our muscles in Jesus so that we are well prepared to use his strength as needed. There is no time like the present to get going, for the stronger we are in Jesus, the more confidence we have to start each day, ready for whatever may come.

January 13. Tough Stuff

> "Lord, save us! We're going to drown!" He replied, "You of little faith, why are you so afraid?" Then he got up and rebuked the winds and the waves, and it was completely calm. The men were amazed and asked, "What kind of man is this? Even the winds and the waves obey him!"
>
> —Matthew 8:25–27

I was having dinner last night with one of my precious friends, and we started talking about the trials of life and how nobody really wants to go through a difficult time. Sometimes our trials are short, bringing resolution in a relatively quick time frame. Sometimes they are drawn out a little longer, but then resolution comes. Yet other times the storms in our life go on and on and on, leaving us to wonder when this difficulty will end. The one thing that we can always know is that no matter the length of time, whether it be short or long, God is with us. This is one of the gracious gifts that he brings us through his birth. He is right there in the middle of the storm, making a pathway through the driving rains and pelting ice to lead us to a place of comfort and peace. He will bring moments of solace right in the middle of these storms, continually reminding us that he knows what we are going through and that he will end this hardship with blessings beside. Our trials are no challenge for him. Like the storms of nature that obey him, so do our storms of life. No matter what, we can stand on his promise that after the storm, blessings flow. Nature's storms blow in, often bringing driving rain and gale-force winds and sometimes sleet and snow, chilling us to the bone. So do the storms in our life. But God's word says that these storms will bring me glory. We can handle anything if we remember this truth. Are the storms uncomfortable? Yes. Are they tough? Yes. Sometimes lengthy? Sigh-producing? Yes, yes, yes! But Jesus says that we can know that each and every moment that we suffer will draw us closer to him. He calls us to be strong in his love, find solace in his love, and trust in his love. Through his promise that he is with us always, we can rest in his message of hope that he is always by our side, even in the darkest of storms.

January 14. Walking on the Ledge

Lord, you have assigned me my portion and my cup;
you have made my lot secure.

—Psalm 16:5

I was walking my dog, Mojo, a few days ago, and he loves it when I give him a little leeway so that he can explore, finding new scents and grasses to eat. This particular day, we were walking in an alley, and he found a ledge running alongside the concrete. He immediately jumped up on it, and it continued to get higher and higher as he walked. Of course, I talked to him as if he could understand me, saying, "How do you do that?" He was having absolutely no difficulty keeping his paws firmly planted on the top of this narrow rim of concrete, balancing perfectly, seemingly without any effort. Then it hit me: *This is what the Lord does for all of us. We walk along ledges of varying heights each and every day, balancing so many things that come along. It is through the power of Jesus that we are able to manage life, for life is a balancing act in itself.* Just seeing Mojo walk that ledge with complete confidence, never stumbling nor hesitating as he went along, painted a mental picture in my mind of Jesus providing this same confidence for us as we move along life's ledge. What more can we ask of a Savior than this, to give us what we need to meet each and every day with confidence and complete assurance that no matter what ledge we may be on at the moment, he will provide. That's it. He will provide. Nothing can compare to the security in knowing that no ledge is too narrow nor too high for the Lord.

January 15. The Treasure of Jesus

> And the Lord has declared this day that you are his
> people, his treasured possession as he promised.
>
> —Deuteronomy 26:18

If someone asks us what it is that we treasure most in this life or what one thing we would grab if we had a catastrophe, most of our answers would refer to a worldly possession: pets, photos, wedding rings, art, and so on. In relation to this thought is the reality that our greatest treasure is not of earthly form but is Jesus. It makes perfect sense that we would all grab one of the things listed above, but our greatest treasure lives within us through the gift of the Holy Spirit. So here's the good news for all of us. We don't even have to think about grabbing Jesus, for he is always with us. In fact, he has gone before us to provide safety and recovery from whatever it is that we are facing. No ring, nor silver, nor chair—not even a photograph—would have any value at all if we could not know that Jesus will always be part of our lives, not only here but also for all eternity. Let us fall to our knees this day and thank God for the greatest treasure known to man, and one that didn't cost us a cent, Jesus Christ. They say that he is our all in all and, truly, without him all is lost. It's through his love for us that we can really know the meaning of something of value.

January 16. Say Cheese!

> I am the vine; you are the branches. If a man remains
> in me and I in him, he will bear much fruit;...This is
> to my Father's glory, that you bear much fruit,
> showing yourselves to be my disciples.
>
> —John 15:5, 8

Photos—so many photos being taken these days, sealing forever the memories of our lives. We are collecting photos for the slideshow for our daughter's wedding, and it is great fun to go back over all the years since she was born, reminiscing about different places and times spent together. I am absolutely horrible about taking pictures. I either forget to even take the picture or I cut off someone's head or it's not centered. Yet the photo that is most important is the one that we are in with Jesus. Just as we have been grafted in to his family, we can know in our hearts that all of us are in his family photo. He has chosen us to be his own, and he would never leave us out of a picture of his family. Knowing that we, all of us who believe in him, are part of his family gives us comfort and peace, for he will take care of us no matter what. So as we look through photos of times past, think upon that photo of our family, the family of Jesus, where we are gathered around our perfect Savior, smiling and sharing life to the fullest!

January 17. Infinity and Beyond!

> Do not let your hearts be troubled. Trust in God; trust
> also in me. In my Father's house there are many rooms;
> if it were not so, I would have told you. I am going there
> to prepare a place for you. And if I go and prepare a place
> for you, I will come back and take you to be with me that
> you also may be where I am. You know the way to the
> place where I am going.
>
> —John 14:1–4:

"Infinity and beyond." This is a line from the movie *Toy Story*. I'm not sure why this phrase sticks in my mind. The best guess is that I have a pretty hard time wrapping my mind around the numerical idea of *infinity*. It is defined as *boundlessness*. That doesn't seem so difficult to understand, but when I try to think about something that has no end, that goes on forever, that's when I get a little overwhelmed. In thinking of infinity, I always project my thoughts to heaven and the Lord's promise that we all have a room there waiting on us to arrive. As I think about how many people are in the world, how many more are born each day, how many of these are believers, how many of us will be in heaven, and how many have already gone there, it can get a little over the top in trying to visualize our home there and how vast it must be. But that's the promise, isn't it? The Lord never makes promises that he doesn't keep. It helps me to look at the stars and see how they go on forever and ever as they seem endless, yet I cannot count even the most obvious of them. In the same way, I know with all certainty that each of us has a room in heaven. We can trust that, even though this may be an idea too big to really get our minds around, we can stand on God's promise that we will spend time eternal there, living in the presence of the one who made us, all standing before his throne crying Holy, Holy, Holy is God Almighty, to infinity and beyond!

January 18. It's Almost Here!

> ...but those who hope in the Lord will renew their strength. They will soar on wings like eagles; they will run and not grow weary, they will walk and not be faint.
>
> —Isaiah 41:30

Spring is coming. I can feel that it is on its way. I know that it is only January, but if we look closely at the seemingly dead plants with woody stems, we can see some teeny little buds starting to form, showing signs that they know, too, that spring is coming. We know that, without a doubt, spring will arrive, maybe sooner or maybe later, but it will arrive, bursting out in glorious color, revealing God's glory in all that we see. As children of a holy God, we can also count on the fact that the springtime restored in our lives by the Lord is also always on its way. When times are difficult and we are needing assurance that better times are ahead, we just need to think of our seasons and how winter always turns to spring. Life's tough days will also never fail to turn to spring through the power of the Lord Jesus Christ. No matter what we are facing today, we can remember that he will restore us to sunny days through his mercy and grace. His plan is mighty; his desires for us are precious; and he will renew us through his power in his perfect timing. Just as spring follows winter, he brings restoration from the dry and difficult times of life. So when we go to sleep tonight, let's remember with all certainty that under all of life's withered and brown grass is his precious renewal as promised by Jesus, Lord of all.

January 19. The Doorway of Safety

Teach me to do your will, for you are my God.

—Psalm 143:10

New houses. So many new houses are being built all around us. I have noticed that a lot of people are putting those beautiful metal doors filled with lovely glass panes in their new homes to let in the light of day and yet still be safe. The designs are all so different, giving each home its own unique characteristic. I am thinking how wise that is to be able to enjoy the beautiful sunshine through a lovely door that enhances the front of a home, yet provides protection at the same time. In the same way, we have a beautiful door that opens up to our lives and gives us complete security as well, and his name is Jesus. Each and every day, he provides the clearest of clear glass for us so that we can see life the way that he intended, through his vision for us. His doorway to our soul gives us his perfect light to know what to do, how to live, where to go in the good times and bad. It is through his grace that we can step out of our doorway with complete certainty that he is our Shepherd, leading us in his perfect way. He will always provide us with his clear vision of what this day should be and how to manage life in the light of his plan for our lives, having his safety around us as we step through the doorway to meet the day.

January 20. Prism of Promise

May the God of hope fill you with all joy and peace
as you trust in him, so that you may overflow
with hope by the power of the Holy Spirit.

—Romans 15:13

In reading an article on the psychology of happiness, study author Robb Rutledge, a neuroscientist at the Max Planck UCL Center for Computational Psychiatry and Aging Research in London, had this to say about our happiness quotient: "We're happy when we have a rosy view of the future, but we're also happy when the present exceeds what our expectations were." Since all of us awaken not knowing exactly what our day will bring, the best way for us to greet each morning with a rosy view is to focus on the promises of our Savior, that his mercies are new every morning and that we will never walk alone. Just knowing this gives us the confidence to wake up and go forth with whatever life throws our way. We are able to see the world and its demands through rose-colored glasses with the knowledge that we are loved by the Lord of the universe and that he always wants the best for us. It is through this same prism of promise that we can know that the present, no matter what it happens to be at the moment, is in the hands of the Lord and that he will always exceed our expectations. So stepping out each day surrounded by the love of Christ can only end each day with these words: Oh, Joy! Our Savior lives!

January 21. What a Gift!

The wild animals honor me, the jackals and the owls,
because I provide water in the desert and streams in the
wasteland, to give drink to my people, my chosen,
the people I formed for myself, that they may
proclaim my praise.

—Isaiah 43:20–21

I was cooking the other day, filling a pot with water. The water hit the rice bag that was in the pot, splashing all over the stove. It instantly evaporated, leaving the stove as clean as it was when I started. I immediately thought of how precious the gift of water is from the Lord. It is easy to drink, not having any type of odor, neither being sweet nor sour, so that we can drink as much as we want at anytime. It is refreshing and cleansing for our bodies, leaving us feeling restored after bathing. It is free, given to us freely by the Lord. It keeps our earth filled with beauty through watering our plants and keeping our animals alive. Who but our holy and perfect Lord, who also gave us our living water, the Holy Spirit, could provide a substance as perfect as this? If we are ever wondering if God is here, if he created all things, just think about water. As smart as some men may be and as spontaneous as science is, no way could anyone nor anything have invented such a liquid as this. It's easy to just live each day being washed over with all the good things of life provided by our Father. But as we move forward living life, let's remember how he blesses us in so many ways and thank him for the little things that make life worth living.

January 22. Stepping into the Gap

> The promise is for you and your children and for all who
> are far off—for all whom the Lord our God will call.
>
> —Acts 2:39

I recently read an article about a grandmother whose influence has spanned many generations. This precious grandmother began taking her granddaughter to church because, as she said, "No one else did." Her granddaughter always wanted to belong to a church, for she felt as if she was missing something. And she was. So her grandmother stepped up and began taking her to church each and every Sunday—just the two of them. These are the moments that cannot be bought; these are the moments that span generation after generation, for the granddaughter will never forget the times spent with her grandmother going to church. When asked why she wanted to take the time to take her granddaughter to church, the grandmother said, "That's when the big questions come up. I stepped in the gap." Amazing woman, amazing child. May we all step into the gap with the love of Christ each and every time that we are given the opportunity, no matter when and where that gap may appear.

January 23. Rollin' through the Stop Signs

He who heeds discipline shows the way to life;
but whoever ignores correction leads others astray.

—Proverbs 10:17

Walking a few days ago, Mojo, my dog, and I were right at the edge of a corner, ready to cross the road, when a man drove up to the stop sign and barely tapped his brakes, not really stopping at all. He started across the intersection, then had to quickly stop. A car was coming down the street and he would have plowed right into it. Once this car went past, he sped off. Isn't this what we do sometimes in life? The Lord shows us a stop sign, and we barely touch the brakes, not caring a minute that his sign is there for us to obey. Because of our being in a rush and really wanting to do things our way, we hurry through a situation, almost running smack-dab into an obstacle because we are not willing to slow down and listen to the Lord. It's hard to always listen to his word, it's hard to always see his signs of caution, and it's hard to let God show us the way. But just as with this man in such a hurry that he endangered himself and others in his path, it is better to heed our Father's lead and follow his signs on how to proceed when we are driving so fast down life's highway that we are almost out of control. He will never steer us wrong if we just slow down and pay attention to his signs. When we arrive at wherever it is that we are going, we will get there safe and sound because we relied on him. No more rollin' through God's stop signs. They are there because he loves us so!

January 24. And One More Thing...

In him we have redemption through his blood,
the forgiveness of sins, in accordance with the riches
of God's grace that he lavished on us with
all wisdom and understanding.

—Ephesians 1:7

A chaplain named Matthew Crownover has written an article about what he has learned of faith and life while running sometimes over fifty miles at a time. This article, titled "Pacing Himself with Prayer," has a message that is worth knowing. Near the end of the article it says, "His job as chaplain is not to cure, but to heal. It's all about redemption: That's what happens when we run races. It's not that there's no suffering. It's that it doesn't go to waste." That is the one thought that we need to embrace, that our suffering never goes to waste. God uses each and every moment that we suffer, no matter how it presents itself, for his glory, for our learning, for drawing us closer and closer and even closer to him. Through his running, Crownover has come to know God in a deeper and much more personal way. Running these great distances is tough, it's grueling, he suffers. Yet he learns from his experience that God has a redemptive plan of taking our sufferings and restoring us again and again. He has come to realize that it's not about avoiding suffering but redeeming it. Yes—that's the thing—we need to take all the times that we have been put to the test and use them to know our Father and who he is through them. Being redeemed, being rescued from these sufferings, and finding his mercy at the end of each trial is how we can truly know that God is there for us, each and every moment that we suffer. His plan is mighty, and because he has paid the price, we will and always can be redeemed and restored by the one true redeemer, Jesus Christ. What better ending to our trials than this: to know that through it all, he still remains, lavishing restoration and redemption on us time and time again.

January 25. Fill 'er Up!

Your word is a lamp to my feet and a light for my path.
—Psalm 119:105

Yesterday, for the first time ever, my Jawbone speaker spoke to me and said, "Battery under one-quarter full." Yup, just out of the blue, this peaceful voice began speaking to me, telling me that the battery was running low. Obviously it was encouraging me to plug it in so that it could continue to entertain me with the music that I so love. Once again, I was reminded of our Father who sometimes nudges us, calling us to recharge our batteries for living with his holy word, the holy Bible, so that we can go on encouraging those we see each day with his story. Plugged in! We need to stay plugged in to the Lord by staying in the word and keeping the truths told there ever present on our minds to guide us through life. There is so much, so very much written in the holy Bible that clearly points us to where God longs for us to be. However, it doesn't work if we don't open it! Let us count this among our many, many blessings that we do have the holy Bible right at hand and can use it anytime, any day to hear his word. What better way to spend the day than reading the inspired word of our Father, his book, his holy book. Let's bring new life to our minds, filling up our batteries with words to live by, knowing that remaining plugged in to his word will keep us charged and ready to go, full speed ahead!

January 26. Tag, We're It!

David's Prayer
Praise be to you, O Lord, God of our Father Israel,
from everlasting to everlasting. Yours, O Lord, is the
greatness and the power and the glory and the majesty
and the splendor, for everything in heaven and earth is
yours...But who am I (David), and who are my people,
that we should be able to give as generously as this?
Everything comes from you, and we have given
you only what comes from your hand.

—1 Chronicles 29:10–14

Remember the game that we played as children where we would run after a friend, and when we caught them we would say, "Tag, you're it!"? I was reminded of this game yesterday at a luncheon that celebrated the lives of our homeless population. An outstanding young woman named Liz Murray spoke, retelling her life story of how she grew up homeless on the streets of New York, got out of that state of homelessness, and graduated from Harvard. She spoke of so many messages worth knowing, and I kept thinking, *So this is once again how we know that God has a plan for each and every one of us...a mighty plan of redemption and a future.* It was so evident to see God's hand in her life as he led her through the storms to the clearing, hearing her tell of how she went from starving throughout her young life to living on the streets by herself at the age of fifteen to finding a mentor at a private school who became her guiding light, leading her all the way into Harvard! At the end of her talk, she said, "Tag, you're it!" She left us with a powerful challenge that we should pass along the goodness that we have received from the Lord to others who need a hand up. So that's it. We are the ones that God calls to make a difference somehow, some way, along the way! Tag, we're it!

January 27. Because He Loves Us So

> Come to me, all who are weary and burdened,
> and I will give you rest.
>
> —Matthew 11:28

I really don't like the cold. I would just as soon spring arrive and these chilly days be gone. But the Lord uses these chilly days, many of which make our lives so difficult in the ice and rain, to lead us into those glorious springtime days. He uses the often miserable days of winter to prepare all living things for the arrival of spring *coming soon to a place near you!* It is because the plants and animals lie dormant over the winter months that they can burst forth as the first warm days appear. So life shadows nature, for it is the same with us. We are going to experience some chilly days of life, yet our Father uses them to reveal who he truly is. During life's journeys, we come to know the depth of his compassion, his grace, his comfort, his peace, and his never-ending love. If we had spring all year long, we would never know the excitement of that first tulip popping up through the freshly stirred dirt. If we had spring all year long, we would never step out into the first warm day filled with a brilliant blue sky and feel the light, springtime breeze. If we had spring all our life long, we would never know that first touch of God's grace as we are lifted out of our dormant state and placed gently in the sunshine of life where we will flourish. So as we finish the last days of winter and move forward into spring, let us rest on the promise of our Father that he will deliver us from the challenging journeys of life and place us gently in the sunshine of his love.

January 28. "Make the World Go Away"

> The voice of the Lord is over the waters;
> the God of glory thunders, the Lord thunders over
> the mighty waters. The voice of the Lord is powerful;
> the voice of the Lord is majestic.
>
> —Psalm 29:3–4

Walking outside yesterday, a friend called. As we were chatting, a huge truck drove by, creating a lot of noise. At the same time, dogs in a neighboring yard started barking. A leaf blower was chiming in with its *hrump hrump grrrr*. A cacophony of sounds was keeping me from hearing my friend, so I said, "I can't hear you. The world is in the way." Then it hit me. That's what happens to all of us at some time or another. We can't hear the Lord's voice because we have let the world in and shut him out. The world, with all its pressures on us, is keeping us from our Father's love and from hearing his voice above the loud and disruptive voices of life. If we are so attuned to what is going on in the world and allowing outside influences to shut him out, we will never be able to hear him calling us, guiding and directing us, giving us hope and a future. So here's the plan: When life and all its disturbing sounds from people, places, and things draw us away from focusing on the Lord, let's stop where we are, take a deep breath, tune our minds back to the one voice that really matters, and listen carefully for what he has to say.

January 29. Team In Training

> Therefore, since we are surrounded by such a great cloud
> of witnesses, let us throw off everything that hinders
> and the sin that so easily entangles, and let us run with
> perseverance the race marked out for us. Let us fix our
> eyes on Jesus, the author and perfecter of our faith…
>
> —Hebrews 12:1

Team In Training is the name of an event that the Leukemia and Lymphoma Society started years ago to raise funds for research. It has raised millions and millions of dollars, which the society has put to good use in finding the cure for this disease and its related ones. In essence, people sign up to run in a 5K race and agree at the same time to raise a specified amount that will go toward leukemia research. It is a win-win for all: the runners who love to run and the patients who benefit from the millions of dollars raised. The teams show up at the race of their choice, choosing from races held all over the world. They run in purple shirts that say "Team In Training" so that all who are there can know that they are not only running the race physically but also running the race for the cure of leukemia. It is quite a sight to see so many folks wearing purple shirts, knowing that they are bound together for a common cause. We, as believers, are also a *team in training*, for we are running the race set before us by the Lord. We too are bound together for a common cause: to serve the Lord by serving others. Seeing the Lord's team in action reveals his comforting presence and his love. We are his team, his team in training, whom he sends out to go before him and do his work here on earth. It is because he first loved us that we can now bind together in brotherly love and make a difference in the lives of others. As we step out in faith, letting him lead the race that we are running, let us fix our eyes on Jesus, sharing the restorative love that he washes down upon us with those who need it the most.

January 30. Plugged In

> For you were once darkness, but now you are light in the
> Lord. Live as children of light (for the fruit of the light
> consists in all goodness, righteousness and truth) and find
> out what pleases the Lord.
>
> —Ephesians 5:8–10

No matter where we go these days, everyone, and I mean everyone from young to old, is plugged in, and so am I. When I walk each day, I wear a Bluetooth headset so that I can listen to music easily. It never fails that everyone I pass has their ears and their minds plugged in to some device of some sort, talking or listening to something or the other. In waiting rooms or planes, trains, and automobiles—right?—people are plugged in! How can we transfer this passion for technology to plugging into Jesus? How great it would be if we were this wired into him? Let us think about the ways that we can add to all this newfangled technology that fills our minds with whatever to also being plugged in to the glorious love of the Lord. Make our focus be on Jesus so that his energy and joy will then go forth from us to others, filling them up with his love that fills us all day long. The transfer of knowledge filling our hearts and minds will be about the one who truly matters. It will spill out like melted gold into the lives of those we meet, bringing sweetness and light to their day, and then they can pass it on to others, lighting a string of love for Jesus that circles the globe for his glory.

January 31. Balcony People

> ...how much more will your Father in heaven give good
> gifts to those who ask him! So in everything, do unto
> others what you would have them do unto you.
>
> —Matthew 7:11–12

Balcony people. A dear friend explained that term to me several years ago, and I still think of it often. Actual balcony people, who sit in the balcony of a performance, are the ones who clap and clap with gusto for the performance on the stage, supporting and showing great joy for the person who is performing. The balcony people to whom this term refers are the people in our lives who clap loudly and with gusto for us as we *succeed at life*. We all need balcony people in our lives, those people who truly care about others, being happy for them when they are smarter, prettier, well-liked, and experiencing success in life. The reality for us as believers is that we have a balcony person who is always there clapping for us in our successes. He always knows when the good times come, and he is pleased. He loves to see us shine, and it is because of him that we do. Even if we do not hear the praises of man, we can always hear the praises of the Lord, our balcony person who claps with gusto when we succeed. The Lord longs for us to dance with joy. He longs to see us smile and know that the life that he has given us is filled with goodness. So as we greet another day and share life with others, let's clap and clap loudly when they do good. We can rest assure that when our day comes, our balcony person will be there clapping the loudest of all!

February 1. "Never Give Up!"

May the God of hope fill you with all joy and peace as
you trust in him, so that you may overflow with hope by
the power of the Holy Spirit.

—Romans 15:13

Ever since our children were small, my husband would always encourage them to never give up. Never give up in any sport they were playing, never give up on practicing an instrument, never give up on people. Just never give up! He would send them photocopies of a seagull with a frog in its mouth, the frog reaching out its hands and feet trying its best to get out of the seagull's mouth. So that is exactly the image that I thought of when I heard of a dog whose back had been broken and was left on the side of the road to die. A sweet, sweet woman stopped there and heard a faint cry from this dog. She took it up in her arms and rushed it to the veterinarian for care. The dog's back had been broken for over a month, but due to some loving and caring vets and assistants, they were able to operate and restore this dog back to health. His back had been broken just so, giving them the chance to repair it. After many long months of therapy that included a harness while swimming in a pool, he is now running around chasing leaves and other dogs, just as if he had never been injured at all. The story goes on to say that it seemed to the rescuers that this dog never gave up, that he always had hope that someone would rescue him and restore him to health. Just like this adorable dog, we should never give up, whether we are lying beside the road of life hurt and wounded for a day, a month, or even years. The Lord is bringing restoration and healing to our lives. Never give up hope, because our Savior is on his way. Hope, defined as "to desire with expectation of fulfillment," is the eternal flame that lights our souls within, provided by the only one who could ever fulfill our needs time after time after time, never coming up empty at the well known as hope.

February 2. Home Is Where the Heart Is

How lovely is your dwelling place, O Lord Almighty!
My soul yearns, even faints for the courts of the Lord;
    my heart and my flesh cry out for the living God.
Even the sparrow has found a home, and the swallow a
nest for herself, where she may have her young—a place
near your altar, O Lord Almighty, my King and my God.
Blessed are those who dwell in your house;
    they are ever praising you.

—Psalm 84:1–4

Home. There is something about that word that warms my heart, for my home growing up was my haven. My mom was so much fun, and my dad was the sweetest dad on the planet. My friends liked my mom so much, boys would come over to see her, not me. I would have to sit up all night long while they talked with her. After I married, I would go by my mother's house every day of my life. Even after our children were born, we would always stop by Mom's just to see what was going on. Was it perfect? Nope. Was it always calm and restful? Not at all! But it was where I knew that all of those who dwelled there loved me unconditionally. All of us have this special place, maybe somewhere other than where we grew up. It might be in the company of someone we care about or it could be in a friend's home where we spent our childhood. Many people feel most at home out in nature or at a place where they continue to visit year after year. But each of us can name that place where our heart feels at home. No matter where our hearts have been at home before, the perfect home for our hearts is with our Father! It is with him that we can know without a doubt that he loves us. We can know that he is *in this place* when we go into a chapel and kneel to pray. We know that he is *in this place* when we step outside and view the wonders of his world all around us. We know that he is *in this place* when we share time with him before we close our eyes. Let us seek his face, knowing that we are truly home with him. They say that "home is where the heart is." As our hearts are joined forever with his, let us soak in his love, for he is our home, our precious home.

February 3. Map My Walk

> And now, O Israel, what does the Lord your God ask
> of you but to fear the Lord your God, to walk in all his
> ways, to love him, to serve the Lord your God with all
> your heart and with all your soul…
>
> —Deuteronomy 10:12

A dear friend and I were chatting the other day while I was walking my dog, Mojo. She said that she has a new app for her phone called Map My Walk that tells her many things about her walk. It can send your point of location to whomever you wish, providing a measure of safety and information to anyone you'd like. Now that is some kind of app! Why didn't we think of that? Immediately, this thought came to mind: *How blessed we all are to have a Father who always knows where we are. He never needs to wonder if we need him, nor does he need to look for us to care for us. He knows our every move, going before to clear our path.* Before the beginning of time, our Father, our God, puts his plan in place so that we can walk with confidence the path that he has chosen. Let us rest on the promise that he has set our course for us to walk. This is the greatest app of assurance that we will ever need.

February 4. Rainy Days and Mondays

> But for you who revere my name, the sun of
> righteousness will rise with healing in its wings.
>
> —Malachi 4:2

A few weeks ago, when it was raining on a Monday, I was walking along under my umbrella, having a grand old time singing in the rain. These precious children came out of their house with brightly colored umbrellas and began to dance and play in the rain. They got a little wet occasionally, but they did not seem concerned, for they knew that they had protection from the storm over their heads. They were kicking up the water and splashing around in it, just like baby birds learning to bathe themselves. We too have protection from the storms over our heads. We too can approach the rainy days and stormy weather with childlike faith in the Lord and Savior who guards us closely, no matter rain or shine. The weather may change in a moment to storms and loud claps of thunder, but soon, the day will clear up, and we will feel the warmth of the sun on our faces. Our Father always brings us to this point, for just when we don't think that the clouds will ever clear away again, he gently blows away the clouds and restores our lives to peace and tranquility where we know, without a doubt, that he is our Savior, the one who never lets us down. Let us always look upward to the source of our strength, the Lord and Savior, to feel the warmth of his never-ending care shining down on us!

February 5. It's All in the Timing

But I trust in you, O Lord; I say, "You are my God."
My times are in your hands.

—Psalm 31:14–15

It's all in the timing! This morning, as I awoke, I was asking the Lord in prayer for something, and not ten minutes later it was answered. Be assured that it's not always this way. I have waited years, many, many years for the answer to certain specific prayers. So for me here is a lesson learned.

1. He is always listening.

2. His timing is perfect.

3. His ways are not our ways, and his timing is not our timing.

I am not good at waiting: not in the grocery line, not at the bank, and not for answered prayers. But as the Lord continues to reveal, waiting brings patience, perseverance, and qualities that not only make us better people, but draw us closer, so much closer, to our Maker. It seems that learning to rely on our Father paints the big picture that he has a plan, and the rewards at the end, when the answer comes, are too wonderful for words! As the Psalmist says above, "My times are in your hands," reminding us that all the events and circumstances of life are in the hands of the Lord. So may we continue to pray, and pray mightily, knowing that his timing is perfect, and so will be his answer! What a beautiful quilt he is making out of the pieces of our lives!

February 6. The Best Things in Life Are Free

There is no difference, for all have sinned and fall short
of the glory of God, and are justified freely by his grace
through the redemption that came by Christ Jesus.

—Romans 3:22–24

"The best things in life are free." I think that this is one saying that parents love, for it explains why their children cannot have this or that. Today, I was reading about a ten-year-old boy whose fourth-grade class recently discussed where they would go if they could visit anywhere in the world. The class, I am sure, replied, "Disney World! California! Hawaii!" and so on. But this child answered that he would go to the fire station where he was abandoned as a newborn baby to meet the fireman who found him and found a loving family to adopt him. On the boy's birthday, his adoptive mother planned a visit with the fireman, who had kept his picture in the station ever since. The reunion was one that money could not buy. The fireman took the young boy to his fire truck and let him go for a spin. He told him that he has a big brother for life. How much this fireman must love him, finding a newborn baby and seeing that he got the care and the family that he needed. How much these two people, man and boy, must share emotionally, knowing that the love that they receive from each other cannot be bought but must be freely given. And how much are we also freely given grace, mercy, and love through the redemptive power of Jesus Christ, who gave it all for us. Let's take time to do those things that money cannot buy. Spend time with our Father. Spend quality time with our families and friends. Take time out of our day to visit for a moment with a neighbor or the person helping you at the store. There will be hectic times, but the moments freely given are precious to those who receive them. And the rewards for us cannot be bought, because the best things in life are free!

February 7. Restoring the Goodies in Life

You turned my wailing into dancing; you removed my
sackcloth and clothed me with joy, that my heart may
sing to you and not be silent.

—Psalm 30:11–12

Every day when I walk Mojo, my dog, we go down the alleys in our neighborhood because he loves to chew on certain weeds that he finds along the sides of the fences. He is rather particular, but he always finds some that he likes. However, last week, much to his dismay, all of his favorite weed goodies had been cut down by a mower. I guess most people do not mow in their alleys too often, but this particular week they did. So, here he was, dejected and saddened, not able to find his usual snacks during our walk. Isn't that just how life is? We are going along, and life is good. We are having good days, then all of a sudden, the good days are gone, mowed down by life. They are nowhere to be found. Yet here is the promise of Jesus. He will restore our good days in his precious timing. So just like the weeds of goodness that will grow back soon that Mojo loves to chew on during our walks, so will Jesus bring back our days of joy, because he loves us so, and our hearts will sing and not be silent once again.

February 8. Put to Bed

> And the God of all grace, who called you to his eternal
> glory in Christ, after you have suffered a little while,
> will himself restore you and make you strong, firm and
> steadfast. To him be the power forever and ever. Amen.
>
> —1 Peter 5:10–11

Put to bed is a term that people use when they have finished a project and have turned it over to the next step. It implies that they can rest, as whatever they have been working on is now done, just as we put ourselves to bed after our day's work is done. It reminds us of the times when we have been in the middle of a trial, working hard to get through it. We turn to various solutions, some of which may not work. But the times when we have given them over to Jesus are the times when we can finally "put them to bed." He takes our difficulties from us and gives us rest, precious rest, so that he can then move forward, bringing a resolution and completeness to our journeys. Putting our trials in the hands of our Savior brings rest and restoration to our minds and souls. What better place to leave our struggles than with him, Jesus Christ, so that now we can let go and let God, knowing that he will do the best job possible to restore our lives again. *Put to bed—* where all of our journeys will be restored if we just put them in the hands of the Lord, Jesus Christ.

February 9. Ash Wednesday...the Beginning of Lent

I have declared to both Jews and Greeks that they must
turn to God in repentance and have faith in our Lord Jesus.
—Acts 20:21

Ash Wednesday, the beginning of Lent, is near. Lent is the time in the Christian calendar when we, as believers, are called to solemnly focus on our faith and repent of our sins. The Lord, through Paul in his words above from Acts, says that we must turn to God in repentance and have faith in the Lord Jesus. So there it is, clearly stated. The time is now. The call is here. What blessing there is to be found in this specific time set aside for us to really get it, to really gear down, settle in, and focus on asking the Lord and Savior for forgiveness of our sins. Ash Wednesday got its name from the practice of placing ashes on the foreheads of followers of Christ as a reminder and celebration of human mortality and as a sign of mourning and repentance to God. The word that jumps right out at us is the word "celebration." Celebration of human mortality. Now that is not something that we would think of right off as part of our focus and prayer time during Lent, but what a meaningful thought it is! What glory and praise we should have in thinking that, yes, we are mortal, and yes, praise be to God that we are. Praise be to God that some day, because of our mortality and through his gift of the cross, we will join him in heaven for all eternity, all our sins forgiven. There is peace and joy to be found this Lenten season in remembering and celebrating our mortality as we also mourn and repent of our sins to our Father. To have this special time carved out is so meaningful, encouraging us to lay it all down at his feet. The words of Paul above end with hope. The hope found so simply yet so powerfully in having faith. So as serious and thoughtful and full of mourning we are called to be for the next forty days, we are wrapped in a cloud of hope through faith in the Lord Jesus. Amen!

February 10. Ash Wednesday

> At that time Jesus came from Nazareth to Galilee and
> was baptized by John in the Jordan. As Jesus was coming
> up out of the water, he saw heaven being torn open, and
> the Spirit descending on him like a dove. And a voice
> came from heaven: "You are my Son, whom I love; with
> you, I am well pleased." At once the Spirit sent him out
> into the desert, and he was in the desert forty days, being
> tempted by Satan. He was with the wild animals, and
> angels attended him. After John was put in prison, Jesus
> went into Galilee, proclaiming the good news of God.
> "The time has come," he said. "The kingdom of God is
> near. Repent and believe the good news!"
>
> —Mark 1:9–15.

Today is Ash Wednesday, the first day of Lent as celebrated on the Christian calendar. This day always occurs forty-six days before Easter, never falling exactly on the same date as Easter's date changes yearly. This day is devoted to the beginning of forty days of confession and penitence, signifying the forty days that Jesus spent in the desert to pray and fast. So here we are, praying, repenting, and solemnly focusing on the days to come. Although these are solemn days, days for reflection and prayers for repentance, what inner joy we can find in using this time to worship. Let us spend time in the presence of the Lord and truly worship him for what he has done for us, freeing us from sin and giving us life eternal. With all the business of life, let us step back and cherish this special time to honor and worship the Lord in prayer and supplication for the forgiveness of sins. These are precious days of worship. How blessed are we to be called his, the gift of all gifts. So shall we hold close to our hearts his promise that he will never leave us nor forsake us, for this is the good news, the best news that we could ever hear.

February 11. Things Aren't Always What They Seem

I will ask the Father, and he will give you another
Counselor to be with you forever...the Spirit of truth.
The world cannot accept him because it neither sees him
nor knows him. But you know him, for he lives with you
and will be in you.

—John 14:16, 17

I walk through our neighborhood almost every day, and I guess that my neighbors cannot help but see me. They probably think that I am talking on my phone all the time. While I must look like I am talking to someone, in actuality I am probably singing to the music from Pandora on my phone. How many times are things not what they seem? This truth is proven almost each and every day. The sun can be shining brightly without a cloud in the sky and rain can be falling. We can feel perfectly fine, then all of a sudden we are so, so sick with a virus. To translate this truth to our faith, we will never have this experience in our relationship with our Holy Spirit. He is always what has been promised. The Bible tells us that he gives us joy, he teaches us truths, he convicts, he leads, he strengthens and encourages, he comforts. He is never going to be something that he isn't. He is the perfect third of the Holy Triune: Father, Son, and Holy Ghost. Can we trust him when he speaks to us? For sure! Can we know that he will never be anything except what he is and what God promised? Absolutely! Can we put our complete and total faith in him and who he is? Always! Let us treasure the knowledge that he is exactly, 100 percent what our Father promised, our personal Counselor to be with us forever, the Spirit of truth! And who greater to have whispering in your ear than he?

February 12. The Thorny Rose

Have mercy on me, O God, according to your unfailing
love; according to your great compassion blot out
my transgressions. Wash away all my iniquity and
cleanse me from my sin.

—Psalm 51:1–2

I had the honor of buying flowers yesterday for our daughter's wedding portrait that will be taken today. She asked me to make her a bouquet for the photo shoot, and I was so excited to do this for her. Now, rest assured, I am no florist. In fact, I haven't ever made a wedding bouquet before. The good news is that she is so appreciative and not hung up on perfection that I can go forward feeling that this is doable. So yesterday I was at the flower supplier buying the most glorious flowers ever. One of the flowers that I needed to put in her bouquet is the garden rose. Normally these roses have been stripped of most of their thorns, leaving a clean stem to use so that the holder does not get stuck. But some of the roses that I bought yesterday still had thorns on them, really big ones and lots of them. I had a pair of rose cutters, and I could easily remove these thorns so that she will not stick her finger in the photo shoot today. It made me think, *We are all like these beautiful roses to the Lord…we all came with thorns. Yet because of the celebration of Easter that we will soon experience, we have Jesus, our Savior, who takes us and removes our thorns so that we can live victoriously through his sacrifice on the cross.* He is the perfect one, and the only one who can do this for us. It is only through the power of the cross that we are stripped free from our thorny lives of sin. We are restored by our Savior who came to earth to do this very thing for us through his mercy and grace.

February 13. Because He First Loved Us

We love because he first loved us…whoever loves
God must also love his brother.

—1 John 4:19

In this day and time, people are much more open to speaking with love as to how they feel about those near and dear to them, and it must be so pleasing to our Father. I have seen firsthand recently the love shared among believers, lifting each other up with a love and care that is almost palpable. It is something to take in, for love from another human is something that cannot be replicated. Love can be defined as a deep feeling for or personal attachment to someone close to you, such as a child, a parent, or even a friend. C. S. Lewis talks about love in his book *The Four Loves* in which he looks at the nature of love from a Christian and philosophical perspective. One type that he defines is philia, the love found in friendship—a strong bond existing between people who share a common interest or activity. When we are blessed to be involved in the interaction of this type of love between friends, we bond. We become part of this person, connected by a common thread that brings a strength and comfort with it beyond anything else that someone could find in another. In reading more deeply about our Father's words in 1 John above, we know that "all love ultimately comes from our God, our Father. Genuine love is never self-generated by his creatures. Since our love has its source in God's love, his love reaches full expression (is made complete) when we love fellow Christians. Thus the God whom no one has ever seen is seen by those who love, because God lives in them" (from the *NIV Study Bible*). We are able to show our friends, our fellow believers, what God looks like for he is seen through our loving each other. Knowing this and holding this truth close to our hearts we can love like no other when the opportunity arises, for being able to give the gift of showing to others what our Father looks like is one of the greatest gifts we will ever give to another, and all because he first loved us.

February 14. Lovin' Life

> Dear friends, let us love one another,
> for love comes from God.
>
> —1 John 4:7

As I opened my door this morning, tied to the doorknob was a beautiful red balloon with a red paper heart attached and the verse from 1 John above written on it. Underneath the scripture it said: "Happy Valentine's Day!" I noticed that all my neighbors had one of these special love gifts tied to their doors. I started thinking about how much time and effort it took to share the word of God on this day of love and how special this little act of kindness makes me feel. This family so wanted to share God's word and his love that they honored him and us with this little surprise gift. I am now urged to do something today that will honor the Lord and share his word about love. It's the unexpected that is so fun. To get a little something that you are not looking for warms the heart and makes you feel special. So as you step out into the glorious sunshine on this special day that we celebrate love, soak it in. Let the love of family and friends warm your heart and fill your soul with goodness! Let us know the joy of this day with the assurance that love is from God. It is who he is. He is love, and just as the warm and beautiful sunshine is spreading all over our world this day, let us too spread his love around for all to know him as we do, for love comes from God!

February 15. Opening the Gate

Open for me the gates of righteousness; I will enter and
give thanks to the Lord. This is the gate of the Lord
through which the righteous may enter.
I will give you thanks, for you answered me;
you have become my salvation.

—Psalm 118:19–21

Our daughter's home has a metal gate in front of it that protects the driveway, keeping out unwanted visitors and providing a layer of protection for her. She used to work nights as a nurse and would leave in the dark and come home in the dark, so this gate was put in to secure the area and hopefully keep out any unwanted guests. As her parents, we felt better knowing that she could come and go as safely as possible thanks to this automatic gate. The other day, I went to her home to get something out of her garage, and I too had to get through the gate. Fortunately, I know the code. But in a rush to get this errand done, I kept entering the incorrect code number. The gate would move a little like it was going to open, but then bong back into place, not letting me in. Frustrated, I did this over and over and over again. Relentlessly, the gate teased me by starting to open, but then it would not. Finally, I took my time, entered the right code, and the gate graciously swung open, giving me the right of way to get to the garage. So here is the correlation: Jesus is our code to living, the answer for moving through the gates that we face in life. We try to push through these gates without his help, without his leading us in the right direction. Yet so many times these gates that we push against give a little, tend to swing open a bit, but then slam shut in our faces. We become frustrated and forget that we have the code to open them up—Jesus. He is ready and willing to move these obstacles for us, yet because we don't call upon his name, we bang our heads against these difficult times unnecessarily. Jesus is waiting. He is near, holding the buttons of peace and calm in his perfect hands so that we may get through these difficult times. Instead of continuing to rush headlong into these obstructions, let us punch in the perfect code—J-E-S-U-S—knowing that he will surely open up these gates for us, giving us safe passage to restored joy.

February 16. A Blanket of Snow

> He will cover you with his feathers,
> and under his wings you find refuge.
>
> —Psalm 91:4

A blanket of snow covered all of Dallas, Texas, yesterday, washing our landscape with a glorious dusting of snowflakes. I struck out walking with my dog, Mojo, in the lightly falling snow, both of us full of wonder and delight from sharing in this gift of winter. It brought to mind a time when I was in elementary school and the snow had fallen all night long, covering the ground as it has today with a fluffy overlay of white, glistening snow. Late that evening, my friend and I went out, and it looked like a winter wonderland, for the freshly fallen snow had not been touched by anyone. The full moon shone down on the snow, reflecting the beautiful moonlight for us to be able to see. We fell onto the soft ground, full of excitement to be the first to be in the snowfall. In just the same way, I was the first one out in the snow yesterday, Mojo and I making fresh tracks as we walked. We went a couple of miles, and on our way back on the same route, our tracks had already been covered by more glorious snow, restoring the ground to its original look of pristine and untouched snow. So it is with God. We trek through life, messing up the landscape, tripping on rocks and boulders along the way, and then in a moment's notice, the Lord covers us with a blanket of snow, restoring our lives to the way they had been before we had marched through it, leaving our footprints on the landscape. His blanket of comfort and peace, so like this fresh snowfall, brings the same peaceful restoration that I found as I returned on my walk today, reminding us of his assurance that he never fails to cover over all the tracks in life that need to be restored, just like Mojo's and my tracks today, completely renewed by the fresh-fallen snow.

February 17. Unexpected Gifts

Every good and perfect gift is from above,
coming down from the Father of the heavenly lights,
who does not change like shifting shadows.

—James 1:17

Have you ever come home and found an unexpected gift on your front doorstep when it wasn't your birthday or Christmas or some other occasion? That happened to me this past week, but the gift wasn't one that I could show you nor hold in my hand. It was so much better than that. The gift was an answer from God to one of my life's ongoing situations. Yup, right out of the blue, I was given the perfect answer to a prayer that I had prayed over for many years. The Lord made it clear to me that he is weaving a tapestry together with all of our lives that only he can see clearly. Only he can know when the right stitch needs to be made to sew the piece that connect our lives together seamlessly. Only he can see how to best place each piece of fabric known as our relationships so that the perfect quilt of life is made. We need to wait. Wait patiently on the Lord for his gift of answered prayer. The Lord continues to reassure us that he is answering our prayers in his own time with his perfect answer, and that he knows the desires of our hearts. He's got the plan. He knows the what, the where, and the when of our lives, of all our lives. So we can release the ones we love to him. He's got them. He's got us, all of us, right in the palm of his hand!

February 18. The Tapestry of Our Lives

From heaven the Lord looks down and sees all mankind;
from his dwelling place he watches all who live on
earth—he who forms the hearts of all,
who considers everything they do.

—Psalm 33:13–15

There is a tapestry being woven by our Father, and each stitch is a person whom he created and whose life gives special meaning to his quilt. Each stitch that each life creates reflects God's glory by how they loved and lived and whom they touched. It is a forever representation of his love for us and how our lives are used by him to connect one another as we live each day. It is no accident that we are next to those that we touch and how they touch us throughout our lives, all planned by our Savior. So it is in visualizing this quilt of life that we can find such glorious value in our lives and the lives of those we know who strengthen us by their threads that bind us together. Without these connecting threads, the quilt would fall apart, not being able to reflect God's glorious gift of love and friendship from all those we know. So as we meet another day, let us remember and cherish the stitches that we are making with another and praise our Father for each whom he brings into our lives, creating a magnificent quilt that he has designed before time, and one that will be created for his joy day after day after day. For who can love more than he, the very one who created us and places us exactly where he wants us to be in his precious quilt of life.

February 19. Pillow Talk

Shout for joy, O heavens; rejoice, O earth; burst into
song, O mountains! For the Lord comforts his people
and will have compassion on his afflicted ones.

—Isaiah 49:13

For those of you who don't remember or never knew, *Pillow Talk*
is a movie title from the fifties. A funny thought came to mind.
With texting a predominate form of communication now, a
catchy little noise goes off when we receive a text from someone.
My daughter used to say as her phone binged away, "Somebody
loves me." So it is with the Lord. I feel certain that each time
we talk to him, he hears a lovely little *bing* in our voice that tells
him we care about him, tells him we need him, and tells him
he is important to us. The time that he and I chat the most is
when I am in bed, having pillow talk, sharing thoughts, cares, and
prayers with the one who knows me best! Last night was a lot of
pillow talk, actually, all throughout the night as I had quite a lot
to discuss with my Father. Praise, discussions about others' needs,
going over the past few days, lots of give and take with him. This
pillow talk is something that I look forward to having with the
Lord, for it is a quiet time when I can really share my heart with
him and hear his voice. As we move throughout our days, let us
call on him all the time, the good times and the difficult ones,
and know that we are putting a smile on his face, for what father
doesn't love to hear from his child?

February 20. I Promise!

> We tell you the good news: What God promised our
> ancestors he has fulfilled for us, their children,
> by raising up Jesus.
>
> —Acts 13:32

Do you remember when you were growing up and sometimes a friend would say something and then add the words "I promise!"? Children think that adding those words "I promise" give the statement emphasis and validity, even if what was said could not come to fruition. When we, as children, found out that what was promised sometimes didn't turn out to be true, we were usually very let down. This statement carries great weight. Promises are special. Promises reveal that you care enough about the person to whom the promise is made that you will do everything in your power to make it happen. There is a promise keeper, Jesus, who always keeps his word. He is the promise, the promise that our Father gave to us, whose life we meditate on during this Lenten season, and whose resurrection we celebrate this coming Easter. He will supply our every need. His grace is sufficient for us. We will not be overtaken with temptation. We will have victory over death. Those who believe in Jesus and become baptized for the forgiveness of sins will be saved, and we, who believe, will all receive eternal life. These are promises that we can take to the bank, for our promise keeper always keeps his word!

February 21. Slow and Steady

> And we pray this in order that you may live a life worthy
> of the Lord and may please him in every way; bearing
> fruit in every good work, growing in the knowledge of
> God, being strengthened with all power according to his
> glorious might so that you may have great endurance and
> patience, and joyfully giving thanks to the Father...
>
> —Colossians 1:10–12

Slow, steady rain. What relief we have had with the slow and steady rain that washed our earth over the past few days. This soft, gentle rain reminds us that the Lord knows that sometimes the earth is so dry that, instead of a deluge of rain, it needs this slow and steady rain so that every droplet can be absorbed to benefit nature. Just as when a deluge of rain hits the earth and creates tremendous runoff, all of us have experienced those hard-driving, earth-shattering rains in life. Our Father allows these trials into our lives so that he can refine us like gold. He always reveals much to be learned if we can hear above the roar of it all. So when we are meeting day after long day of continuous rain, whether it is hard driving or just a relentless drizzle, let us try to absorb what he is teaching us. Let us store his insights within, being renewed and refreshed, ready to live life abundantly, just like our earth after a slow and steady rain.

February 22. The Trees of Blessing

The Lord bless you and keep you; the Lord make
his face shine upon you and be gracious to you;
the Lord turn his face toward you and give you peace.

—Numbers 6:24–26

There is a garden of trees provided by Jesus that gives us the peace of the Lord as we need it. This is a garden planted with trees bearing fruit that Jesus is waiting for us to use according to our needs each day. Visualize going into this garden where we will find many trees there laden with precious fruits of all kinds. Some of these trees have fruits on them, and then some of them have bare branches. The gift of this garden is that we may enter it at any time in our thoughts, choosing a fruit from one of the trees named peace, comfort, joy, trust, love—all the attributes of the Lord. He has planted this garden of trees for us because he loves us so. But we may also carry something into the garden to hang on the bare trees found there. Here, we can leave a burr of burden that we are experiencing in our lives, hanging it upon the stripped branches of trees we see waiting there to receive what we need to leave with Jesus. We can step out into this lovely garden and hang up our burrs of worry, anger, hurt, and sadness—all these things that we need to release from our lives. Who of us does not need to remove the challenging burdens of life from our lives at times, the ones that weigh us down? Let's practice giving back these difficulties to the Lord for his care and replacing them with his mercy and grace. It is here in Jesus's garden of life that we may exchange pain for peace, worry for assurance, difficulty for comfort, and hurt for love. All we need to do is follow the call of Jesus to trade these things for his goodness and grace. So the next time we feel the need to let go of something that keeps us from knowing the joy of the Lord, step into his garden and leave your troubles there, feasting instead on the precious fruits of life that only Jesus can provide.

February 23. A Cloud of Witnesses

Be joyful always; pray continually;
give thanks in all circumstances,
for this is God's will for you in Christ Jesus.

—1 Thessalonians 5:16

Walking and talking with the Lord, I was saying that I couldn't imagine living life without all the people I know who pray for me and my family. I started thinking back over the past few years and the times—the countless times—that I have called on them to lift us up in prayer, and what a source of strength and comfort that has always been for me. This visual of the cloud of witnesses popped into my head. Returning home after my pancreatic hospital stay, my husband brought me a prayer card from a church in a small town outside Dallas that one of his associates attends. This card was signed time after time by people I do not even know and I will never know. But these strangers had continually lifted me up in prayer. The Lord heard them and the prayers of others and answered their prayers for me. Those we know who pray for us magnify our cloud of witnesses. Prayer is mighty, prayer is powerful, prayer is our calling. Thank you for praying for others. Prayer is a gift, as they say, that is priceless.

February 24. That's So Squirrelly!

> You are my hiding place; You will protect me from
> trouble and surround me with the songs of deliverance.
>
> —Psalm 32:7

Squirrels, gotta love 'em! Now I am clearly aware that I am probably one of a few people who really love squirrels. Supposedly, they are from the rodent family, but that doesn't matter to me. When our children were little, we found a tiny, baby squirrel in the yard, and, yes, we kept it and fed it out of the tiniest little baby bottle you have ever seen. We named him Nutsy, and he lived with us until he was too large to stay in his box. Then we set him free. Now we have two squirrels that live outside our kitchen window, and they are the cutest couple ever! They run around and chase each other and often look right in at us as if we are in the zoo! When I go out into our backyard, these squirrels dash to the nearest tree, the largest tree that they can find to get away from their predators. This is exactly what we are called to do by the Lord! When trials come and we are under attack by the difficulties of life, the safest place, the only place, the best and loveliest place for us to go is into the arms of our Savior. It is here in this very place where we will find peace, comfort, and security in knowing that he is there, working mightily to resolve our trial and restore us back to life again. Nature is full of God's glory, and if we just take the time to see the connection, we will know with all certainty that he is and will forever be our hiding place!

February 25. Waste Not, Want Not

> Consider it pure joy, my brothers,
> whenever you face trials of many kinds.
>
> —James 1:2

Wow! Now those words above are a BIG order from our heavenly Father through his disciple James: be filled with joy as you go through trials. And pure joy at that? As I was walking today, it hit me between the eyes that we should not waste one precious moment of letting the Lord carry us through the storm. So many times we pray for the trial to end, trying to push through to just get it over with quickly. But then we realize that we might have missed the joy found in drawing closer to Jesus through it all if the Lord had let us decide on the timing. Have we missed the part about finding joy in him while waiting on his perfect timing? We are to use these times of trial as deep, joyous times to celebrate our faith, not turning from the trials but into them! Just as a sailboat gathers speed by turning into the wind, let us also gather speed by turning into Jesus. "Waste not, want not." Waste not one precious moment of our trials, and we will not be left wanting, wanting to know Jesus more deeply, wanting to feel his love and compassion for us. The closer we walk with Jesus, the more we can know what it looks like to walk like him. Let's not waste any more time. Jesus is waiting!

February 26. The Collegiate Day of Prayer

> ...if my people, who are called by my name, will humble
> themselves and pray and seek my face and turn from
> their wicked ways, then I will hear from heaven and
> will forgive their sin and will heal their land.
>
> —2 Chronicles 7:14

Soon it will be the collegiate day of prayer. This day of prayer on college campuses has been revived by twenty-four collegiate ministries where 873 churches and communities will pray for 1,062 college campuses from 578 cities, fifty states, and five countries today. We are called upon to select a campus over which to pray and ask for God's Holy Spirit to protect the hearts and minds of those students who attend college there. This idea of praying over these students who will become the leaders of our families and our country began in 1823, when every major university in America decided to choose the last Thursday of February as the day to blanket the country's students in prayer, calling on the Lord to lead them and guide them on this journey. There were two goals stated at that time for which to pray:

1. A spontaneous movement of the Holy Spirit throughout the student body of America.

2. The triumph of the gospel throughout the unreached world.

Still today, this is our prayer. Students can learn everything there is to know academically, but if they are not led by faith in the Lord Jesus Christ, the most important part of their education will be missing. It is an honor for us to be able to pray over these students, asking our Father to lead them by the power of the Holy Spirit, a power that they will not find in college any other way. Let us go to our knees in prayer, covering our precious students of all ages today. Let us pray that our Father will stir in their hearts a love for him and rest in the certain knowledge that this is where the power of our country lies, in his precious hands that lead our students into the future.

February 27. Acidic to Alkaline

> The Lord is my shepherd, I shall not be in want.
> He makes me lie down in green pastures,
> he leads me beside quiet waters, he restores my soul.
>
> —Psalm 23:1–3

Apple cider vinegar. Over the years, I have had people suggest that I consume two teaspoons of this vinegar with the "mother" in it to create an alkaline system in my body. The medical world suggests that keeping our bodies in an alkaline state is best for resisting all kinds of diseases. So each day I take a cup of hot water, add two teaspoons of apple cider vinegar, and drink it down. It makes me feel amazing! In this same way, reading and absorbing the words of Jesus will change us for the better, taking us from an *acidic* frame of mind to an *alkaline* one of peace. It sounds counterintuitive to use an acid to change our systems into alkaline, but that is just the way it works. Jesus works this way also, pouring his words of joy into our bodies and minds, providing us with his kindness and sweetness. As important as drinking this apple cider vinegar may be for our health, even greater is dwelling on the words of the Lord, letting them sink deep into our minds and souls. He is the one who can return our hearts and minds to a place of comfort and restoration. Let us drink away each day the vinegar that brings good health and daily absorb the words of Jesus that restore our soul.

February 28. He Lives

> I know that my redeemer lives.
>
> —Job 19:25

Walking the other day, I started thinking about Jesus and what happens to us when we hear his name or someone speaks about him. What is the first thing that comes to our minds? Do we automatically think of a man who lived millennia ago, making him seem distant to us the same way another famous person would be, say Abraham Lincoln? When we think of Lincoln, I am sure that all of us instantly visualize what he looked like and what he did for our country. Although we may read about him and know a lot about his life, we don't really know him. We never will, because he lived quite a while ago, in a different time and way of life known to us now in America. So it may seem to some with Jesus. People may read about him and process all that there is to be known about him in text, but you and I, having been called to his side, we know him. He is not just some name in history nor a person about whom much is written yet no one will ever know in real life. He is here, in the here and now. He is present and accounted for, and we truly know him because he does still live and will continue to do so for all eternity. Remember a time recently when he spoke to you. Remember a time recently when he provided for you, protected you, and comforted you. Who beyond Jesus could still be doing these things almost two thousand years after he died? No one. Not one single, solitary person. Not even someone as amazing and admirable as Abraham Lincoln. Let us give thanks that Jesus is still here among us, providing everything that we could ever need, just as he would have done when he walked in Jerusalem, for our redeemer lives!

March 1. "From Nowhere to Somewhere"

I will lie down and sleep in peace, for you alone,
O Lord, make me dwell in safety.

—Psalm 4:8

On the program *60 Minutes* was a piece on the Lost Boys of Sudan. These young, African men were just boys when Civil War in their country broke out, killing too many people to count and leaving them homeless. A large group of these boys started out walking to freedom, traveling over a thousand miles on foot, shoeless, and without any help whatsoever. It took them—get ready for this—five years, yes, five years to arrive in Kenya, where they found refuge and safety. While in Kenya, the United States became aware of all these precious young men who had no home, no family, no identity, and started bringing them over, one by one, to America, land of the free and home of the brave. Interviewed by *60 Minutes* were several who have remained good friends, finding out how they are doing today in America. One of these young boys, now a young man, is named Abraham, and we cannot escape the irony in his name. He had a Bible that he took with him from the Sudan, five years of walking to Kenya, and on to America. This is what he said when asked about his Bible, "It's my life." Most of us today have Bibles at our fingertips, ready at a moment's notice to open and to hear from the Lord. Hearing Abraham describe his Bible as his life just says it all. He is right. The Bible is our life for it contains the inspired word of God, our Father, and what could be more important to us than that? What a group of witnesses these young men are. They love the Lord and give him the glory for their safe arrival here in the United States. The title of this piece on *60 Minutes* "From Nowhere to Somewhere" is the perfect definition of where we were—nowhere—until we accepted Christ as the Lord and Savior, and now we are somewhere, safe in his care. Let us think on these things and be glad.

March 2. Two Words

For nothing is impossible with God.

—Luke 1:37

Our minister at our church has been doing a sermon series entitled "One Word," and each week for several weeks he has preached on one word that he feels could impact our lives for Christ if we just implemented it into our minds. Tonight at church, the one word was *laughable*. Now at first thought, it is hard to grasp how the word *laughable* could possibly play into our spiritual lives. Yet the sermon was so inspiring, calling on us to think of the things all throughout our lives that we have thought laughable, never gonna happen, never thinking that anyone, maybe not even the Lord, could make this one thing come to pass, and then it does. So this is how God works. He takes our laughable thoughts and turns them into reality. We then begin to know that nothing is impossible with God. We have read about these impossible moments in the Bible becoming possible moments. Saul, slayer of Christians, becomes Paul, one of the Lord's greatest apostles. Lazarus is raised from the dead. Mary, a simple child of maybe twelve years old, has the virgin birth and delivers Jesus, and on it goes. But the two words that have made all the difference, without which none of the one words would matter, are the words we uttered when we first accepted Jesus Christ as our Lord and Savior, "I believe." That's it, "I believe." It is from these two simple words that everything changes. Our lives belong to Christ; our lives become better. Not only can one word make a huge change in our lives, but also these two words become our lives through believing in our one true Savior, Jesus Christ.

March 3. The Best Value for the Money

Freely you have received; freely give.

—Matthew 10:8

An article put out by the *Princeton Review* lists the colleges, public and private, that are the best value for the money. They have researched all the data and have come up with a viable group of schools from which to choose if you are looking for value. The University of North Carolina at Chapel Hill and Williams College are the public and private top-ranking schools, respectively. But here's the important truth about relative value: The only true best value for the money is the free gift given to us by our Savior, Jesus Christ, who freely redeems us from sin. It cost nothing. Absolutely nothing. What is surprising is that many people in this world think that if something doesn't cost anything, there's either a catch or it's not worth it because it is free. We paid nothing, yet we have everything in him. He gives this to us with no cost, absolutely nothing asked except to believe in him so that we may know him and stand on his promises here on earth. But then, even better than what he gives us each and every day that we live is that, as we are delivered home, we will live eternally in heaven, forever and always, free, freely given. He paid the price and gave us this gift. Now that is what we can know as the best value for our money, hands down, and we don't even have to poll others to know it's true, for he shows us this time and time and time again.

March 4. Thank You, Jesus

Jesus called out with a loud voice, "Father, into your
hands I commit my spirit." When he had said this,
he breathed his last.

—Luke 23:46

Thank you, Jesus! One of my dear friends had a precious, precious woman who worked for her for many years, helping take care of her children and her home. These are the people we cherish. The people who love us enough to come to our homes and care for those we love the most. She was a fairly young woman when she went to work for this family, and she worked there for many years until she grew too old to care for the children. The good news is that by this time all the children were grown and she could go to work and just be an inspiration to this family. She had the most precious spirit and was one of the strongest believers that I have ever had the blessing to know. The cutest thing is that when something good happened, she would always say, "Thank you, Jesus!" Hearing those precious words come out of her mouth with a grin as wide as the Mississippi River was a treasure that I still carry with me to this day. These three words, "Thank you, Jesus" carry such weight, for it is through them that our Lord and Savior can know that we truly thank him, thank him for the blessing that we are witnessing, thank him for who he is, thank him for loving us enough to die on a cross for our sins. It doesn't take much. It only takes these three little words to let Jesus know how grateful we truly are for all that he has done.

March 5. Spring Is Breakin'!

Because of the Lord's great love, we are not consumed,
for his compassions never fail. They are new every
morning; great is your faithfulness.

—Lamentations 3:22–23

I am pretty sure that all you have noticed that spring is on the way. The green tufts of grass poking their heads out the ground, the bushes starting to bloom with their buds getting ready to pop, trees with blossoms hanging on the ends of their boughs. Is there a better time of year than this? New beginnings, new growth. How evident is God's presence in our world. All we have to do is just look around at the beauty of this season to know that he is present. As the grass turns to green and the birds begin to chirp in the trees, we can be reminded day after day that he is here. He is with us. I was reading about the financial crisis our country is facing in the paper today, and I was comforted and inspired by what one journalist wrote, saying that our schools will still open, our military will still function, and each day will continue to unfold. Is our country facing difficult times? For sure. Does our country need to face the existing situation and do something about it? No doubt! But we can always count on our certain rock on which we stand, Jesus. He is still in the mix. He is still on the job. And if we doubt for one minute that he has left us to fend for ourselves, just go outside and soak in the wondrous gifts given by our Father through the rites of spring. It is through the glory of this time of year that we can rest assured that our Father never tires of caring for us. Whether we are actually going away on a spring break trip or staying home this time, springtime is breaking out all over, revealing with brilliant beauty the certain truth that God is on the job! We are not alone!

March 6. Selfies

> The Lord himself goes before you and will be with you;
> he will never leave you nor forsake you. Do not be afraid;
> do not be discouraged.
>
> —Deuteronomy 31:8

Isn't it just so much fun to live in the 2000s, the century of the smartphone, the fastest-moving computers, and so many other technological discoveries that keep us well-informed, fascinated, and completely entertained whenever we have a free moment to enjoy one of these? I took our granddaughter and her friend out of town for spring break, and it was so cute as they started taking selfies wherever we were. A selfie is a photo taken by the person holding the phone of herself or with someone next to her. Our granddaughter and her friend had a pictorial collection of our trip, using their cell phones to take selfie images of the two of them. When we take selfies of ourselves, we are never the only one in the photo. Our Lord, Jesus, is right there beside us, loving being a part of our lives, the most integral part of our lives. He is always in our sight, always in our selfies, for he never leaves us alone. He walks with us through every minute of every day. So when we take our next selfie, whether alone or with a friend, if we look closely, we will see the glory of Jesus standing right there beside us, sharing life with us all day long!

March 7. Apple from the Tree

> I will be a Father to you and you will be my
> sons and daughters, says the Lord Almighty.
>
> —2 Corinthians 6:18

Here I am, in the middle of spring break week. Our four-year-old grandson is in town, so I offered to take him to Jumpstreet, a place where kids of all ages can go and jump on trampolines to their hearts' delight! I always take my iPad along to entertain myself while he jumps for two hours. As luck would have it, my iPad's battery ran out. So for lack of anything else to do, I started watching the moms and grandmothers there with their children. It became so obvious which child belonged to which mom or grandmother, usually put together in my mind by the hair color, the facial features, or even the personalities. The redheaded ones were obvious, and the dimples always helped. As I sat there, my mind connected this thought to whether people we meet can know who our Father is. Do we have his warmth? Do we share his peace? Do we reflect his love for others? Can those folks that we meet day after day know that our Father is the Lord of the universe? That our Father created all that we see and all that we know? That our Father gave us a new heart for loving others as he loves us? Let us remember that those with whom we interact can catch a glimpse of God's majesty through just a smile or a simple but heartfelt hello from us, his children. As we bask in the glory of this day, given to us by our Father, God of all, may we give to those we see a tiny reflection of who our Father truly is. Just as he fed the thousands of people with a few loaves of bread, may we spread his joy one by one, until the whole world can experience his grace through us, proving that the apple truly does not fall far from the tree.

March 8. Outside the Tent

Accept one another, then, just as Christ accepted you,
in order to bring praise to God.

—Romans 15:7

A show updating the election of Pope Francis was on recently. The program made reference to the fact that he thinks outside the tent, longing to draw in those who do not feel connected, those who feel lost or not a part of something greater than themselves. What a lovely thought, this idea of being inclusive, of loving all people, even those outside the tent. This is the very call made by our Savior, Jesus, as he walked this earth and drew people to himself, all people to himself. This thought is a really good one to focus on as we go through Lent, thinking on Jesus and what this season means to us as believers. Pope Francis says, "Lent is a season that prepares us for the saving mysteries of Christ's passion, death, and resurrection...a moment of renewal which allows us to look at the needs of others with new eyes and grow in love." So as we who have been called to our Lord's side continue to reflect and pray and think on these things, let us share the complete and total joy that we know in loving him with others, those who may feel outside the tent, whether in their faith or in their daily lives. This time of renewal that we experience during Lent is reflected in the Lord's renewal of our earth as it comes back to life through the beauty of spring. As we are experiencing renewal today, may we also renew the love for life in others by touching them with our joy. Let us see others in the same way that the Lord sees us, beautiful and lovely, each and every day.

March 9. At the Foot of the Cross

Praise be to the Lord, to God our Savior,
who daily bears our burdens.

—Psalm 68:19

Comparing the children's relay game in which runners take turns running with a ball to a line ahead of them, placing the ball there, and returning to touch the hand of the next team player reflects what Jesus calls us to do time and time again in life. He calls us to pick up our balls of heavy burdens and lay them at his feet. He does not want us to pick them back up. We are to lay these burdensome trials there, right where he is standing, and leave them there. Yes, leave them there. His rules call for us to do it time and time and time again, every time that we meet one of life's troubles that is far too heavy for us to carry, and there are many to be certain. Just like the school children running this relay, some of us will easily place our load at his feet. Yet others will struggle and be tripped up, finding it much more difficult to lay them down. Jesus has promised us that he will take those right out of our hands and give us his peace, if we only let him. As we think on Easter and what it means to us as believers, let us answer his call to lay our burdens at his feet, at the foot of that glorious cross, where he is waiting, always waiting, to lighten our load.

March 10. The Shrouded Cross

> As evening approached, there came a rich man from
> Arimathea, named Joseph, who had himself become a
> disciple of Jesus. Going to Pilate, he asked for Jesus' body,
> and Pilate ordered that it be given to him. Joseph took
> the body, wrapped it in a clean linen cloth, and placed it
> in his own new tomb that he had cut out of rock.
>
> —Matthew 27:57–60

A neighbor who lives near us puts a cross in the yard every Christmas, and over it hangs a shroud symbolizing the shroud left behind by Jesus when he arose from the dead and ascended into heaven. I always find this so powerful and interesting, for they do it at Christmas and not at Easter, which is the time that might make most sense to most people. But the fact that they do it at Christmas speaks volumes to me, for it makes me remember year after precious year that although Christmas is the beginning with Jesus's birth, the true beginning for us, as believers, is Easter. Easter is when our Lord and Savior rose from the dead, leaving his tomb empty to ascend into heaven and sit at the right hand of God, the Father Almighty. This is when he went to prepare a place for us to live with him eternally, forever and forever. It is his journey through life and his rising from the dead that says it all. Christmas and Easter are forever linked in holy perfection, his birth and his ascension into heaven, and it is from these two perfect gifts given to us freely by our Father that we can know the hope found in his name—the name of Jesus.

March 11. Beauty among the Thorns

And surely I am with you always,
to the very end of the age.

—Matthew 28:20

I was walking a few days ago, just as this cold front was blowing into Dallas, turning our beautiful, springlike days into another round of blistery weather. I walked past a rose bush not yet recovered from the icy blasts of our winter past, and sitting there on one branch was just one gorgeous red rose, in full bloom, among the thorns and withered leaves left by the cold days of winter. This rose reminded me of Jesus, our beautiful Jesus, who blooms no matter what the season, who brings a beauty to our world even though it may seem dark and dreary. Just as this rose was growing so beautifully, as if it were the fullest days of spring and the earth had been revived from the winter hush, our Lord and Savior is always in full bloom, filling our hearts with his glorious warmth and beautiful grace that can only be found in his presence. He promises to be with us always, and as we gaze on something as stunning and perfect as this one single rose, we can know his promise is even more glorious than anything found here. He never fades away, no matter what the season, no matter where we are or when we need him, for he knows that we need his love and his guidance all the days of our lives. As the days of winter fade away and spring begins to burst upon the earth, let us soak in the beauty that will soon emerge from the flowers and trees and be reminded of our Savior's promise. His love for us will never fade away, just like the beauty among the thorns in the red rose that I saw today.

March 12. Enough Provides Great Wealth

> But he said to me, "My grace is sufficient for you,
> for my power is made perfect in weakness."
>
> —2 Corinthians 12:9

I recently heard this idea that if one has enough, then he or she is wealthy. How simple this thought is, grounded in truth. *Enough* is defined as "sufficient, an ample supply." This is a great thought for us to carry with us each and every day. As we apply this thought to our faith, how grand it is to know that Jesus is enough. He provides great wealth to our lives, all the wealth that we will ever need coming from his deep and abiding love for us. His grace is sufficient for every day that we live, and that is the promise he made in 2 Corinthians above. We do not have to ever wish for more than Jesus. We do not ever have to worry that we might be shortchanged by the Lord. He never fails us with his grace and mercy, always providing just the right measure of what we need. So when we worry that our needs are too big for him to handle, we can know deep in our hearts that whatever the task is, he will always provide just what we need, leaving us covered over with his love, just enough!

March 13. A Story to Tell

The angel said to the woman, "Do not be afraid, for I
know that you are looking for Jesus, who was crucified.
He is not here; he has risen, just as he said."

—Matthew 28:5–6

A friend and I were talking about writing the other day and
how we both liked thinking about words and then using them
to express our thoughts. She looked at me and said, "I need your
help. I have a story to tell." I told her, "Great! I will help you. You
tell me the story, and I can help you write it—a ghost writer so
to speak." We laughed and went on sharing time together. Later,
I thought about our conversation and thought to myself, "Every
believer has a story to tell, a story of how their Savior went to the
cross and gave his life so that we can live and live life abundantly."
Right then and there I realized that we all do have the greatest
story in the world to share, and what better time to do it than
with Easter approaching. How we each tell his story will be a
different way, our own special way, maybe with words, maybe
with actions, but always encompassed in his love. What we need
for others to know is how he loves us all, each and every one of
us, and because he loves us so, we can give love and know love. So
as we approach this Easter season and we think on Jesus and his
walk to the cross, let us begin to tell our story, his story, of how his
life changed ours, and know that our words and our actions will
open up the storybook of life and its true meaning for another
who longs to know his love.

March 14. One at a Time

> Your word is a lamp to my feet and a light
> for my path.
>
> —Psalm 119:105

I have been reading through these reflections, getting them ready for print, looking for typos or places where I have misused a word or written down the wrong resource. In doing this, I spent the last two weeks just rereading the Bible verses at the top of each of the entries, being certain that they are typed just as written in my NIV Study Bible. Although I did reread more than one verse each day, it brought me such delight to read one verse at a time, without any commentary or any other input connected to it, leaving me to digest God's words and seal them close to my heart. So often when I read the Bible I read lots of passages, not just one verse. But having the opportunity to read one verse slowly, absorbing its power, has brought clarity and a much deeper meaning to me than any other process could. So, here's my suggestion that has evolved from my own editing process. During one part of each day, read just the verse at the top of the reflection for that day, reading nothing else with it, and let it sink in, bringing your own insight and love for God's word with it. It is amazing how just these few minutes spent absorbing just one verse at a time will provide such a closeness to our Father and reveal a thought or two that we might not otherwise find any other way. What joy to be found by drawing near to our Father's heart through his very words written just for us!

March 15. "Message Failed to Send"

Then he continued, "Do not be afraid, Daniel.
Since the first day that you set your mind to gain
understanding and to humble yourself before your God,
your words were heard…

—Daniel 10:12

Whenever we get a chance to notice cell phone usage and how this one device has taken over our lives, we realize that it is a phenomenon that will define the first part of this century in the years to come. It is fascinating to notice all the people everywhere who are on their cell phones maybe talking, maybe reading e-mails, who knows, but on the phone in some manner. Cell phones have such widespread usage that we are able to use them almost anywhere we are. But lately, I have been in a few spots where I was not able to use my cell phone for texting, and this message kept popping up on my screen: "Message Failed to Send." I surprisingly find this message written in red, no less, letting me become aware that whatever I was trying to relay had not been received by my recipient. But here's the good news, news from many, many years ago and yet still true today: Messages that we send to Jesus never fail. No matter where we are or how we send them, he always receives them and hears our call. It can be a quiet whisper or the very loudest shout. He is there on the other end to receive what we need him to know. We will never have to wonder if he heard our words. We will never have to question whether or not he knows what is in our hearts. He is there—always at the other end of the line—listening, loving, and working mightily in our lives to make it better as only he can do.

March 16. Background Music

And now these three remain; faith, hope, and love.
But the greatest of these is love.

—1 Corinthians 13:13

This is a sure sign that I am getting older. Wherever I go, music of various genres is playing, usually quite loudly. Shopping, dining, doctors, it really doesn't matter the location. The world seems insistent on playing music over speakers so that everyone who is in the particular area can hear it. Now no one loves music more than I do. But it is becoming increasingly more difficult to think clearly and enjoy what we are doing because we are being inundated by music, music, music! The most interesting part of this background music is that it is not the sort of instrumentals playing softly to enhance our experience. It is up-tempo, loud, lots of words and sounds, music that keeps us from being able to hear one another. So this brings me to an aphorism that I keep running across: I have loved and been loved, all the rest is background music. Upon reading this, I immediately thought of the words written above, "And now these three remain; faith, hope, and love. But the greatest of these is love." Because God is love and he has commanded us to love one another, loving Christ, loving others, and loving ourselves is the most important part of life that we should live and act on, for love outlasts everything else. There are many kinds of love, calling us to love and be loved above all, leaving the rest to become background music. Let us start each day with that thought at the forefront of our minds. "Love one another. As I have loved you, so you must love one another" (John 13:34). And all the rest will fall in place.

March 17. Standing Firm

> But we ought always to thank God for you, brothers
> loved by the Lord, because from the beginning God
> chose you to be saved through the sanctifying work of the
> Spirit and through belief in the truth. He called you to
> this through our gospel that you might share in the glory
> of our Lord Jesus Christ. So then, brothers, stand firm
> and hold to the teachings we passed on to you,
> whether by word of mouth or by letter.
>
> —2 Thessalonians 2:13–15

Today, I started thinking about a trip that we took several years ago with our children to the Bahamas. They all know that I have an aversion to water unless it is coming from a showerhead. But two of them decided to go parasailing, and my husband and I were offered the opportunity to go out in a dinghy to follow their boat and watch this exciting flight. When we returned, the little boat that we were in pulled up onto the shore, but the waves kept rolling in, lifting it up every few minutes or so. The kind man who had been assisting us on the boat ride held out his hand to help me out of the boat. I had not noticed that the boat was being ever so slightly lifted periodically by the gentle waves. So step out of the boat I did. However, at that very same moment, the boat lifted up, I missed my footing, and I face planted right into the sand and surf and all those things that I am not too fond of touching. I feel pretty certain that this will remain one of our children's greatest memories of their mom—biting it in the ocean. It reminds me of some words spoken by our president Abraham Lincoln: "Be sure you put your foot in the right place. Then stand firm." Oh, how true his words are on many levels, literally and figuratively. In applying them to our faith, we have been given the gracious gift by Jesus of placing our feet in the right place, in his perfect care, because he loves us so. We can now stand firm in our faith, knowing that it is through the power of the Lord that, no matter what waves of life come along and try to knock us down, we will stay upright through his power. He has given us this free gift of faith through which we can withstand all the waves of life, standing firm in his footsteps.

March 18. Eggs Galore!

How great is the love the Father has lavished on us,
that we should be called children of God!

—1 John 3:1

I have been spending the last few days getting our eggs ready for our grandchildren to hunt on Easter morning, as our family gathers for a sweet time together. I have spent some time trying to decide what to put in these plastic eggs that the children would actually want and their parents would be happy to take home. That's the trick. In the past, I have filled them with tiny trinkets and small candies, and, most of the time, I am left with tiny trinkets and small candies. Two of our grandchildren have outgrown this fun, so I am hoping that I have enough eggs to make it fun, yet not so many that I am eating tiny candies until summer! I realized that the greatest thing that they could find in their eggs this year was the confirmation of how much they are loved, loved by me and my husband. But more importantly, they are loved by a father who will always keep them by his side and carry them through life as the cherished people that they are to him. As we read above, our Father lavishes love on us, and don't we know that is so? This year, not only will they find treats, but also messages of love from their Jesus, the one who loves them most. They will be reminded this Easter and going forward that the greatest love of all is the love of the Savior, whose greatest gift was what he did for us on Easter. As long as we all remember that Jesus loves us, this we know, then all our lives will be filled with the loveliest surprises we could find, just like Easter eggs on Easter morning!

March 19. The Golden Egg

> If you love me, you will obey what I command.
> And I will ask the Father, and he will give you another
> Counselor to be with you forever—the Spirit of truth.
>
> —John 14:15–17

It's Easter week. Praise be to God for all that he is and all that he has given us as we celebrate the Risen Lord this Sunday. Jesus has prepared an Easter egg basket for each of us. This basket, however, is filled with eggs that will never melt, never spoil, and never be used up in any way. These eggs are forever eggs, available to all people who love the Lord, given freely by him. Inside our basket lay beautiful, brightly colored eggs. As we open up the eggs, inside we find the fruit of the Spirit: love, joy, peace, patience, kindness, goodness, faithfulness, gentleness, and self-control. These special eggs filling our Easter basket are pure and perfect gifts given by our Lord and Savior for us to treasure. But then, as we finish opening these wonderful eggs, we find nestled down in the middle of all them the golden egg. Yes, that's right. Jesus gives each of us the golden egg—that most treasured and sought-after prize. As we gently pick it up, turning it around in our hands and wondering what precious gift is inside, we carefully open it up to see what he has given us that could be more precious than the ones that came before. Inside our golden egg is the gift of the Counselor, the Holy Spirit that Jesus promised us in John 14:15–17. Jesus says that he petitions his Father on our behalf to send the Holy Spirit to dwell in us and with us forever to teach us everything and remind us of what he has told us. This golden egg is a gift that we could not even have ever imagined, a gift too grand to conceive in our human mind. To think that our Lord and Savior, Jesus Christ, thought of me and you as he made his way to the cross brings us to our knees. He reminds us of whose we are, encouraging us to enjoy those brightly colored eggs known as the fruit of the Spirit. As we go through this Easter week, may we remember how wide and how deep the love of Christ is for us that he would die on a cross for our sins. Let us call upon our Counselor, the Holy Spirit, found in our precious golden egg, each and every day to help us on our way.

March 20. Hosanna in the Highest

> The crowds that went ahead of him and those that
> followed shouted, "Hosanna to the Son of David!"
> "Blessed is he who comes in the name of the Lord!"
> "Hosanna in the highest!"
>
> —Matthew 21:9

Palm Sunday was last Sunday, and now we are looking to Easter, the day our precious Lord arose from the dead to sit at the right hand of his Father, our Father, our God. In church on Palm Sunday, our minister did a lovely service on "Jesus—I am." During it, he mentioned the word "Hosanna" several times. I decided to look into it and try to have a deeper understanding of this word used so often on Palm Sunday. An Internet search shows, "Hosanna was the shout of praise or adoration made in recognition of the messiahship of Jesus on his triumphal entry into Jerusalem." It goes on to explain that it stems from the verb originating first in Latin, then Greek, then Hebrew, meaning "Save now, we pray." In picturing this precious scene of Jesus's triumphal entry into Jerusalem on Palm Sunday, we can visualize the crowds calling his name, crying out "Hosanna in the highest." We can almost feel the energy and excitement of that day, knowing that Jesus, their Jesus, was on the way to giving us eternal life through his walk to the cross. Our Savior, the one and only one who deserves our shouts of praise, "Hosanna, praise in the highest," had come then and is still here today to save us from ourselves and our sin. Then as is now, all of us, his people, cry out to him for his mercy to wash over us and "Save now, we pray." That is the message of Easter. He has come now, he has saved us now, and he will continue to guide us, save us, and love us no matter what. He paid the price, and we are the victors, now and forevermore!

March 21. Quack! Quack!

Be imitators of God, therefore, as dearly loved children,
and live a life of love, just as Christ loved us and
gave himself up for us as a fragrant offering and
sacrifice to God.

—Ephesians 5:1

Rabbits, ducks, and chicks, oh my! Easter will be here soon, and when I think of Easter I can't help but remember those brightly dyed chicks and ducks that we used to see being sold on the side of the road when I was growing up: hot pink, blue, and green. Being the animal lover that I am, I got a baby duck one Easter when I was in middle school. Now I don't remember exactly how this duck was able to live in my room, but that he did. He even slept with me on my pillow. We were close, this duck and I. It is almost like he was imprinted on me, you know, when an animal at its earliest age believes that someone else other than its mother is its mother. That was how my pet duck was. And that is how we first come to know God as our Father. He imprints us with his love and we are never the same. We grow closer and closer to him as our faith matures, for our hearts are tied to his. Just like my duck that followed me around and always wanted to be near me, we long to cling to our Father and have him near. As we draw closer to Easter, if by chance you see a duck, a rabbit, or a chick, think on that imprinting capability and know with certainty that God is our Father. Let us remember that his fatherly love has been imprinted on our hearts forever, and we don't even have to be dyed a bright color for him to find us!

March 22. Come as You Are!

I delight greatly in the Lord; my soul rejoices in my God.
For he has clothed me with the garments of salvation and
arrayed me in a robe of righteousness.

—Isaiah 61:10

Parties—so many parties, so little time! Usually at the bottom of a party invitation is the directive of what your attire should be: formal, casual, festive cocktail, come as you are. Now there is a directive that really works for me. Those parties where you get to just drop on over and have a great time, not worrying about what you have on, makes life easy, breezy! I love to look around and notice where the party people have been prior to arriving: tennis game, luncheon, exercising, or a sporting event for a child. You see anything and everything. That is exactly what the invitation from the Lord says to those he has invited to come to his party—come as you are! Thank goodness we get to come as we are, with the tears in our clothes, the stains on our shirts, and even our messy hair, for we are all earthly messes. But here's the good news: We look perfect in his eyes. He has cleansed us of our sins and removed them as far as the east is from the west! He has dressed us in robes of white, the garments of salvation, and arrayed us in robes of righteousness. We know without a doubt that there are no finer garments than these; nothing that we can borrow nor buy to wear to his party is more precious than these perfect gifts of finery. So as we enjoy the festive events, let us know with all certainty that we are always invited to his party, and he has even provided the perfect party clothes!

March 23. Built with Love

> And he is the head of the body, the church; he is the
> beginning and the firstborn.
>
> —Colossians 1:18

Looking out of our back window, you will see the most intricately built bird's nest gently sitting under the eaves of our garage right behind a drainage pipe. In watching what happens there, we have seen the mother bird bring pieces of wood, strips of paper, and strands of who knows what to build this precious home for the eggs that she would soon lay there. As I looked at that nest and watched the time and effort that it took for her to build this special place for her family, I was reminded of how Jesus takes us, each of us, just like the broken bits of wood, the twigs, and leftover parts in this nest and gathers us together to become his church, his nest of believers where we are comforted and cared for by our Savior, our Lord, Jesus Christ. How blessed we all are to have been carefully found and placed in the nest of the Lord. So let us go forth this Easter season and worship the one who made us, the one who knows us, and the one who loves us as the body of Christ Jesus, our Lord and Savior.

March 24. They Have Been Adopted!

> Praise be to the God and Father of our Lord Jesus Christ,
> who has blessed us in the heavenly realms with every
> spiritual blessing in Christ. For he chose us in him before
> the creation of the world to be holy and blameless in his
> sight. In love he predestined us to be adopted as his sons
> through Jesus Christ, in accordance with his pleasure and
> will—to the praise of his glorious grace, which he has
> freely given us in the One he loves.
>
> —Ephesians 1:3–6

A sweet friend of mine knows how crazy I am about dogs, and she feels the same way. As we were together one day, she said that two precious dogs had been on her front porch that morning, and they seemed to be lost. She rushed back to her house in hopes of finding them still there so that she could take care of them. These precious pups were still in her front yard. One of them was walking on three legs, holding her paw up, not wanting to step on it. My friend took the injured dog to the veterinarian to check on her paw. All the bones on the top of her foot were broken, so the vet set her foot. Then she was able to walk on all four feet. Not being able to keep the dogs herself, my friend took them to the SPCA, where they assured her that these dogs would be adopted, and adopted quickly. Indeed they were! Even the one with the broken foot got adopted the very first day! Such good news for all us dog lovers to hear: "They have been adopted!" Sweet, sweet words, and the very same sweet words that we know when we become adopted into our Father's family of faith through accepting Jesus Christ as our Lord and Savior. He takes us where we are, whether we come walking on all four feet or with a broken paw. As it is written in Ephesians above, we are his sons and daughters—holy and blameless—whom he loves. We have been adopted by the Lord of the universe, forever and ever. Amen!

March 25. Time in a Bottle

> There is a time for everything,
> and a season for every activity under heaven.
>
> —Ecclesiastes 3:1

Time—the one thing in life that we cannot buy, we cannot borrow, we cannot own, we cannot get back. It is simply a gift from the Lord, twenty-four hours a day that we have to live life and know him as our Father. All of us use time so differently, and as I think on this, I realize that how we use time relates to our personalities and our interests and our gifts. These sunny days are the ones that we would love to put in a bottle and save for another time when the winter winds are blowing and we are chilled to the bone. Seeing young love in full bloom, seeing the sweetness as it unfolds into a relationship. If only they could put these special days in a bottle to use when life gets hard and times get rough. Yet the Holy Spirit tells us that it is only through trials and hardships that we can draw closest to the Lord and know the gifts of grace and mercy that he has given us by his life, death, and resurrection. So, knowing that "there is a time for everything," let us thank God for all the times of our lives, the good, the bad, and everything in between. For all our times come wrapped in the love of the Lord.

March 26. Peter Pan

> Just as Moses lifted up the snake in the desert,
> so the Son of Man must be lifted up,
> that everyone who believes in him may have eternal life.
>
> —John 3:14

Last week before our daughter's wedding, she and I were up in our attic looking for something she needed. A dear friend called at that time, but my phone was downstairs and I did not hear it ring. I sent my friend a text when I got downstairs saying that I was sorry that I had missed her call and explained that we were up in the attic. She asked if we were looking for something old in reference to brides and the saying that they need "something old, something new, something borrowed, and something blue" on their wedding day. I jokingly replied that I am the something old. Laughing to myself later about my joke, I realized that believers are never truly old, for we will spend eternity with our Lord and Savior forever and ever. What an empowering thought for us to hold on to, knowing that we will be spending eternity with Jesus, thanks to his death on the cross for our salvation. Things of this earth have a life span, so to speak, yet we, as believers, have an eternal expiration date. For us, we are given renewed strength and joy with which to live each day. We will live forever with the one who loves us the most. So as we move closer and closer to celebrating the Risen Lord this Easter, we know the joyous gift to come that only God can give—eternal life with our Savior.

March 27. You Get What You Pay For

Let us fix our eyes on Jesus, the author and
perfecter of our faith, who for the joy set before
him endured the cross, scorning its shame,
and sat down at the right hand of the throne of God.

—Hebrews 12:2

"You get what you pay for." It seems that these types of catch phrases were more prevalent during my youth, coming from my parents and other adults that I knew, words of wisdom, so to speak. You do get what you pay for, meaning that generally speaking greater value comes with greater cost. Now many times we can get a deal, finding something that is worth more than we are being asked to pay for it. But usually we really do get a better job if we are willing to pay a little more for quality work. I had my windows cleaned a few weeks ago, and the crew who came to do the work did cost a little more but, boy, was the job superb! It was so worth the extra expense to get a job done well. Here is something that we, as believers, get that we didn't pay for: eternal life given freely to us by our Lord and Savior who paid it all. He went to the cross to pay for our sins, and we don't have to pay a thing. He paid and we get. It's that simple and that amazing! He paid it all so that we can have it all. Let us praise him and worship him this Easter for giving us a gift freely given yet worth more than all the gold on earth!

March 28. Too Small

> How great is the love the Father has
> lavished on us, that we should be called
> children of God! And that is what we are!
>
> —1 John 3:1

So many times in life we make a mistake in thinking that something is too small to be what we need it to be. Perhaps we are having a party and believe that the party room will not hold everyone, but then the guests arrive and they have plenty of room to enjoy themselves. Or perhaps we think that last year's clothes will be too small this year, but they fit just fine. So on it goes in life. We underestimate different situations in our minds, sometimes even the power of our God. We guess at things, and mistakes are made. This is exactly what happens when we guess that our God is too small to handle our problems. We think that no one, not even God, could possibly handle what we have going on in our lives. Nothing could be further from the truth. God is bigger than anything—yes, anything—that we will face in this lifetime. He can handle anything that comes our way. So as we face difficulties, let's not make our God too small, for he is bigger than life—your life, my life, all lives—and there is nothing that he cannot handle through the power of the cross.

March 29. It's Never Over

> Now that same day (after Peter had found Jesus's tomb
> empty) two of them were going to a village called
> Emmaus about seven miles from Jerusalem. They were
> talking with each other about everything that had
> happened. As they talked and discussed these things with
> each other, Jesus himself came up and walked along with
> them; but they were kept from recognizing him.
>
> —Luke 24:13–16

Easter day has recently passed, when Christians all over the world celebrated our Risen Lord. What a day of rejoicing, to thank God for the life of his Son, giving up his life to save us from our sins. It's almost hard to wrap our minds around a gift such as this. We had an Easter egg hunt here at our home with our grandchildren. I had bought twelve golden eggs for them to find, and as the hunt progressed, I counted them to see if these eggs were all found. As the day ended, I realized that one of these golden eggs was still somewhere in our yard, possibly hidden from sight, yet still there. So I went about, looking for this one egg but not seeing it anywhere. Then as I looked more closely, I saw a peeping of gold where the golden egg had accidentally been stepped on and driven deep into the ground. Some days this is what it feels like for us with Jesus. We need him and we look for him, yet we cannot find him. We start frantically searching, spinning around and losing our calm. Then he appears. He was there. He was always there, just like this golden egg on Easter. Yet often we cannot find him for we let the world and its pressure distract us from seeking his face. Once we focus on him, we are covered with his calm and peace like never before. Did he just show up? Not hardly! As our lives move along and we need Jesus, may we remember to first seek his face. Even though Easter is officially over, it's never truly over, for he came so that he will forever be here, there, and everywhere to provide us with his mercy and grace.

March 30. Deal Maker

> God is not a man, that he should lie, nor a son of man,
> that he should change his mind. Does he speak and then
> not act? Does he promise and not fulfill? I have received a
> command to bless; he has blessed, and I cannot change it.
>
> —Numbers 23:19–20

I was walking at the mall last week, and a guy passed me in a T-shirt that simply said "Deal Maker." That's it, Deal Maker. I was in the T-shirt design business years ago, so I always find screen-printed T-shirts interesting on some level. Now I didn't stop him and ask exactly what these words on his shirt meant, but the word "deal" has many definitions in the dictionary. In reference to the phrase "deal maker," it probably means to trade, do business, a transaction. It seems to me that humans are the deal makers. We are the ones who do deals, and sometimes these deals fall through. Because we are human, things don't always go right on our end. But Jesus isn't a deal maker, for his promises never fail like human deals can and will. He doesn't bargain with us nor make transactions with us. We can stand on the promises of our Lord and Savior, for never once has he not upheld his end of the deal. His deals really aren't deals at all, they are promises made by the Savior of the universe, the one who made us, who knows us inside out, and who is always there to guide and direct us in the way we should go. So as we move about our day and deals are made, some good and some not so good, let us rest easy tonight knowing that Jesus makes promises that he will keep, no matter what comes our way, no matter what deals make or break, all day long.

March 31. Spring, Magnificent Spring

> Blessed be your glorious name and may it be exalted
> above all blessing and praise. You alone are the Lord. You
> made the heavens, even the highest heavens, and all their
> starry hosts, the earth and all that is on it, the seas and
> all that is in them. You give life to everything, and the
> multitudes of heaven worship you.
>
> —Nehemiah 9:5–6

I love the spring months, when everything begins to bloom, revealing God's majesty. Just as certain as I am that the sun will rise in the sky tomorrow, I know that spring is right around the corner. It is so exciting to watch spring slowly begin to reveal its glory as the bulbs in the ground peak their heads out of the dirt, letting us know that a beautiful bloom will soon arrive. We have a pink dogwood tree in our backyard that, once it blooms, has breathtaking flowers for only a week, possibly two. Then the blooms turn to leaves for the rest of the season. I love waiting on the arrival of the flowers of this precious tree. It doesn't cost us a thing to receive these special gifts from God. He just lays them at our feet, giving us gifts of delight all day long. There are no sweeter days than these spring days. The sky turns a brilliant blue, and we know that we are loved by the Father of the universe. In this same way, we know his love each and every day that we live in the smile of a stranger, in the laughter of a child, in the hug of a friend, in the sweetness of life that our Father so graciously provides day in and day out. These are the gifts that matter. These are priceless gifts from our Father who loves us so. So as spring begins to creep our way, let us sit back and enjoy each of his radiant glories coming soon to you and me.

April 1. Time Well Spent

> ...for it is time to seek the Lord,
> until he comes and showers righteousness on you.
>
> —Hosea 10:12

Solitude. This is a word that is hard for people to discuss or even know how to process in their lives. A famous astronaut claims that even he is uncomfortable with solitude, and we can all imagine that he has experienced plenty of it. That pretty much sums it up, it seems, for many people. Not only finding solitude but being able to appreciate solitude is problematic for some people. There are all kinds of people in this world, and some of them can be defined as being people persons. They love being in the presence of others all the time. Then there are those people who long to be alone, thriving on solitude, being alone, only with themselves. As believers, we all know for certain that while we may be physically alone in our solitude time, we are truly never alone. Our Father, our heavenly Father, is always with us even in the quietest or loneliest moments of our lives. Whenever it is that we find solitude, whether for several days or a part of a day or even a few moments in time, we cannot put a price on this priceless time in solitude. As we sit and observe his world and talk to the Lord about whatever it is that we need to say, we can come into his presence and know him for who he is, our Creator, our Maker, the one who made us and loves us and calls us to be his own. What more could we possibly want than to spend time in the presence of God, feeling his love wash over us, stripping away the pressures of the world and all its difficulties for a time, time well spent, in the solitude of God's love.

April 2. *The Giving Tree*

> Whoever does not love does not know God, because
> God is love. This is how God showed his love among us:
> He sent his one and only Son into the world so that we
> might live through him.
>
> —1 John 4:8

I am sure that most of us have read the book *The Giving Tree* by Shel Silverstein. This is a book about a tree that is a person, if you will, for it can speak, has feelings, and reveals a loving spirit. I am going with the interpretation that I best remember. It is a story of a tree that continues to love a small boy as he grows up, longing to give him anything that he asks for that the tree can provide. As the boy gets older and older, the tree, having a heart full of love for this boy and wanting to give him his heart's desire, finds creative and precious ways to supply whatever the boy is asking for. Some of us can find this story relatable to Jesus's love for us, the one who loves us beyond anything that we could imagine. Jesus loves us even when we may seem unlovable, just as the boy in the story becomes at times. The tree, named The Giving Tree because his whole existence is spent giving unconditional love and comfort to this boy, leads us to remember that this is how the Lord loves us. The boy in the story could not have lived without the love of his tree, and we too cannot live the life we are called to live without the love of Jesus. Jesus gave, gives, and will continue giving for all eternity a love that is hard to even wrap our minds around, just as the love we read about given by this tree to the boy who means everything to him. So no matter how you interpret this well-known and highly thought of children's book, *The Giving Tree*, it is always inspiring to find a story written for any age that points us to Jesus, even if it is a tree that leads us there.

April 3. You Got This!

> Great peace have they who love your law,
> and nothing can make them stumble.
>
> —Psalm 119:165

A commercial came on the television last night that teaches you how to invest your money and make a profit from it. The advertising line used is "For all the confidence you need…You got this!" They go on to say that they will deliver tools, education, and support to help you develop your plan. This, to me, sounds exactly like the life plan laid out for us by Jesus. Believing in him provides us with all the confidence we need to face whatever may come our way. He has given us the tools, education, and support to help us develop our plan. Through knowing his word and seeing his care for us in all things, we can rest assured that we are completely prepared with all we will ever need to live life. We have been educated through studying his word as to how to live and go through each day. Best of all, Jesus provides us with his perfect support to deal with the daily pulls of life. Just like this company ends its advertising with "You got this," we got this! And it's all due to the love of our Savior, Jesus Christ. We got him, and with that comes everything necessary to wake up each day and live in his light, bringing with it a confidence like none other.

April 4. As the World Turns

> Look at the birds of the air; they do not sow or reap or
> store away in barns, and yet your heavenly Father feeds
> them. Are you not much more valuable than they?
> Who of you by worrying can add a single hour to his life?
>
> —Matthew 6:26

When I was in college, I lived in my sorority house, and some of my sorority sisters were completely addicted to the daytime TV show *As the World Turns*. Not being one to add unnecessary drama to my life, I wasn't interested in this show. I would come back from class to find hordes of them gathered around the television in the living room, obsessed with each word that was being said. Oddly enough, I woke up last night, thinking and praying about the events of late in the world, and the title of that show came to mind. I was reminded that no matter how our world turns, our Father is still on his throne. At times it seems as if we are spinning out of control, and it becomes difficult to visualize how to get it back on track. But we must remember that nothing escapes the hand of the Lord, for he made this world and everything in it. He will never take his eyes off it. We should not forget that he was, is, and will always be moving his hand over the universe, involved in each and every aspect of what is going on here. So when things seem to be spiraling in a downward circle, whether it be in world events or in our own lives, let us count on his promise so well told by Whitney Houston in a song, "His Eye is on the Sparrow," based on a hymn by the same name by Civilla D. Martin: "Why should I be discouraged / Why should the shadows come /.../ When Jesus is my portion / A constant Friend is He / His eye is on the sparrow / And I know He watches me."

April 5. Perfect Vision

> This is what the Lord says: "Let not the wise man boast
> of his wisdom or the strong man boast of his strength or
> the rich man boast of his riches, but let him who boasts
> boast about this: that he understands and knows me,
> that I am the Lord who exercises kindness, justice, and
> righteousness on earth, for in these things I delight,"
> declares the Lord.
>
> —Jeremiah 9:23–24

Walking today, my contact became cloudy and I was not able to see very well. This created somewhat of a problem for me because I like to save worms that are stuck on the concrete, picking them up and returning them to the grass where they will thrive. Somehow this act reminds me of how our Savior has saved each of us. These worms get onto the concrete and cannot seem to maneuver themselves back to the grassy areas where they can live without struggling. That is how some of us have felt before. Yet Jesus always picks us up and restores us to the grassy area of our lives. So here I am today, walking along, picking up sticks that look like worms and probably skipping over some of the worms looking like sticks that needed help. How blessed we are that we have a Father who has perfect vision and never loses sight of us and where we are, especially when we are in need of help. No matter where we may walk this day or tomorrow or the next, how precious to know that he never glances away and will always see us. He sees with perfect eyes, no blurry vision with the Lord, Jesus Christ!

April 6. Flip the Switch!

> But you are a chosen people, a royal priesthood,
> a holy nation, a people belonging to God,
> that you may declare the praises of him who called
> you out of darkness into his wonderful light.
>
> —1 Peter 2:9

The garage to our home is connected to our house in the back, and we have a garage door that goes up and down electronically. The other day it was making a funny sound, and I went out to see what was the matter. Whenever I open the door leading into my garage, it is as dark as the darkest night. I started thinking about how I always know right where the light switch is, even though it is so dark in our garage that I cannot see to turn it on. I can immediately touch the switch for the light, flipping it on, flooding our garage with light. I never miss, not even once. We all have this same opportunity in turning on the light of our world, Jesus, every time that we need him. Because we know him and love him, we can immediately flip his switch on and have his light brighten our lives. What glory to be found in the truth that he is right there, whether we are in the dark or not, ever present, ever ready. Let's make that our first objective, flooding our lives with the light of love that only Christ can bring.

April 7. Safety Net

I will lie down and sleep in peace, for you alone,
O Lord, make me dwell in safety.

—Psalm 4:8

Walking yesterday through the neighborhood, I saw multiple tree limbs that had recently fallen. These were not just tiny limbs but big, thick limbs off big, thick trees. The limbs had fallen unexpectedly without warning due to a sudden storm. So often life's limbs come crashing down around us in much the same way. But we have a safety net that keeps us from being crushed beneath the weight of these limbs—Jesus. Because of his unfailing love for us, we can walk with complete confidence knowing that when the limbs of trials do come falling down, often very unexpectedly, we have Jesus who will keep them from pinning us under their weight as he pulls us free from the difficulties through his never-failing mercy and grace. We do not have to walk through life looking all around nor worrying about what may come our way. Jesus has gone before us, enabling us to walk in a limb-free zone. How great it is to have a Savior whose power is mighty and can clear our path of all life's limbs so that we can walk without fear again and again.

April 8. Sweet Surprise!

> But each man has his own gift from God;
> one has this gift, another has that.
>
> —1 Corinthians 7:7

Surprises! What is more fun than receiving a surprise when you least expect it? It really doesn't matter how old you are to love a surprise. I am not sure which is more fun, being the recipient of the surprise or the one who gives it. So here I am, the week of our daughter's wedding, and much to my surprise, our azaleas had budded out and were getting ready to burst into full bloom! I couldn't have planned it better. Azaleas have a very short blooming cycle, revealing their glorious flowers for only a short while in a blaze of glory. The day of the wedding, the bushes were full of gorgeous, hot pink blooms. This sweet surprise for me made me realize how many times the Lord showers us with these joys when we least expect it. They will not always come in the form of blooming flowers. They will be revealed in various ways through every aspect of our lives. He delights in loving us in this way. What a Father to surprise us time and time again!

April 9. You're in the Street, Son

I am the Lord your God, who teaches you what is best
for you, who directs you in the way you should go.

— Isaiah 48:17

I was just about finished walking Mojo, my dog. As we stepped off a curb and into the street, he balked. He stopped right in the middle of the street, not wanting to move in any direction. I looked at him and said, "You're in the middle of the street, Son." I couldn't figure out what he was trying to do. Then all of a sudden, I realized that he had found some food that was smashed on the street, right in the middle of where we were crossing. He tried so hard to get some of that food off the street. I managed to get him to keep walking, fearing that a car would wheel around the corner and hit one or both of us! How many times have we heard these words from Jesus as we are walking through life, "You are standing in the middle of the street, Son"? Just as any of us would be concerned for someone we love who is standing in the middle of the street, even more so our Savior loves us and wants to keep us from harm, getting us out the street to safety. We need to have ears to hear and hearts to believe that when he speaks to us, it is out of love and complete concern for our well-being. May we respond with thanks to the one who made us for keeping us out of harm's way. When we hear him say that we are standing in the street, let's heed his precious words of caution and get moving in the right direction. Then we will always end up on the right side of the street!

April 10. You Light up My Life

> ...if you spend yourselves in behalf of the hungry
> and satisfy the needs of the oppressed,
> then your light will rise in the darkness,
> and your night will become like noonday.
>
> —Isaiah 58:10

Fireflies have always held a fascination for our youngest child. When she was around four, she could not wait for early summer to arrive, for she knew that the fireflies would soon light up the night as their lightbulbs twinkled in the dark of night. So many spring evenings we would spend outside just as darkness would consume the day. Having jar in hand, she would use her tiny, tiny hands and snatch a firefly in flight as soon as its light blinked on and off. I don't do too well with trapping anything in a jar. So once she had plopped three or four into her jar, delightfully watching their lights illuminate the dusk, I would encourage her to let them go so that they could continue on, lighting up the night for others to enjoy. I love to imagine our Father watching us in the same way. Somehow I can envision God sitting in heaven, and as soon as we act kindly or help someone, our spiritual lights blink, and he smiles. Similar to watching the lights of a city pop on during a winter's evening high on a hill, let us blink our spiritual lights for his enjoyment often and with love as we go about our lives, doing random acts of kindness that light up the lives of others. Random acts of kindness, so easy to do, so important to God. Blink on today. Let the light show begin!

April 11. Hot and Cold

> Because God wanted to make the unchanging nature of
> his purpose very clear to the heirs of what was promised,
> he confirmed it with an oath.
>
> —Hebrews 6:17

Texas weather—it truly defines in realistic terms the saying hot and cold. One day, we wake up and it is sunny and seventy-five degrees outside. The next day, we awaken to a blustery day of winds and forty degrees of chilly weather. But I do believe that the weather is one thing that we Texans love about living here. We never really know what's coming next, weather-wise! The phrase "hot and cold," is often used in reference to people and their approach to something. One day they will be hot about an idea, then the next day they will have turned cold to it, changing their minds as quickly as our Texas weather. Hot and cold, an ever-changing approach to things. We are blessed to have a Savior who is never hot and cold. He is never one to change his love for us nor his passion for caring for us. We can rest securely tonight knowing that, as the sun rises in the sky, the Lord will be the same tomorrow and forever, never deciding that he has better things to do than to shepherd us, than to love us, than to care for us and to provide exactly what we may need each day. Let us give him the glory for always thinking of us, his children whom he loves.

April 12. Patience Is a Virtue

> But the fruit of the Spirit is…patience.
>
> —Galatians 5:22

I am just crazy about my cell phone. But I have found lately that cell phone usage can really try my patience, especially when I am waiting on someone to back out of a parking space, whose backing car lights are on, yet no movement is forthcoming. So I wait, and I wait, and I look around for other potential parking spaces. There are not any. Sitting there, I am absolutely certain that the driver has popped into the car, turned on the motor, and is now checking e-mails or texts. Remembering that I am just as guilty of this as the next, I continue to try to be patient. How glorious to have a Savior who never becomes impatient, who never gives up on us and moves on to another when we are not relying on him. His patience in waiting on us to talk with him, to share our lives with him, to love him is never-ending, for he loves us more deeply than the human mind can imagine. As we pull out those phones and begin another message of some sort, let us first chat with the Lord who deserves our undivided attention and can't wait to hear from us, even if we just say "hello!"

April 13. Life Is Good!

> The Lord is my Shepherd, I shall not be in want. He
> makes me lie down in green pastures, he leads me beside
> quiet waters, he restores my soul. He guides me in paths
> of righteousness for his name's sake. Even though I walk
> through the valley of the shadow of death, I will fear
> no evil, for you are with me. Your rod and your staff,
> they comfort me. You prepare a table before me in the
> presence of mine enemies. You anoint my head with oil;
> my cup overflows. Surely goodness and love will follow
> me all the days of my life, and I will dwell in the house of
> the Lord forever.
>
> —Psalm 23

Many years ago, a friend and I decided to go into business screen printing T-shirts and other promotional items. Because of this, I always seem to notice what is on a T-shirt that someone is wearing. A line of screen-printed goods just came out with this catch phrase written on them: Life Is Good. Hopefully these products will inspire us to remember that life is good. But as we all know, life does have its ups and downs. So the question is, *Is life really good all the time?* The unspoken yet critical part of this message is that no matter what journey our life is taking today, life is good as long as we know Jesus. Having Jesus in our hearts is what makes life good each and every day. If our lives are going along smoothly for a time, then thank you, Jesus! If our lives are on a bumpy road, making this journey one of difficulty, then thank you, Jesus! He is traveling the road beside us, providing strength, comfort, and love along the way. All our journeys lead us to cling to Jesus and know him for who he is, everything that we could ever need. And to know that he has gone before us with each step we take assures us that, yes, life is good, for Jesus will provide. He is the good news, after all.

April 14. Nailed It!

As iron sharpens iron, so one man sharpens another.

—Proverbs 27:17

Walking, walking, and it seems that I am always looking, looking to be sure that I do not trip on the uneven sidewalks. I find small things along the way: pieces of glass, rubber bands, nails— lots of nails. So about those nails. I always pick them up, not wanting to leave them behind for someone to run over, for I have experienced many a flat tire produced by a nail along the way. Picking up a wayward nail, I looked at it and thought of what the Lord says about iron sharpening iron. Just as a nail can be sharpened by rubbing it against another, we will be sharpened by others, refining our character. This will lead us to become better—kinder, more loving, more helpful, more like Jesus. We are blessed to be able to grow through the love of others who sharpen us each day through their love for the Lord.

April 15. Faithful and True

The Lord, the King of Israel, is with you;
never again will you fear any harm.

—Zephaniah 3:15

So there she is, this mother bird of ours, sitting on that beautiful nest that she has painstakingly made. She has laid her precious eggs, and she is sitting, and sitting, and sitting, all day long, never leaving except for a quick drink of water or a quick bite to eat. All around her is chaos, for Mojo, my dog, is going crazy at the moment due to the never-ending construction of the new house next door. We can learn so very much from observing nature, and here it is at its best! This mother bird reminds us of who we can be, who we are meant to be, thanks to the call of the Lord to be his own. We too can now sit among the chaos, calm and steadfast, assured that everything will be all right because he loves us so. Our bird has been given the ability to persevere by her maker no matter what may come, and he has given us this same perfect gift. We can rely on him to protect us, strengthen us, and encourage us whatever comes our way. We can hear his reassuring voice speaking to us this promise that "the Lord, the King of Israel, is with you; never again will you fear any harm." Let us think on this promise as the days unfold and step out with the same faith and strength seen in this precious mother bird. We will never again fear harm, for he is with us, our Protector, our Savior, our Lord of Lords!

April 16. Treasures of Gold

> The Lord your God is with you, he is mighty to save.
> He will take great delight in you, he will quiet you
> with his love, he will rejoice over you with singing.
>
> —Zephaniah 3:17

Each day as I write, I turn to my Bible to find a verse that relates well to what I am thinking about that day. It is always there in the Bible, not very hard to find. God has given us all the words that we need to know him, to love him, and to trust in him. I came across this verse from Zephaniah. When I read it, I felt complete. We are empowered by that first thought: "The Lord your God is with you." He is stepping in tandem with us throughout each and every day. We can know that no matter what any day brings, God, the Lord of the universe, is with us! It goes on to say that "He is mighty to save." Mighty to save us! This adds another layer of peace to what we already know, that he is with us and he is mighty to save us. The next sentence gives us such joy to know that he takes great delight in us. In us? Yes, us! Then he assures us that he will quiet us with his love. Reading the last thought has to bring a smile to our faces, to know that our Father who made us will rejoice over us with singing. We can thank our Father for these precious words in Zephaniah that comfort us, encourage us, wash over us with his love, fill us with joy. Treasures of gold brought to us by our Lord and Savior whom we celebrate as our Risen Lord! Praise be to God!

April 17. Love for Love's Sake

> God is love. Whoever lives in love lives in God, and God
> in him. In this way, love is made complete among us so
> that we will have confidence on the day of judgment,
> because in this world we are like him. There is no fear
> in love. But perfect love drives out fear, because fear has
> to do with punishment. The one who fears is not made
> perfect in love. We love because he first loved us.
>
> —1 John 4:16–19

I read an article in our local paper recently about an amazing, nineteen-year-old young man who was called to donate his bone marrow for another who was battling leukemia. He had signed up in a drive last summer in the hope of becoming the bone marrow match for a local woman. But the call for him to be an actual donor was not for this woman, it was for someone whom he had never met—a total stranger. This young man probably never expected to get the call that he was actually a match for anyone. He says, "It's a huge blessing to have the opportunity to show people that you don't need a reason to love someone." Now that is a powerful statement coming from a nineteen-year-old, or anyone else for that matter. Loving for love's sake—that is our call from the Lord. That is exactly what Jesus does for us. He loves us, not because he has to love us, but because he is love. He just loves us, every tiny bit of us. As John says above, because God loves us, we love him and reveal our love for him by loving others, and love is made complete. Complete love: nothing is better than this. Whether we have the opportunity to show this love in such a powerful way as this young man or show our love with simple gestures throughout our day, we reveal to others the love of Christ by loving without a reason—just because!

April 18. Roundabout Way

Ask and it will be given to you; seek and you will find;
knock and the door will be opened to you. For everyone
who asks receives; he who seeks finds, and to him who
knocks, the door will be opened.

—Matthew 7:7–8

I have to share this fact—I was not an athlete growing up. I always wanted to be one, but my daddy was very artistic and loved music, so he had me taking piano lessons when I was very young. Six, I think. It seemed like I took piano lessons my whole life. Because I could play pretty well, I was the pianist for Lads and Lassies, the select choral group at my high school. Midyear my junior year, however, I was over the piano. So the choir teacher asked me to join the group as a singer. I was thrilled. Somehow, in a roundabout way, I got to join this elite singing group. I love to sing, so I finished out my high school career singing with joy. The lesson that I took from this is that it doesn't matter how you get in, just that you get in. That is exactly how we, as believers, feel. No matter how we came to know our Lord and Savior, we are all grafted in as sons and daughters of the Risen Lord. Each of us came to faith in different ways, different times, and different journeys. But however we got here, we are now residing in the family of the Most High God. So we may sing and dance with unbridled joy, even if we came in a roundabout fashion. The welcome sign is always up and shining, *Come On In*.

April 19. Bigger Than Life

> Now, brothers, I want to remind you of the gospel I
> preached to you, which you received and on which you
> have taken your stand. By this gospel you are saved, if you
> hold firmly to the word I preached to you. Otherwise,
> you have believed in vain. For what I received I passed on
> to you as of first importance: that Christ died for our sins
> according to the Scriptures, that he was buried, that he
> was raised on the third day according to the scriptures.
>
> —1 Corinthians 15:1–4

Think about it—we have all known people whom we would consider bigger than life. This phrase is often used to describe a person with a big personality who enters a room and owns it. Some of us have been given what is often described as outgoing personalities—the ability to carry the conversation in a big way no matter where you are. We can know without a doubt that the one who really owns the show is Jesus. He is truly the one who is bigger than life. He is the one who was born, walked among us, and went to the cross because, in truth, he is bigger than this life. He transcended this earthly life by leaving the tomb and joining his Father, our Father, in heaven. Yet he lives among us, "the way and the truth and the life" (John 14:6) to life eternal. He left this life to be bigger than life for us so that we can know him, walk with him, call on him to help us in our daily walk, and then when this life is over, join him in heaven, our home—home at last. May we cherish this thought that Jesus gave us his mercy and grace to live our lives through losing his so that we may know life and know it abundantly.

April 20. Believe It!

You did not choose me, but I chose you and appointed
you to go and bear fruit—fruit that will last. Then the
Father will give you whatever you ask in my name.
This is my commandment: Love each other.

—John 15:16–17

"The body achieves what the mind believes." I recently heard
this quote from an intellectual speaker, and haven't we all seen
that this can be true? Otherwise, how would people accomplish
some of the amazing things that they do, when in actuality these
feats should not be possible? How does someone actually run a
hundred miles a day? I read about someone who does this, and
I stand amazed. He says that he sets his mind to it—that's it—
he sets his mind to it. This is his response to what he believes
he can do: He believes that he can, his body responds, and he
does it. Impossible feats like these done because someone sets his
mind to it. Our minds are powerful things. The Lord our God
has not given anything else such a mind as ours. People prove
each and every day that any of us can achieve what we believe
in our own minds. We are only limited by our imaginations or
what our minds say that we can or can't do. We are called by the
Lord to use our minds to glorify him in all that we do. He has
commanded us time and time again to love one another. What
does this look like for each of us? Only we can decide in our own
minds how we answer his call to love, and love, and love again.
He said it, we believe it, let's do it!

April 21. Mosquito Mister

> You are my hiding place; you will protect me from trouble
> and surround me with songs of deliverance.
>
> —Psalm 32:7

Several years ago we had a mosquito mister installed in our backyard to prevent those pesky mosquitoes from eating us alive. My husband is especially susceptible to them, and, boy, does it help. A few mosquitoes get by, for sure, but nothing like their presence when that mister isn't working. Last week, we kept pushing the button to dispense more and more of the juice but the mosquitoes were everywhere. The tank needed a refill, and sometimes this is how it goes with our faith. We get complacent, expecting God to always be there, forgetting to thank him for his continual spray of protection. We go along, living life, and forget to refill our tank with our thanks for his minute-by-minute mist of protection from life's knocks. Our Lord, our Protector, never fails. He never runs out of grace. His protection always covers us with a mist of safety and mercy even when we don't think to refill the tank. It is in our Father's care that we can abide in his never-failing protection, calling us to sing for joy over his deliverance from the bites of life.

April 22. His Perfect Hands

> For he guards the course of the just and
> protects the way of his faithful ones.
>
> —Proverbs 2:8

Here I am sitting, watching our robin who has built her nest in the drainage pipe running down the side of our garage. She laid her precious eggs a few weeks ago and has been faithfully sitting on them day and night, waiting on them to hatch. Hatch they did, and three of the most precious little beaks have appeared, demanding food day and night from their parents. To sit and watch this sight is seeing God manifested in the sweetest of nature's glory. We can't help but be reminded of how Jesus holds each of us in his mighty hands, just like this beautiful and sturdy nest built by these robins to hold their young. As I watch them fly back and forth, back and forth, fulfilling the demands of their children with food all day long, so are we being held in the hands of Christ, calling on him all day long to feed us, to provide for us. He never fails to do so. Jesus will never stop caring for us, responding to our call for his constant and loving care. We too, like these young bird fledglings neatly tucked in their protective and well-built nest, sit in his protective hands, knowing that he will never disappoint, giving us even more than we deserve.

April 23. Happy Feet!

> You made him ruler of the works of your hands;
> you put everything under his feet.
>
> —Psalm 8:6

Feet—now there is something that I know a lot about from experiencing two foot operations about two years ago. I inherited from my mom a condition where the main foot bone of both my feet collapses, causing huge bunions to grow inside the feet, leading to great discomfort. Pain is pretty much the rule of the day with shoes on and even off. So realizing that two operations, one at a time, could get rid of the pain and allow me to wear shoes again—flat shoes, tall shoes, wedge shoes, shoes and more shoes—I jumped on that quickly. Now, sitting here today, I am pain-free and wearing big ol' heels again. So yesterday, when I heard a beautiful godly woman give the closing prayer at a luncheon by saying, "Thank you for giving feet to our faith," I loved it! I love that phrase, for what better describes who we are called to be than people who put feet to their faith? What better use for our feet than to serve the Lord through where we go and what we do. As it says in Psalm 8:6 above, God our Father has put everything under our feet. So with a spring in our step, may our feet take us where he calls, giving us happy feet for Christ!

April 24. The Rainbow Connection

Now Israel [Jacob] loved Joseph more than any of his
other sons, because he had been born to him in his old
age; and he made a richly ornamented robe for him.

—Genesis 37:3

In the Bible, there is a story about a man named Joseph, who was the youngest son of Jacob. Jacob loved Joseph and gave him a special coat, a coat of many colors. This coat was beautiful, made of bright colors, colors of all sorts. We all have our own coat of many colors, Jesus Christ, that we too can wear each and every day. He provides us many colors throughout our lives:

Jesus reflecting the color blue: Jesus is steady, someone we can trust, bringing harmony and loyalty into our lives. He gives us sincerity and quietness when need be.

Jesus reflecting the color yellow: Jesus illuminates our lives and offers hope, cheerfulness, and joy.

Jesus reflecting the color red: Jesus brings warmth and a positive spirit to us, offering us motivation to be the best we can be through leadership and confidence.

Jesus reflecting the color green: Jesus brings balance and harmony and helps us to grow through renewal and rebirth. He calls us to love and nurture ourselves and others.

Jesus reflecting the color pink: Jesus creates love, insight, and openness through thoughtful, caring living and being tender and kind to those you meet.

So as we dress for the day, let's put on our very own coat of many colors, Jesus, revealing all of those vibrant and color-specific qualities found in him to show the whole world how bright and beautiful he is! What color of Jesus will you wear today?

April 25. "Seismic Shifts"

After the Lord Jesus had spoken to them, he was taken
up into heaven and he sat at the right hand of God.

—Mark 16:19

The phrase "seismic shift" kept coming to mind today and I have no idea why. I was pretty sure that I knew what a seismic shift was, but just to be sure I typed it into my search engine. An editorial review popped up on a book by Kevin Harney entitled *Seismic Shifts: The Little Changes That Make a Big Difference in Your Life.* Lo and behold, right there in front of me was a review of a book that applies the idea of seismic shifts to our faith walk—who knew? Harney defines a physical seismic shift as "A small movement in the crust of the earth that can send out shock waves that have radical and far-reaching effects, redefining an entire landscape." We can take this definition of a seismic shift on earth and relate it to the birth of Jesus, which brought the most important seismic shift that will ever be—to our lives, to the whole world, and its future. This is the seismic shift that wraps up the whole idea in one—Jesus! He is the one who has shifted our lives from sinner to redeemed. No one, nor anything, could have ever done this for us. Our Lord and Savior came to earth to be the seismic shift for sinners in need of a Savior, all of us. Jesus has been the one and only thing that has made all the difference, having far-reaching effects, redefining our entire landscape, and shifting our lives from sinner to redeemed!

April 26. God of Surprises

> My heart is steadfast, O God; I will sing and make music
> with all my soul. Awake, harp and lyre! I will awaken the
> dawn. I will praise you, O Lord, among the nations;
> I will sing of you among the people. For great is your
> love, higher than the heavens, your faithfulness reaches to
> the skies. Be exalted, O God, above the heavens,
> and let your glory be over all the earth.
>
> —Psalm 108:1–5

I attended a luncheon a few days ago where I heard the loveliest woman speak. She works with an agency that restores the lives of women who have been living on the streets, and she started by saying that we worship a God of surprises. How right she is! To know and to believe that God, our Lord, is a God who has so many good and glorious surprises in store for us makes each day the special gift that it is. I was walking last week, and, boy, was I surprised! I had my dog, Mojo, and we were walking down the street, minding our own business, when I saw something—not sure what at first—coming directly at us in midair. It was coming fast, right about the level of my head. Then, all of a sudden, I realized that it was two ducks in furious flight right over us! Was I expecting that? Not at all, yet it was a fun surprise to see these beautiful ducks on their way to who knows where. We can walk through our days expecting God to surprise us with so many gifts of glory. Let's be on the lookout for them. It may be a beautiful rose just getting ready to be in full bloom, it could be running into an old friend that we haven't seen in a while, or it could be a bright and beautiful clear Texas sky. Whatever the case, he is always gifting us with surprises, because he loves us so!

April 27. Press Pause Please

> I baptize you with water for repentance.
> But after me will come one who is more powerful than I,
> whose sandals I am not fit to carry.
> He will baptize you with the Holy Spirit and with fire.
>
> —Matthew 3:11

For the last three years, I have had the honor to sit on a board with sixteen Christian women whose mission is to select one or two Christian groups to whom we give funds for their work in bringing people to Christ. In one of our meetings, a precious woman on our board made this comment: "That gives me pause." Not having heard that phrase before, I was so enamored that I could hardly keep my focus on what we were discussing. That gives me pause. I instantly thought to myself that there were so many times that I wish that, when something had actually given me pause, I had taken a moment or an hour or a day or two to think before I said or did something. It reminds me of the pause button on my remote. This pause button gives us the opportunity to keep a show on hold until we are ready, and that is what our pause button can do for us in our lives. There are so many times that we need to push that pause button to stop, think, and make the right decision or say the right thing or weigh in on something with thoughtful obedience to our faith and what we know to be right. Armed with this phrase, we can now think to use our pause button, that tapping on the shoulder by our own special pauser himself, the Holy Spirit. Press pause please. Not quite ready to go forward!

April 28. As Good as Our Smartphones

> As the body without the spirit is dead, so faith without
> deeds is dead.
>
> —James 2:26

Watching recorded television recently, I saw a story about a phenomenal young man named Jack Andraka, who at the age of eleven became interested in developing a test for pancreatic cancer. Of course, having survived pancreatic cancer, I was glued to this story on many levels. He started researching everything he could about this disease, even during the school day. At one point, his biology teacher caught him red-handed, thinking that he was goofing off. Obviously, this isn't your average eleven-year-old. Due to his unbelievable intellect and thirst for knowledge, he began to see a pattern in what he was studying, and a few years later came up with a simple blood test that would indicate the beginning stages of pancreatic cancer in people. Now that he has developed this test, he has released it to drug companies for clinical trials, testing its accuracy on thousands of people. We are still years away from its widespread use, but this is a breakthrough of epic proportion. The whole story was almost too amazing to comprehend, but I loved it when he said, "Intelligence without creativity means that you just have a bunch of knowledge. You're just as good as your smartphone." Immediately I thought of how that compares to our faith in Jesus Christ. To believe is everything. It must come first. But faith without deeds is dead. This young man's comparing having intellect without using it in a creative way just made me think of our having faith in Christ, but we need to use it creatively, doing good works with it, whether that is being kind, sharing with others, or going to another country to build homes. What a gift Jack has been given by our Father; what a gift we have been given by our Father, belief in Jesus Christ. Let us use it in creative ways, just as this amazing young man has taken his gift of intellect and combined it with creativity to save the lives of so many, and the glory goes to God!

April 29. Way off Course

Folly delights a man who lacks judgment,
but a man of understanding keeps a straight course.

—Proverbs 15:21

A group of friends and I were deep in discussion on a topic that was of interest to everyone. As they were weighing in with interesting insight, I kind of veered off on another subject that was relevant but not exactly on point. After a few minutes of these thoughts, I made the statement, "I have gotten way off course," meaning that I had left the original topic and segued into another. I thought to myself later that day that many times we do get way off course. Life has a way of doing that. There are countless ways to veer way off course, literally in a different direction from where we meant to be going, changing the direction of a plan for the day or the year or your life, going with a totally different idea from what we had originally thought. Sometimes the end result is good, sometimes difficult. So here's the good news! Jesus never lets us get way off course if we let him lead us through our days. We need to give him the control. That's the hitch, giving him the control. So often we want to charge on without seeking his will first, turning to him in prayer, or listening for his direction. If we seek his face in all that we do, we will stay on track, his track. And where else would we want to be when we arrive at our destination?

April 30. A Brighter Tomorrow

> I lift my eyes to the hills—where does my help
> come from? My help comes from the Lord,
> the Maker of heaven and earth.
>
> —Psalm 121

Disappointment—defined as the condition in which an expectation, hope, or desire is unfulfilled or fails to come to fruition. We have all experienced it. We have all planned on something being one way, and much to our chagrin it turns out another. We appoint a situation to be lived out with one expectation, yet it doesn't come to pass. Why not, we ask? Seriously, why not! We wonder, we are sad, we cry out and ask our Father for the answer. It is in these times that we must not be confused. Our Father is working mightily day and night, night and day, always, on our behalf. He never tires nor grows weary of taking our disappointments in life and setting us back upright at the appointed time, his appointed time. We set a schedule that meets our desires, but it is his greatest joy to return our joy to us in his framework for our lives. While we don't like to experience disappointments, he always uses them for good—our good—as we release them into his perfect hands to mold, reshape, and send us on our way. It is through these times of disappointment that we know with all certainty where our strength comes from—our Father of goodness and grace. These times truly show us the power, the strength, the love of our Lord whose goodness will always bring a brighter tomorrow.

May 1. "He Knows Our Name..."

> Before I formed you in the womb I knew you,
> before you were born I set you apart.
>
> —Jeremiah 1:5

I started thinking about how significant it is when people we see know our names and use them in speaking to us. Hearing a friend or acquaintance use our name makes us feel special. Most of us can remember a face, but remembering someone's name is just that much better. Remembering people's names and then using them as we see them again takes practice and focus. But it is so worthwhile to be able to do this. It makes us realize how priceless it is that our Father knows our name. Yes, he knows each and every one of us by name. We are his children, and he knew us before we were even born. As we go about our day, saying hello to someone we know and saying their name brings a sweetness that cannot be bought. But even sweeter is hearing our name called each and every day by the one who knows us best—our Father— who will never forget our name!

May 2. The Perfect Carryall

> Listen to me...you whom I have upheld since you were
> conceived, and carried since your birth. Even to your old
> age and gray hairs I am he, I am he who will sustain you.
> I have made you and I will carry you. I will sustain you
> and I will rescue you.
>
> —Isaiah 46:3–5

My purse is my lifeline. As I got into my car today, I started to clean my purse out. Yes, at that very moment! It must be a woman thing—when we have a minute when we don't have something to do, we start cleaning out our purses, no matter where we are. The thought crossed my mind that my purse is my worldly lifeline, but my Jesus is my true lifeline. Just as we continue to put things into a purse—things that make us happy and things that we also need—let us also put happy things and necessary things into Jesus, not only praises for the blessings that he continually pours out but also requests and cries for answered prayers to life's trials that we desperately need. He is our all-in-all, our perfect carryall, for he carries our joys and sorrows, never running out of room for anything that we ask him to carry for us. Just as promised in Isaiah above, he carries not only everything we ask him to carry, but he also carries us every day, all throughout the day, never wearing out nor getting tired of being loaded down with all that we hand to him. I can't think of anywhere that we could buy a carryall more valuable than the one we already have—Jesus!

May 3. The Two Hundred-Mile Trek Home

How lovely is your dwelling place, O Lord Almighty...
blessed are those who dwell in your house;
they are ever praising you.

—Psalm 84:1–4

I never cease to be amazed at the will of a pet to return to its family, no matter what the cost. Last week, I heard the story of a cat that had been on vacation with her family, traveling two hundred miles away from their home. At one of their stops, the cat, for some unknown reason, jumped out of their car and ran off. After looking for their cat for quite a while, the family returned home. Certain that they would never see their beloved cat again, two months later they received a call that she had been found by someone very near their home. This causes us to wonder what would cause this cat to travel over two hundred miles to get home to the people she loved? The family surmises that their cat's deep and abiding love for them is due to the fact that they nursed her back to health after a terrible accident when she was just a newborn. Correlating this precious story to the love of Jesus, he has nursed us back to health time and time again. With the same passionate love for our Savior as this cat has shown her family, let us never miss a chance to know his love and find him in any situation. Praise be to God that we dwell with him daily, and we will never have to travel two hundred miles to find his never-failing love.

May 4. Humpty Dumpty!

> Restore us, O God; make your face shine upon us,
> that we may be saved.
>
> —Psalm 80:3

"Humpty Dumpty sat on a wall, / Humpty Dumpty had a great fall." In this well-known and well-loved nursery rhyme, Humpty Dumpty is an egg. That's right, he's pictured as an egg person. As the poem progresses, he falls off the ledge and shatters to pieces. Just like the egg in this nursery rhyme, we, too, are broken. Many times we are broken into a million pieces. Life has a way of breaking us apart at times, and we do not know how to put our lives back together again. But unlike Humpty Dumpty, who is never put together again in the poem, we will always be restored by the love and saving grace of God. In Psalm 80:3 above, we know with all certainty that God restores us. His face will shine upon us and make us whole once again.

May 5. The Best for Last

> Then he (Jesus) told them, "Now draw some out (water
> he had turned into wine) and take it to the master of the
> banquet." They did so, and the master of the banquet
> tasted the water that had been turned into wine…he
> (the banquet master) called the bridegroom aside and
> said, "Everyone brings out the choice wine first and then
> the cheaper wine, but you have saved the best till now."
>
> —John 2:8–10

While Jesus is attending the wedding of a friend, he is told that the wine had run out, and there was no more to serve. Jesus calls the servants to his side and tells them to draw water into the jars that were empty. He then has the servants take these newly filled jars to the one in charge of serving the wine. Upon pouring the liquid, the servants realize that Jesus has taken water and turned it into wine. The banquet master tells the groom that the best wine has been saved for the end of the party, unusual for hosts to do. Isn't this exactly what Jesus has done for us? Just like the servants who saw Jesus turn water into the best wine, we can know with the same certainty that he has prepared a place for us in heaven, saving the best for last! This story assures us that we will have the best of everything when we arrive home to heaven. Although our earthly dwelling place is beautiful and full of God's glory, it will pale in comparison to heaven, where we will not only live eternally, but we will also see Jesus face to face. It's just like our Lord and Savior to give us everything we could need here on earth, and—better yet—saves the best for last.

May 6. Go Ahead, I'm Coming!

...we have sought the Lord our God; we sought him,
and he has given us rest on every side.

—2 Chronicles 14:7

I remember so vividly the challenge of getting our four children
to a restaurant at the same time when all of us were getting ready
to go somewhere as a family. This was at the time when the two
oldest ones were already grown and the two youngest were in
high school. Now their father is very punctual, always ready
and waiting for us. This is a quality that I greatly admire. He
would wait on the one lagging behind, either myself or one of
our children. Whether a call came from upstairs or on the phone
from one of our grown children, he would hear, "Go ahead. I
am coming. I will meet you there." It was very helpful to let us
know that we should go ahead. This way, we could wait on the
one running behind at wherever we were going rather than make
the entire family late. In the same way, the Lord always knows
that we are coming because he knows our every move. He has
gone before us to prepare the way, especially in a trial that we
are facing, and the way will be filled with his glory. The Lord is
ready. He is always ready, and he is never late. He has prepared
victory after victory for us as we journey through a difficult time
and arrive at the end because he was ready and waiting for us. Just
as in life when we know that someone is on the way, we can trust
that Jesus has gone before to prepare the way, his perfect way.
Lord, we are coming, thank you for preparing the way.

May 7. Happy Mothering Day!

When Jesus saw his mother and the disciple whom
he loved standing nearby, he said to his mother,
"Woman, behold your son." Then he said to the disciple,
"Behold your mother!" and from that hour the disciple
took her into his own home.

—John 19:26–27

Mother's Day is fast approaching. This year, our little goat that lives at our place near Hillsboro has put a new slant on this Mother's Day for me. This goat slipped through our fence about a year ago. As we don't raise goats, my husband tried his best to catch this little visitor. Being unsuccessful, we wondered how he would fare living among the white-tailed deer that we raise. No need to worry! The deer took him right in as their own. They have been mothering him ever since, and he feels loved and safe. Observing nature can teach us so much. Mothering goes on quite often in nature as species take care of others who are not like them. We humans need to follow this example of mothering so that we can love others as Christ loves us, providing friendship, caring, and love along the way to someone in need. Any of us can do this mothering. It does not take a mother to carry out the important task. Christ, as he was on the cross, asks his disciple to mother his own mother, honoring her until his last breath. So may we also follow his perfect example and become experts at mothering. It just could be the greatest Mother's Day gift we could ever give or receive! Happy Mothering Day!

May 8. Wow!

"The most important one," answered Jesus, "is this: 'Hear,
O Israel, the Lord our God, the Lord is one. Love the
Lord your God with all your heart and with all your soul
and with all your mind and with all your strength.'
The second is this: 'Love your neighbor as yourself.
There is no commandment greater than these.'"

—Mark 12:29–31

This Sunday is the day designated as Mother's Day. But Mother's Day is not a day celebrated exclusively for women who have had children; it includes all those people everywhere who have loved with a mother's heart. Jesus calls us to love like this, completely, sacrificially, generously, and genuinely, giving all that we have to another to strengthen them and fill them with joy. Time after time, we see the love of a person for someone else creating a bond that cannot be broken, for it is bound through the deepest love there is. It is this love through which Jesus calls us to mother those we meet. He calls us to be that mom to someone who can know the joy of being loved completely and unconditionally. It is a love that stems from knowing the love of Christ in us, the love that he gives us each and every day. We don't need to wait on a special day to love like this. How do we know that love? From the love that we have been given by the one who loves us most, from the one who is love himself, Jesus, Savior, Lord. If we turn the word *Mom* upside down, it becomes *wow*. And *wow* is exactly how we can make someone feel if we love them with the greatest love of all—the love of Christ.

May 9. Bingo!

Let us fix our eyes upon Jesus,
the author and perfecter of our faith.

—Hebrews 12:2

The game of bingo, in which small balls with numbers on them spin round and round in a hopper, reminds us of the game of life. In bingo, the balls are randomly selected one by one, and no one ever knows which number will be coming out next. In the same way, as we go through life, the challenges we meet are like those balls in the hopper of bingo, and sooner or later our number will pop up. We have no idea when our number will be called, but we can play with all certainty because we have the winner on our side, Jesus. He will take our number when it is called and exchange it for victory, calling out "Bingo!" for us as he conquers our difficulties through his mercy and grace. Let us live life abundantly knowing that Jesus knows the rules and has the perfect number to play when we need it, leading us each and every time to play a winning game, for he truly is the author and perfecter of our faith.

May 10. All Things Bright and Beautiful

He has made everything beautiful in its time.

—Ecclesiastes 3:11

Walking today, I saw the most gorgeous bright blue butterfly, floating through the air on its gossamer wings. Then I saw a precious squirrel running through the grass with a nut in his mouth. God's beautiful creatures out and about living gloriously in this beautiful weather on God's great earth. And then comes winter, the temperature drops, trees lose their leaves, flowers wilt, and it's time for all of nature to draw in, resting and restoring until spring returns again. These gorgeous electric-blue butterflies hibernate, and the squirrels huddle up trying to survive on the hidden nuts they have stored for this wintry time of life. Sometimes we meet such a season as this, a wintry freeze of life where we need to pull away from the world and surround ourselves with God's love and protection just as his precious animals in nature do during the winter months. There are just such times as these, no matter what the month of the year may be, when we must draw ourselves to the Lord and rest there until we move through the frozen and debilitating challenges that life brings. During this time, our Father wants us to draw near to him for warmth, letting him deal with the icy, freezing weather we are facing, leaving us wrapped in the warmth of his protective arms. We are covered for protection by the Lord's love as he goes forth to bring resolution to whatever it is that we are working through during this time of cold and barren living. How great it is to have a Father who will always be there to deal with those times of life that take us to a wintry place where we don't want to go and certainly don't want to stay. He knows that it is only a matter of time until he warms everything up, and we can fly again in his beautiful world, just like that magnificent butterfly I saw today.

May 11. Hope and Promise

But now, Lord, what do I look for? My hope is in you.

—Psalm 39:7

My husband and I attended the high school graduation this past weekend of twin boys whom he has mentored for nine years. What a sight to look in the faces of all these excited and hopeful young people graduating who have accomplished a great dream, some of them being the first in their families to graduate from high school. The valedictorian and salutatorian were both articulate and respectful of this day and all that it represented to them and their classmates. To see the faces of all the graduates in that large auditorium with excitement written all over their faces gave me a renewed sense of what they were feeling about life. It made me realize that all of us have a new opportunity to start each day full of hope and promise. Even though our high school graduations could have been a few years ago or a distant memory, we can still face each day with this same excitement and enthusiasm found in the students this past weekend. We, as believers, can choose to open our eyes each day with hope and promise because we are loved by Jesus, the one who brought the best of both words into our lives. Without his loving us, hope and promise would not have the same meaning as it does for us now. Sharing this attitude of hope and promise given freely to us by our Savior is a gift that costs nothing. Let us extend this approach of living to everyone we interact with daily, taking the joy found in these graduates and passing it on through the love of our own, Jesus Christ.

May 12. Stop, Look, and Listen!

If from there you seek the Lord your God,
you find him if you look for him with all your
heart and with all your soul.

—Deuteronomy 4:29

Remember the phrase Stop, Look, and Listen that we all learned as children? This phrase cautioned us to stop (stop at the corner before crossing the street), look (look for oncoming traffic), and listen (listen for cars coming to be sure that no one is in the road). As I was walking today, all of a sudden I was overwhelmed by the most beautiful fragrance, wafting by me from no obvious source. I was just taken mentally to the loveliest place, and I knew that God was present. Then I remembered how often I feel this cool and refreshing breeze on a trail where I walk, and it reminds me that the Lord is near. To hear his voice in the delicate sound of the leaves of the ash tree in Colorado or the wind ruffling the palms at the beach lets me know that he is near. So these experiences make me think of stop, look, and listen as the Lord passes by, whether in a beautiful fragrance that cannot be explained, in a cool and delightful breeze that rushes past me from no known source, or in the rustling of leaves from verdant trees. He longs to delight us with boundless gifts, and, if we are thinking on him, we will be blessed by his presence and feel his love. Let us stop, be still, and know that he is God; look, look for him with all your heart and soul; and listen, listen for his voice whispering, "I love you, for you are mine."

May 13. Wonderful Counselor

> Counsel and sound judgment are mine;
> I have understanding and power.
>
> —Proverbs 8:14

Whenever I hear the word "counselor," I am reminded of the comic strip *Peanuts* and Lucy, who would set up shop with a sign that said, "Psychiatric Help 5¢...The Doctor Is In." This was to imply that Lucy was a counselor available to help out anyone needing sage advice from her. All through life, we meet counselors—school counselors, legal counselors, religious counselors, you get the idea. Even some counselors we meet are like Lucy, not really qualified but certainly wanting to help. But the first counselor whose advice we should always seek is our counselor, Jesus. His name, Wonderful Counselor, reveals his infinite wisdom and knowledge that will lead us through even the toughest of times. As the godly people who knew Jesus turned to him for direction, teaching, and wisdom in how to live their lives, so shall we likewise do the same. It makes perfect sense to go to the source of all wisdom and knowledge, the one who knows us inside out. Although chatting with Lucy about our troubles in her box of an office might be interesting, we would certainly get some out-of-the-box advice. Rather, let's seek out the wisdom and guidance of our Lord and Savior, our wonderful Counselor, whose guidance is not only free, but the best advice that we will ever receive!

May 14. Miracles Still Happen!

You are the God who performs miracles.

—Psalm 77:14

How mighty is God who rescues! I was reading about this young woman in Bangladesh, around twenty-two years old, who was buried alive under mounds of rubble after an earthquake and found still breathing after seventeen days. Just imagine, seventeen days alone under literally tons of concrete and dirt. She did not believe that she would ever see daylight again. These seventeen days are the longest that anyone has survived being buried alive. After these long, soul-crushing seventeen days, people above ground trying to clear the rubble finally heard her beating on a pipe and dug and dug until they reached her. Metaphorically speaking, we have all been buried under the mass of a trial, feeling as if we are under so much dirt and concrete that we will never be free to enjoy daylight again. Yet in the midst of this trial, we have a Savior. We have Jesus who always hears our voice on the first cry. We have Jesus who knows exactly where we are and what our needs are, and he promises that he will lift us up and carry us out of this mess of concrete. Whether he slowly, one by one, lifts the blocks of broken concrete that are too heavy for us to lift by ourselves, or he quickly sweeps them away with one movement of his mighty hand, he never forgets us and always hears our cries for help. Miracles still happen. He restores the daylight with joy, for he is truly the Miracle Maker!

May 15. Fence Me In

> So do not fear, for I am with you; do not be dismayed,
> for I am your God. I will strengthen you and help you;
> I will uphold you in my righteous right hand.
>
> —Isaiah 41:10

We have a small place here in Texas that is high-game fenced, and we raise white-tail deer there. When they hear or see something that scares them, they stop in their tracks and become as still as stones, hoping that the suspecting predator will not see them. Mojo, my dog, and I always walk for a while. So here we are, walking alongside one of the deer pens, and the deer in the pen freeze, sensing danger is near. They start to run alongside the fence, trying to find the safest place to be. They become confused, not knowing that there is no way that Mojo could reach them even if he tried, for they are safely fenced in. We are so much like these beautiful deer. We sense danger, but not remembering that our Father has fenced us in with his protection and his promise to keep us safe, we also start to run, often banging against our fence trying to figure out how to escape from our danger. Just like Mojo appears frightening to the deer, our troubles sometimes become much bigger and scarier than they truly are. Our Father longs for us to remember that he has fenced us in with his promise that he has gone before us, paving the way with peace and answers to whatever danger we face. Nothing can penetrate the Lord's protection if we only choose to remember that he has us right where he wants us, in his impenetrable fence of perfect love. The perfect fence to withstand any enemy.

May 16. Can You Hear Me Now?

> When he cries out to me, I will hear,
> for I am compassionate.
>
> —Exodus 22:27

I often think of that ad for a cellular network with the man standing in a field saying, "Can you hear me now?" Lately, I have said, "Can you hear me now?" while talking on my cell phone as I lost the connection trying to talk. There are two sections of road as we drive to our place outside Dallas where I always lose the connection. Both are valley areas where the road dips down, leaving me with a weak connection or no connection at all. Such is life as we know it. Many times we feel as if we are getting a weak signal from the Lord or possibly no signal at all. Nothing could be further from the truth. The absolute reality is this: He is always with us. His signal is ever present. In those valley times of life, it is our golden opportunity to establish a lifeline of communication with our protector and Savior that cannot be broken, no matter where we are nor how far we travel in life, deep in a valley or high on a mountaintop. The sign on our journey is clear: All networks work here. For they are powered by our Almighty Lord, in whom there are no power outages!

May 17. "He Has a Future"

"For I know the plans I have for you," declares the Lord,
"plans to prosper you and not to harm you,
plans to give you hope and a future."

—Jeremiah 29:11

The title of an article in our paper this morning is "Given a Real Life." This is the story of redemption, a story that we know so well, as believers, but do not get to hear often enough. The young man written about in this article is named Lester. The apartment where Lester lived was right behind a golf course, and to get away from the chaos and confusion of his life, the thirteen-year-old would slip through the wrought-iron fence and just sit on the driving range, watching a man hit ball after ball after ball, never saying a word. Then he would leave. As time went by, this man, a golf pro at the driving range, developed a relationship with Lester and began teaching him how to play golf. Then things happen, and Lester's life gets off track. After skirmishes with the law and actually ending up in a detention center, the young man and the golf pro are reunited, and the golf pro adopted Lester, who is now eighteen. He has become an excellent golfer and hopes to play in college. These are the words written by his golf coach: "He has a future." That's it. That is all he says. But that is enough. Four simple words, but such power found there. This young man, now adopted, says, "They [his adopted family] have given me"— and he pauses, drops his head, and lowers his voice—"a real life." Here is a young man, like so many of us, meeting challenge after challenge, finding chaos at every turn, longing for help. He finds a family who loves him with warts and all, giving him a new life. So, then, does our Father give us new life, a real life, as he picks us up out the muck and mire, clears away the chaos, and replaces it with a life of love, calm, and security, just like the special people in this story. Just like them, we have a new life and a future, a future of spending life eternal in the loving arms of our Father.

May 18. Days Like This

Finally, my brothers, rejoice in the Lord!

—Philippians 3:1

I am sure that all of us can relate to this from "Mama Said" by the Shirelles: There'd be days like this. We can't help but think how true they are. There will be days like this. What does that mean exactly? Some days just don't go as planned. Some days do not evolve in the way that we thought they would. Something doesn't get done, we forget an appointment, a fun event gets cancelled, and on and on it goes. These, then, become days like this. But these types of days that have a little blip on the radar can still be glorious days if we remember that each and every day is a gift, a precious gift from our Jesus. Sometimes we tend to let the little things drive us nuts, but if we just keep it in perspective, realizing that there are going to be those days that don't go off seamlessly, then we can expect the unexpected and always stay positive through the ever-present love of Christ. When we find that we are in the middle of a day like this, we can look at the big picture and remember that we are loved by the Lord of the universe, and what could make for a better day than that?

May 19. A New Perspective

The Lord does not look at the things man looks at.
Man looks at the outward appearance,
but the Lord looks at the heart.

—1 Samuel 16:7

These days of amazing weather in Dallas, Texas, have been unbelievable. I have been spending a lot of glorious afternoons and early evenings on my downstairs patio. But the other morning as I was getting ready to go somewhere, I opened the door to my upstairs patio to let in the gorgeous weather. It's funny that I never go out there, but I did step out to enjoy the day and realized what a different perspective I had on the world around me. I felt as if I was in the trees, surveying all of nature and what it holds. It was a delightful change from being downstairs, and I didn't want to go back in. The view was so fascinating and uplifting, drawing my eye to all sorts of things that I could not see from below. Isn't this true in all things that we know? When we have the opportunity to view something from a different perspective, things change for the better. When we step outside our comfort zone and look at life through a different set of eyes, situations become enhanced, beautified, easier to comprehend. We can see the world in a different light, especially if we are looking through the lens of Jesus. When we turn to him and use his eyes, our world is a kaleidoscope of colors that bring a freshness to all that we see. Jesus can change the landscape of our lives by our just looking with eyes that he has provided, taking a loftier view from where we sit. There's no telling what lies ahead to inspire us, to bring us joy, to see life through a better lens with a new perspective, and to remind us how blessed we are to be loved by Jesus and all that he is.

May 20. The Greatest Gift of All

> Be devoted to one another in brotherly love. Honor one
> another above yourselves. Never be lacking in zeal,
> but keep your spiritual fervor, serving the Lord.
> Be joyful in hope, patient in affliction, faithful in prayer.
>
> —Romans 12:10–13

In thinking on the past few weeks and the many tragedies surrounding us in this world today, I could not help but think of how best we could help these people in so many different places without being able to actually be there. We long to be able to wrap our arms around these three women found after ten long years of being held captive in a house and say, "Praise be to God for your rescue. We celebrate your lives with you and thank him for his providing the way." We long to hold each and every person in Moore, Oklahoma, hugging on them as we wrap them in blankets for warmth and to keep them dry, saying, "God loves you, and so do we." All the food, water, and hands to help clear the way are so important and necessary for them to move forward and find their footing again. But not being there and not being able to physically help in any way, we still have the greatest gift of all to give, and that is the gift of prayer. All of us know the gift of prayer, for we have given it and received it, showing us time and time again that there is power in prayer. Wrapping all these people in our blanket of prayer provides a comfort and warmth that they will find no other way. Let us continue to cover them with prayer day after day, week after week, as we have been doing. Shall they know the comfort and strength to wake up tomorrow, having slept under the sweetest blanket there is, the blanket of prayer.

May 21. A Sliver of Sunlight

> But may they who love you be like the
> sun when it rises in its strength.
>
> —Judges 5:31

A young woman who was held captive for 410 days in an Iranian prison talks about how she was able to get through this ordeal and come out on the other side. She was held in solitary confinement for the whole time—410 days—with no one to talk with nor share even a moment of time in her cell. She reveals how such an experience can deeply affect your psyche, and she says, "Whether or not you have five minutes of sunlight can make the difference between a day where you fall into a deep depression or one where you are able to constructively get through the day." Most of us will never experience anything even remotely close to her experience. But we can take away some very important thoughts. Just as she longed to enjoy just a sliver of sunlight on any given day, we awaken almost every day to all the sunlight that we could ever want, the light of our world, Jesus Christ, Lord and Savior. We don't get just a sliver of him. He provides us with his sunlight each and every day to guide us, to comfort us, to let us know that he is always with us, now and forever. He loves us in a way that is immeasurable, washing over us minute by minute, hour by hour, day by day, with his love. Near the end of the article she says, "Everything means more if you can share it with someone else." So that's the call. That's Jesus calling us to share his complete and life-changing love for us with others. Then not only are we being fed with the complete restoring love of our Savior, but we can also give his bottomless love to others, filling them to the top with all they will ever need—the love of Christ.

May 22. "Watch Where You Are Going!"

He will not let your foot slip—he who watches over
you will not slumber.

—Psalm 121:3

Walking these days has proven to be precarious for me, for as I am walking I am thinking of ideas to write about, and I use my smartphone to take notes. As of late, I have been walking along, not paying attention, and all of a sudden I look up and I am literally looking face to face with a large machine of some kind that is pulling up trees or a truck parked on the grass where there is construction going on. I remember so vividly saying this to our children as we were walking somewhere or shopping or just out and about, "Watch where you are going!" Now here I am, needing to heed my own advice! Our Father's eye is always on us. He never takes his focus off us. It is just downright phenomenal to know with all certainty that his love for us is clear and direct and all-encompassing. Let us find comfort, peace, and joy in knowing that Jesus will not let our foot slip. He is always watching our every move.

May 23. Are You There?

You know with all your heart and soul that not one of
all the good promises the Lord your God gave you has
failed. Every promise has been fulfilled;
not one has failed.

—Joshua 23:14

I remember vividly my experience with pancreatic cancer and the pure, body-trembling, all-controlling fear that I felt as I continued to go through testing, looking for more carcinoid tumors shortly after my initial surgery. Although I knew that God was in control, that I had given my outcome to him, and that I trusted completely in his going before me, I still could not get a grip on that body-shaking fear that I had as I lay in that CT scanner multiple times. I was shaking so much that I was worried I would have to repeat this two-day, three-hour test. You must find it strange to hear that I was that fearful after reading my writings on how to get a grip on fear, how to not worry, and on and on. But the truth is, I had it. Even though I was standing on the promises of God, I was shaking uncontrollably. The only way that I can understand why I couldn't stop the trembling is that I am human. And so are you. So was David, as he faced that giant on the hill with just a slingshot. So was Abraham, as he poised himself over his son with knife in hand. In these situations, we know in our rational mind that the Lord has gone before. We trust completely in his sovereignty. And we tremble. But the hand of the Lord is reaching down to steady us. He is holding on with a grip that cannot be broken, and this is a promise that will not fail. This is what we can know as standing on the promises of God!

May 24. Glow Little Glowworm

> Jesus did many other miraculous signs in the presence
> of his disciples which are not recorded in this book.
> But these are written that you may believe that Jesus is
> the Christ, the Son of God, and that by believing you
> might have life in his name.
>
> —John 20:30–31

I was attending a high school spring intersquad football game last week, and a precious young man that we know came into the stadium. I was sitting next to a dear friend, and we had been talking about essential oils and how they really make a difference. I introduced her to our young friend, and as she watched him go past us, she said to me, "He glows." I immediately responded without any forethought, "That is because he is Christ centered." I had not put that adjective with this young man in all the time that we have known him. After I said it, I realized that this is exactly who he is. He is a young man of solid faith whose life is centered on Christ. She leaned into me and said with great sincerity, "I want that glow." We all want that glow that comes from within that reveals a heart centered on Christ. The glow that we desire can only come from a life that has been given to our Lord, Jesus Christ. Let us set our hearts on Christ, our Savior and Redeemer, and spend each day reflecting his glorious glow.

May 25. Falling Short

> This righteousness from God comes through faith in
> Jesus Christ to all who believe. There is no difference, for
> all have sinned and fall short of the glory of God, and are
> justified freely by his grace through the redemption that
> came by Christ Jesus.
>
> —Romans 3:22–24

Over the weekend we went out of town with friends, and we were playing the game of horseshoes with them. We had teams, each taking turns throwing the horseshoes. Now, if you haven't thrown horseshoes in a while, or possibly never, they can actually seem quite heavy. It looks fairly easy, but to toss the horseshoe into that box becomes a challenge for some of us. You have to get a rhythm going, sort of like swinging a pendulum, and then at just the right moment, you let go and hopefully get a *ringer*. Many times I would shank it, and the horseshoe would fall short, terribly short. But the good news for all of us playing is that everyone fell short at one time or another, no matter who was throwing. Even the best athlete among us threw it short a couple of times. This game is just like life—we all fall short. Isn't it comforting to know that we all spin one down the hill now and then? We need to remember that falling short is not the end result. We can and will fall short, but our Savior picks us up and makes us a ringer for his glory!

May 26. Problem Solved!

> Finally, brothers, whatever is true, whatever is noble,
> whatever is right, whatever is pure, whatever is lovely,
> whatever is admirable—if anything is excellent or
> praiseworthy—think about such things. Whatever you
> have learned or received or heard from me, or seen in
> me—put into practice. And the God of peace will be
> with you.
>
> —Philippians 4:8–9

Yesterday I had the great privilege of attending a symposium in which three well-respected and top medical scientists spoke on various issues regarding the health of women. One of the speakers gave this quote from Albert Einstein: "We cannot solve our problems with the same thinking that created them." As we apply this quote to life, we, as believers, know that we will have problems. We have been promised that. Some we may have created and some we haven't. But in order to solve them, we need to always think on these things: "Whatever is true, whatever is noble, whatever is right, whatever is pure, whatever is lovely, whatever is admirable...if anything is excellent or praiseworthy... think about such things." As we move from focusing on our problem to focusing on Jesus, we can then shift our thinking to the one who has the answer, our Savior, the problem solver. It is here in his hands that we can know his peace and begin to reverse the situation. Now we have a new way of thinking, enabling us to bring a fresh look and approach to our problems. As we hand them over to the Lord, we have successfully moved in a new direction—his perfect direction.

May 27. Be Brave

> Be strong and courageous. Do not be afraid or terrified
> because of them, for the Lord your God goes with you;
> he will never leave you nor forsake you.
>
> —Deuteronomy 31:6

I have been praying and thinking on a decision in my life that has me in sort of a scaredy-cat state, so to speak. In the whole scheme of things, this decision ranks up there for me, and I do not know what to do. Not knowing what to do brings a timid and questioning state of mind, at least for me. But the two words that keep coming into my mind are be brave. Just be brave. All of us have these times when we are not sure of which way to go. All of us have journeys that bring us to a fork in the road, creating confusion and a sense of insecurity. Yet our Lord is here, right beside us, saying "be brave." Be brave in his love, be brave in his care, be brave because we know that he will never forsake us nor leave us. So as I awoke this morning, I was brave, remembering that he is with me now and forever. He has this situation in the palm of his hand, and I need not be afraid. No matter what life may bring our way, remember to be brave because we are being led by the bravest one of all, our Lord and Savior, Jesus Christ.

May 28. Changing Your Mind

Your love, O Lord, reaches to the heavens,
your faithfulness to the skies.

—Psalm 36:5

Sometimes, I think very differently from most people, and this may be one of those cases. I find value in people who can assess a new situation and change their minds about something. This switching to a new way of thinking is referred to as *flip-flopping* by politicians, and they use this term in the most negative way. I, however, find that curious, because I think that being able to change our minds is one of the gifts that we have been given. As I think back over the years on various topics, I have changed my mind countless times. I used to love to swim, now not so much. I used to like wide-legged pants, now not so much. I realize that these are pretty mundane subjects compared to the seriousness of others where the topic of changing one's mind is discussed. But I still admire a person who thoughtfully listens to the pros and cons of a subject and then decides to change his mind based on new information or a different set of circumstances. Many times this takes great courage to alter your mind-set in the face of criticism. Sometimes it is as easy as deciding that you really don't like snow skiing after all. The good news in all of this is that the Lord never changes his mind. In the verses from Psalms above, we are assured that God never changes. His faithfulness reaches to the skies. With the world as we know it changing constantly, what more could we ask for than a Father who never changes his mind?

May 29. When the Time Is Right

> Whoever obeys his command will come to no harm,
> and the wise heart will know the proper time and the
> procedure. For there is a proper time and procedure for
> every matter.
>
> —Ecclesiastes 8:5–6

Today is the day. I just know it! I can tell that this is the day that our fledgling robins are going to leave their protective nest. One in particular keeps standing on the edge, ready for flight, standing in all his glory. He flaps his wings and acts as if he is leaving. He can hardly stand there, for his head keeps pressing against the top of the drainage pipe under which his mom built their nest. I wait and watch, and wait and watch, but I know without a doubt that he will leave at the appointed time—the very time that he is ready. When the time is right. How comforting for us, as believers, to know that when we are on a journey and God has pulled us in for a time, he will restore us to complete joy when the time is right. We are just like these precious robins who know instinctively when they are to leave the nest. They will get a little nudge from their father, sending them on their way, willing and ready to be in the world. And so will we get a little nudge from our Father at the perfect time that we are ready to complete our journey and go back to living, restored and ready to take each day as it comes. Isn't it just the best to have a Father who protects us, feeds us, and cares for us just like the father robin? Then when we are ready, he sends us off with complete assurance that today is the day. We can just know it!

May 30. America the Beautiful

> Then the land will yield its harvest, and God,
> our God, will bless us. God will bless us,
> and all the ends of the earth will fear him.
>
> —Psalm 67:6–7

Memorial Day arrived, and in our church service yesterday one of our choir leaders sang "America the Beautiful," a patriotic hymn whose final version was completed one hundred years ago in 1913. It was originally a poem written by Katharine Lee Bates, whose heart was moved as she traveled across the United States. Here is the first verse of the lyrics that we sing today.

> O beautiful for spacious skies,
> For amber waves of grain,
> For purple mountain majesties
> Above the fruited plain!
> America! America!
> God shed his grace on thee
> And crown thy good with brotherhood
> From sea to shining sea!

Let us think about this gift that we have been given, this America, and the men and women who fight for our freedom that we hold so dear. Without their service and love for America, we could not sit here today and share special times with family and friends. To them we give our deepest thanks. America is the greatest country in the world, a place where we can worship freely and live gloriously. Thanks be to God, our Father, who has shed his grace on thee, who has given us this great land with neighbors who are a brotherhood of citizens with whom we share the great and wondrous gift of freedom. Our freedom and our lives of joy are protected and guarded by these dedicated warriors who love our America and preserve our inalienable rights as found in our Declaration of Independence, the right to life, liberty, and the pursuit of happiness. That's our America! That's our land we love so dearly! Somewhere found there between the shining seas, among the mountains and plains of waving grain, under God's spacious skies, is that special place that each of us calls home, somewhere where we can just be us. So God Bless America, and God bless you!

May 31. A Little Bit of Heaven

For by him all things were created, things in heaven and
on earth, visible and invisible, whether thrones or powers
or rulers or authorities; all things were created by him
and for him.

—Colossians 1:16

I went to see the movie *Heaven is for Real*. The story is that of
a four-year-old boy named Colton who has emergency surgery.
While he is on the operating table, he goes to heaven. He sees
Jesus, people in his family, angels. Colton survives the surgery, and
in the ensuing months tells his parents about his visit to heaven.
He reveals tidbits to them that he could not possibly know about
living here on earth. To see his view of heaven is so comforting
and affirming. We too see heaven each and every day that we
live here on earth: in the cry of a newborn baby, in the smile of a
stranger, or in the hug of a friend. The Lord provides us with a
little bit of heaven all the time if we keep our eyes open and see
his glory right before us. His magnificence is revealed in nature
as flowers open up their gorgeous blooms, trees put on bright
green leaves, soft breezes blow, and sunsets glow stunning shades
of orange and pink. Tiny birds and baby animals are born, and
nature is at its best! Let us give thanks for the promise of Jesus,
that as heavenly as these things of earth are, heaven is infinitely
better. We will walk, talk, and share the rest of our lives with
Jesus. Heaven—better than anything we can imagine!

June 1. Inside Out!

> The Lord your God will circumcise your hearts and the
> hearts of your descendants so that you may love him with
> all your heart and with all your soul and live.
>
> —Deuteronomy 30:6

I have some jeans that I bought a couple of years ago that I just love to wear. They have silver paint applied down the sides of the legs. They came with washing instructions that said, "Turn inside out to wash." I have followed these instructions since the beginning, and they are as good as new. Other items that I have not taken such care with have lost their color, becoming faded and dingy with time. Inside out. These are the washing instructions of the Lord too. He wants to take good care of us by changing us from the inside out. He starts with our hearts, washing them gently so that when he is done, we always remain good as new. This gentle care by our Maker leads us to a life that celebrates him and always points to his glory. Because he loves us so, he wants to use the very best washing instructions. After he is done, he will have given us hearts that allow us to live, and live abundantly so that we may love him with all our hearts and with all our souls. Now isn't that just like a Father who loves us, his own children, so much that he takes special care when dealing with our hearts? That's who he is, our Father, the one who always knows the best way to change things—from the inside out!

June 2. The Calm after the Storm

Then they cried out to the Lord in their trouble,
and he brought them out of their distress. He stilled the
storm to a whisper; the waves of the sea were hushed.
They were glad when it grew calm, and he guided them
to their desired haven. Let us give thanks to the Lord for
his unfailing love.

—Psalm 107:28–30

So much of our lives are paralleled in nature. I was sitting outside yesterday morning after a refreshing rainstorm blew through. There is nothing quite like that calm that pervades the air after a thunderstorm. The birds were chirping, the clouds had begun to break up, and the bluest blue was peeking out through the still-dark clouds in the sky. A soft breeze gently goes by, and the world is at peace again, refreshed and washed clean by the stormy waters that fell from the sky. Our lives are just like this. Trials build up like storm clouds, foreboding and serious in nature. The thunderclouds of our lives back us up with the hail and winds, driving rain pours down upon us, causing worry and stress. But then the storm of life rolls through and the peace of Christ is revealed, reminding us that he is always there, even on the darkest of days. Just as blue skies are always behind those dark and foreboding ones, so the Lord is always behind our suffering, holding us tightly in his grip until that storm passes through, and our skies are blue once again.

June 3. Jesus Loves Me, This I Know

Tell it to your children, and let your children tell it to
their children, and their children to the next generation.

—Joel 1:3

I have a secret. But before I share the secret with you, I need to tell you about a party that I attended last summer for a dear friend's daughter who was having a baby. At the baby shower we were asked to write down on a piece of paper the one thing that we wanted this baby to know when she was big enough to read and understand what we wrote. Now, this is somewhat of a daunting task when you first think about it. I wish that I had written down what I am about to tell you, for this secret is the perfect response. Later, we were at dinner with another friend and asked to see the picture of his new grandson. Our friend said, "I wish that he could talk as I have so much to share with him. The very first thing that I whispered in his ear when it was my turn to hold him was 'Jesus loves you.'" Wow! I had to soak his words in. How profound is that? These three precious words spoken to this gift from God just says it all. How very simple yet how very impactful. Really, isn't this all we really need to know? If we stand on these three words, the rest falls into place—Jesus loves me. And he loves you and you and you! That's it. That's the secret. It is the secret to life. Jesus loves me, this I know. We can be sure that this secret is one for the whole world to know. So when you are chatting it up with someone today, ask them if they want to know a secret. Then smile and say, "Jesus loves you, this I know."

June 4. Walk This Way

> "…I was blind, but now I see."
>
> —John 9:25

I read an article today about this amazing nine-year-old boy named Zach who is going blind from a rare and incurable eye disease that is gradually killing his retinas. To quote his mom, "Ever since, he's been preparing to be blind, including orientation mobility lessons that will help him get through a world he will someday no longer see." He was participating in an event in downtown Dallas for blind or nearly blind people to become more adept at using their white canes to navigate the city. Many participants, including Zach, wore T-shirts that read "Fearless" on the back. There is so very much to learn from this boy in relation to our own faith walk. The reality for us is that we also cannot see, metaphorically speaking, what tomorrow will bring. Although in the verse above Jesus actually heals the blind man and gives him his sight back, praise be to God that we also have Jesus to give us our sight for each and every day—our white cane to guide our way. We must trust in the mightiest stick of all, our Lord, who will guide us through the unknown, just as Zach's white cane leads him through the perils of Dallas traffic and pedestrians. As believers, we have been preparing to be blind ever since we accepted Christ as our Savior. Although the future is unknown to us and we cannot see what tomorrow will bring, we have that perfect power, Jesus Christ. Let us know with all certainty that no matter what we cannot see coming in the future, God, our protector, will guide us through. So may we also walk this way as this child who can teach us so much about life, fearlessly!

June 5. Charmed for Sure!

> How lovely is your dwelling place, O Lord Almighty!
>
> —Psalm 84

Charm bracelets were all the rage in the fifties and sixties, and my mother had several that she wore all the time. The bracelets were packed with charms that her friends and family had given her, things of love and precious memories attached. As I look up *charm* and *charming* in the dictionary, the one word that jumps out at me is delightful. Yes, delightful! I know for sure that these charms brought delight into my mother's life, and now I am filled with delight when I wear one and think of her and her contagious spirit. Charms remind me of the friends with whom I have shared a special journey, a time when we walked through a trial together. They have become a charm that I get to wear on my charm bracelet of life. I love thinking of the memories that each represents: a heart, a bright sun, a blanket of peace, a teaspoon of joy. All the things that resulted from these walks of faith. But how can I think of these times as good times? Each of these situations has been traveled with the strength of the Lord leading the way. Each of these situations has been experienced with the love of the Lord right in the middle of everything. This dependence on Jesus is what, in the end, no matter what the outcome, makes sharing these times together delightful, for we are able to see the Lord at work in a mighty, mighty way. Charmed, you say? Yes, we are charmed, for we know that each of these charms are soldered onto a golden cross to signify the love of Christ—our peacemaker, our joy, our rescuer, our Mighty Lord! Let us find great delight in letting our minds dwell on the greatest charm on our bracelet of life—Jesus Christ our Lord. When we hear the phrase "a charmed life," may we remember that we are the ones who get to live that way, with the most precious charm there is!

June 6. Revisiting with Thanks

> Give thanks to the Lord, call on his name; make known
> among the nations what he has done. Sing to him,
> sing praise to him; tell of all his wonderful acts.
> Glorify his holy name; let the hearts of those
> who seek the Lord rejoice.
>
> —1 Chronicles 16:8–10

I am one of those people who really only likes to do things once. Just doing something one time is enough for me. I only like to see a movie once, I only like to visit a certain city once, I only like to go to a museum once. The thought came to mind right out of the blue last week that I should revisit right then and there all of the times that the Lord has brought me and my family through the fire. I started reeling off these times in my mind, and even I was surprised and thankful, so very thankful, to remember and revisit these times of trial from which my Savior has saved me and my family time after time. As clear as day, they ran through my mind, reminding me of the difficulty of each experience, but more importantly of my Lord's ever-present redeeming grace. I was reminded of his mercy in bringing me to this place of peace. As we remember his mercy and grace, let us praise him and thank him for these tough times, one by one. As much as some of us don't like returning to places we have already been, we know that he was at that spot when we arrived, the protective doorman, waiting for us with open arms. The best part is that our doorman, map in hand for the journey ahead, is there when we do arrive, and his map always leads us to a place of comfort and resolution, if we only give him the lead.

June 7. He's Not Afraid to Be Great

Therefore, since we have a great High Priest who has
gone through the heavens, Jesus the Son of God, let us
hold firmly to the faith that we possess.

—Hebrews 4:14

Last week, I read an article about a new Dallas Cowboys player who has joined the team. A former Cowboy was talking about this rookie, saying that he is not afraid to be great. This caught my attention. In applying it to our faith, let us not be afraid to be great. This will mean different things to different people. But here are some ways that we can be great for Jesus. Let us be willing to put ourselves out there, sharing our faith with those we are with, even if it might feel awkward or make us uneasy at times. Let us reach out a helping hand to someone who needs a hand, even if this means that we sacrifice something that we may want. Let us take time out of our day to spend time with Jesus, even if we still have a magazine that we want to read or a television show that we want to watch. Let us be great for the Lord, and however that looks for each of us personally, we will not look back and wish that we had. Jesus loves us with the greatest love there is. May we take his love and implement it into the lives of others, revealing a heart that is *great-full* for his love.

June 8. PLZ...O RLY? LOL

> My command is this: Love one another
> as I have loved you.
>
> —John 15:12

2day I got a text from my grandchild, and it went like this: "JK...
plz...IDK, do you? OIC, you are a noob, now I am ROTFL."
Whoa? What? Have I just dropped into a foreign land somewhere?
I was conversing with one of my grandchildren, yet he was speaking
a totally different language from the one I know. This, my friends,
is a snippet of words from the new and ever-changing texting
glossary. These letters represent a litany of phrases so that people
who text can use them as shortcuts and do not have to type so
many letters. The ones in the know understand these symbols and
know exactly what is being said. However, some of us, including
me, are lost souls at this. But there is a universal language that all
of us can speak, and even those around the world will recognize
this language. It is the language of love—agape love. What kind
of love language is this? It is unconditional, selfless love of acting
with no benefit to self. We humans can show this kind of love to
one another because we receive this love from our Father, who is
love. His love is the highest type of agape love, his unconditional
love for his children. So if we want to speak a language that is
instantly recognizable by everyone we meet and the language that
all people everywhere desire to hear and know for themselves, let
us speak agape love. It speaks to the very soul of us. Even this new
generation of young people, who speak this unfamiliar texting
language, will embrace this love. 2day let's plz try speaking the
language that we have learned so well from our heavenly Father.
As it says in 1 Corinthians 8, "Love never fails." How great to
know a language that will never be misunderstood, much unlike
the RU, JK, O RLY, LOL form. And just for the record, for those

of you who think that LOL means "lots of love" like I did, it really means "laughing out loud." LOL at myself and ROTFL—rolling on the floor laughing!

June 9. Row, Row, Row Your Boat!

In my distress I called to the Lord; I called out to my
God. From his temple he heard my voice;
my cry came to his ears.

—2 Samuel 22:7

We are headed to Florida, and while we are there we can use all kinds of boats: paddleboats, rowboats, canal boats, and YOLO boards. I can only imagine my trying that YOLO thing. You stand on something similar to a large surfboard and use a long paddle to row yourself through the water. YOLO stands for "you only live once." There are so many clever people in this world! I am pretty sure that I will leave that YOLO activity to the younger ones on the trip. Recently a friend and I started talking about all the wonderful people we know and the journeys that they are going through right now. I said to her, "We are all in the same boat, but we are just rowing with a different paddle." Yes, that is it! We are all in the boat named life, yet each of us is holding a different paddle with various names on them relating to the journey that we are on at the moment. One paddle is named "financial," for some of us are dealing with money matters. Some of us are rowing with a paddle named "family," for our family is facing a difficulty. Some of us are paddling as hard as we can with that paddle named "health" as we deal with medical situations. There are many, many paddles rowing our boat of life. The reality is this: We are all living life and calling on our Lord and Savior to help us row through the turbulent waters. He is providing each of us a tarp of care around us to keep us warm from the chilly waters that are splashing up from beneath our boat. Although trouble will come as we all know from looking at the names on our own paddles, the blessing is provided by the gift of our Savior, Jesus Christ, who knows our troubles and has gone before us to warm up the waters of life and calm down the surging waves. Our rudder, Jesus, is always underneath our boat, keeping us steady and moving in the right direction!

June 10. Lost and Found

> If a man owns a hundred sheep, and one of them wanders
> away, will he not leave the ninety-nine on the hills and go
> look for the one that wandered off? And if he finds it,
> I tell you the truth, he is happier about that one sheep
> than about the ninety-nine that did not wander off. In
> the same way your Father in heaven is not willing that
> any of these little ones should be lost.
>
> —Matthew 18:12–14

I am fascinated with the whole idea of a lost and found. I have on occasion needed to visit one of these looking for items that one of my children has lost, either at school or at the pool or even at a restaurant or two. Lost and found. I love that term. It precisely describes what it is: a place for items that are lost to be found. Having visited many of these places, however, this does not seem to be the case. Yes, the items there have been lost by their owners, but rarely it seems they are then found. I am not sure why this is. I have found, so to speak, unbelievable things that people obviously have chosen not to recapture. The good news is that the Lord doesn't just leave us in the lost and found, unwilling to search for us when we go astray. He longs to bring us back to his fold, calling our names and seeking us out to restore us to him. We are his sheep whom he loves. He searches day and night for us, unwilling to leave us in that cold and unprotected place where we have roamed. What a relief to know that we are loved beyond measure by God who will not rest until he finds us. Even if he cannot hear the sound of our voice, he knows how and where to find us. Now who could ask for more than that?

June 11. Have You Taken Your Vitamins Today?

So Abraham called that place The Lord Will Provide.
And to this day it is said,
"On the mountain of the Lord it will be provided."

—Genesis 22:14

Daily vitamins—we have all been encouraged for years to take vitamins daily. Many companies offer a daily pack of the vitamins that one needs, to be taken all together so that you will live a healthy life. I wish it were this easy. I think that we are all at the mercy of the people we know who give us advice on what to take daily. The good news is that our Great Physician provides the true daily vitamins we need to live a life that brings him glory. He supplies vitamins for our every need through his grace and love. These include vitamin A (abundance): He gives us life abundant through his love and mercy. Vitamin B (beauty): His beauty found in all things of this beautiful world. Vitamin C (compassion): He delivers a daily dose of compassion for each of us as we travel through this life. Vitamin D (direction): We never need to feel lost or ask for directions again, for he is always there to show us the way. Vitamin E (empathy): Jesus knows our situation and empathizes with us. What vitamins from the Lord do you need to make you feel better? Have you taken your vitamins today?

June 12. Clearing the Clutter

> He says, "Be still, and know that I am God."
>
> —Psalm 46:10

It's June already. How can that be? It seems as if I was just putting up the Easter bunnies last week. But here we are, rolling into summer, and I am still planning on clearing out the clutter. I have been longing to unclutter for a while. When I am with friends, we all talk about scaling down, reducing the clutter, making our space cleaner and less filled with stuff. We are all called to reduce the clutter, the clutter of our minds, by Jesus who longs to fill this space with his words, his guidance, his glory. In the same way that it is hard for us to remove items in our lives that take up space and create confusion, often we have a hard time slowing down, clearing our minds to be with our Lord who longs to spend time with us. It is much more difficult to hear his voice as we scurry about our day, doing errand after errand, not able to stop and hear what he has to say. So as we think of removing clutter from our spaces, let us also unclutter our minds and free up some of our time to spend with Jesus. Just as we often feel so much better when we get rid of the stuff, we will know the freedom found in sharing time with the Lord, clearing our minds of what we need to do next, letting his precious words replace the clutter found there.

June 13. A Snail's Pace

> It was the Lord our God himself…who protected us
> on our entire journey and among all nations
> through which we traveled.
>
> —Joshua 24:17

Snails—now there's a critter that most people are not crazy about, for they eat their way through our vegetation, wreaking havoc wherever they go. Walking my dog last week, I kept passing these great big snails, slowly moving along the sidewalk. I jumped and skipped lightly over them, for the sight of a smashed snail is not one that I like to see. But my dog stepped across one, knocking it sideways, kind of tossing its shell to the side. I quickly got it upright, and with no harm done the snail was on its way again. I noticed that its shell was able to take quite a blow and that this protective covering was all that it needed to fend off danger and keep on going. Like these snails, we also have that protective covering, provided by our Father who gives us protection from hard knocks every minute of every day. He has given us Jesus, under whose protection we can hide and recover from life's blows as they come unexpectedly toward us. There is not one of life's knocks that we cannot withstand with Jesus by our side. He gently reaches down, uprights us, dusts us off, and sends us on our way. Traveling life's journeys is so much easier with the Lord there to fend off the blows of life. What more could we ask for than this shell of protection? What a reassurance to know that he's got our backs, no matter what comes our way today!

June 14. Brain Freeze

> "For I know the plans I have for you," declares the Lord,
> "plans to prosper you and not to harm you, plans to give
> you hope and a future. Then you will call upon me and
> come and pray to me, and I will listen to you. You will seek
> me and find me when you seek me with all your heart."
>
> —Jeremiah 29:11–13

Here we are in the Texas heat in June. On a little weekend trip with our daughter and her husband, we found a shaved ice stand right in the middle of the town that we were driving through and decided to stop. Our son-in-law is crazy nuts over shaved ice, and there were over a hundred choices of flavors from which to choose. As I began to eat mine, I got what is commonly known as a brain freeze. The coldness of the ice went straight to my head and instantly created a crushing blow. I started thinking about other types of brain freezes, such as the ones that come in life and stop us in our tracks, so impactful that we don't know which way to turn. This is the time in our lives to turn it all over to Jesus. He is prepared to stop the pain and move us off square one where we are stuck, frozen in time and space. Jesus can unfreeze us and get us started again, moving us in the right direction. His ever-warming presence in the midst of an uncertain situation will restart us and melt away the fear of the unknown through his mercy and grace. There is never a frozen time in life that he cannot handle. Just take a deep breath and place it all in his hands where he can and will bring warmth and joy back through his power and might.

June 15. The Flytrap

> The path of the righteous is level; O upright One,
> you make the way of the righteous smooth. Yes, Lord,
> walking in the way of your laws, we wait for you; your
> name and renown are the desire of our hearts. My soul
> yearns for you in the night; in the morning my spirit
> longs for you.
>
> —Isaiah 26:7–9

Twelve of us in our family rented one house in Florida. It was great fun, blending all the adults and kids into one big house. One of the most special parts of the trip, oddly enough, was the huge front porch of the house that had a very large and sturdy swing and Adirondack chairs on it. As we sat there on that swing throughout the early mornings and late afternoons, we shared our lives and talked about everything and nothing, learning a lot and learning nothing about each other. Our son named it *the flytrap*, for we were literally stuck to it as if we were flies on a sticky pad, caught and glued securely to its surface. The beauty of this swing was that it drew all of us in, creating the perfect environment for loving each other and spending time together that would otherwise not have happened. Doesn't this swing so remind us of Jesus, who draws us to him as if we were moths to a flame, calling us to share time in his presence and swing gently to the rhythm of his love? As much as everyone in our family wanted to pack this meaningful swing into our suitcases, it wouldn't fit. But we did return with Jesus in our hearts. All of us, you and I, have every opportunity to sit by the side of our Savior, enjoying sweet family time in his ever-present company. He sticks to us like glue and will never be pulled away from us for any reason! As we yearn for him early and late, let us draw close to his side and hear his words of love softly floating to our ears, filling our souls with his precious and ever-present goodness.

June 16. Snack in Between

Let them give thanks to the Lord for his unfailing love
and his wonderful deeds for men, for he satisfies the
thirsty and fills the hungry with good things.

—Psalm 107:8–9

I have a clever little flip-book with all kinds of inspirational sayings in it, and the one that I read today says this.

Hope for the best

Plan for the worst

Snack in between

As lighthearted as this may sound, it has some significant implications for us to use as we go about our daily lives. "Hope for the best"—good idea here. Hope is always in style, for Jesus came to give us hope in all situations. "Plan for the worst"— another good idea, for that Boy Scout motto *Be Prepared* has seemed to be invaluable throughout the years for all of us who know it. So plan for the worst and be prepared for it. The only way to plan for the worst is to live each and every day with the assurance that no matter when that worst happens, and it will, Jesus, our Savior, will see us through to the end of that worst, whatever it may be. Now the last sentence, "Snack in Between" is so grand, for snacking is one of my favorite things to do. In applying this in a more important way, let us snack on the words of the Lord throughout the day, supplementing our daily meals with his words of joy, comfort, trust, and love so that we are never hungry for direction nor lack being fulfilled with his word. We can draw on our reserve of snacks, keeping us full of his promises, filled to the brim with his snacks for living!

June 17. Can You Define That?

Let us fix our eyes upon Jesus, the author and perfecter
of our faith, who for the joy set before him endured the
cross, scorning its shame, and sat down at the right hand
of the throne of God.

—Hebrews 12:2

When writing, I often think that I know the definition of a word, but sometimes I like to look it up anyway to be sure that I am using it in the right context. Then when I reread a sentence that I have written, I realize that I need to replace one word with another that is closer and clearer in meaning. We also are defined in various ways. People may connect us to our parents or to one of our children or through the job that we have. But to know who we are with the clearest and most precious definition is to look to the words of the Lord. Jesus says, "I am the vine; you are the branches" (John 15:1); "But I have called you friends" (John 15:15); "We are fellow heirs with Christ" (Romans 8:17); "We are a 'new creation'" (2 Corinthians 5:17). As we are the children of the Most High God, we can set our lives in the context of his words, finding a more understandable meaning for ourselves. He is the one who sets the tone for our knowing who we are. We belong to Jesus. He has chosen us for always, we are his and loved completely by him, the author of our faith. This defining knowledge assures us that we have been claimed by him, encouraging us to live accordingly. We have now been completely made new by his loving us. It is in him that we can understand clearly and certainly our definition of who we are and shape our lives according to his perfect and holy plan.

June 18. The Lucky Children

> Jesus said to them, "My Father is always at his
> work to this very day, and I, too, am working."
>
> —John 5:17

Father's Day, once again, will be celebrated soon. The speaker at a recent meeting was talking about decorating with a Chinese theme, using huge representations of the Lucky Children worshipped in China. Having never heard of this term before, I turned to the Internet to reveal anything of interest. The most applicable explanation revealed that the Chinese believe good fortune can be cultivated or carelessly lost. It is all in the hands of the god of luck. The term comes from a tale long, long ago of two fierce green lions that preyed on the children of China. The locals prayed to gods for deliverance of these children. The celestial Jade Emperor sent two spirits manifested in the form of children to the earth, and they vanquished the lions through cunning and skill. Thus, these two children are referred to as Lucky Children. We, as believers in our most high God, know that we are the lucky children, the blessed children of our Father in heaven! We are the children whom he calls his own. Our future is in his hands, and luck has absolutely nothing to do with it. He has called us to be his, forever and always. Our future belongs to the one who called us to be his children, our heavenly Father. We who call him Father are his blessed children and know beyond a doubt that he loves us as only a Father can.

June 19. That's What Fathers Do

> For you did not receive a spirit that makes you a slave
> again to fear, but you received the spirit of sonship.
> And by him we cry, "Abba, Father."
>
> —Romans 8:15

Killing the Monsters

Father's Day has rolled around again, and I read something the other day that took me back, way back, to when I was a little girl. My daddy was sweet, calm, and patient beyond measure, especially with a little girl who was afraid of the dark. I was terrified, actually. Every time that light would go off, my mind would start to imagine terrible monsters and creepy things either under my bed or coming out of my closet. Experiencing a few minutes of this unexplained terror, I would start calling out my daddy's name: a whisper, then a gentle sound, until it grew into what sounded to my ears as a terrified scream, although I am sure that it wasn't. My precious daddy would come quietly into my room, and somehow he could fix it for me. I came across this quote about fathers by Fiona Wallace that could have been written about my daddy:

> "The monsters are gone."
> "Really?" Doubtful.
> "I killed the monsters. That's what fathers do."

This defines exactly what the Father of us all does. He takes the monsters in our lives and kills them. He fixes things. We, as believers, are loved by our Father who kills the monsters and rescues us from our fears. Let us fall to our knees in grateful thanks knowing that we have the perfect Father who never fails to come when we call, killing all the monsters and leaving us comforted in his perfect love.

June 20. Too Hot to Handle

...the Lord knows how to rescue godly men from trials...
                                        —2 Peter 2:9

The days of summer are getting hotter, and as I step out to walk, I remember that I need to go earlier to be able to stay cooler and not get caught under the hot June sun. When I do go out a little too late and the sun is high in the blue, summer sky, I know that I have waited too long, for Mojo, my dog, and I start to get hot really quickly. Many times, however, to my great delight, I will be walking, getting warmer by the minute, and then all of a sudden a cool breeze wafts across my path, bringing such delight with it. I always think of Jesus when this happens, for so many times in my life he has done this very same thing. All of us have had this experience during a time when the fires of life are getting hotter and hotter and we have no idea how to cool them down. But with prayer and trust in the Lord, we find that he sends his cooling touch right down upon our trials by fire and relieves us from the heat of the moment. We all have plans on what our days will look like, but so often these plans go awry and we find ourselves in the middle of a difficult situation, feeling its heat. The Lord knows that we need his help to bring a cooling presence, and he longs to provide just what we need at just the right moment. The next time that we are out and about, sweating under the hot Texas sun and a cooling breeze comes our way out of the blue, we can know and remember how Jesus is always there to bring his merciful relief to any situation that is too hot for us to handle!

June 21. Will Wonders Never Cease?

As far as the east is from the west,
so far has he removed our transgressions from us.

—Psalms 103:12

Having just returned from a vacation in Florida, I never cease to be amazed by the majesty and power that I find in the ocean. Even just enjoying its beauty from the shore belies its strength and true magnitude as one of God's greatest wonders. All of God's gifts to us affect us in just the same way: the magnificent sky full of twinkling stars and glowing planets, the majestic mountains with their snowcapped peaks, the glorious sunrise on an early winter's morning, and the peaceful sunset at dusk as fall begins to come. These are God's assurances in nature that he loves us and wants us to know him through these gifts. The phrase, "Will wonders never cease?" reminds us of the Lord, who made all the true wonders of this world for us to enjoy and glorify his name. Will his wonders never cease? No, never. Just as certain as we can be that the sun will rise tomorrow and the oceans will send the tide to the shore, so can we trust in his certainty that he has removed our transgressions from us as it is written in Psalms above. How *wonder-full* is that? Not only has he covered the earth with his wonderful gifts, he has wonderfully removed our sins by dying on the cross in our place. Will wonders never cease? No. Not now, not ever, because of Jesus.

June 22. *The Landfill Harmonic*

> So he (the angel) said to me, "This is the word of the
> Lord to Zerubbabel: 'Not by might nor by power,
> but by my Spirit,' says the Lord Almighty."
> —Zechariah 4:6

The indomitable human spirit—once again a story proves to us that we have been given an indomitable human spirit by our Father that no circumstance can stop if we choose to grab life with God's hands and use it for his glory. The story, now a movie, is called *The Landfill Harmonic*. It is set in Cateura, Paraguay, a poor area of the world where people are living off the refuse of others—women, children, and men, all living off trash. The men in this place found an old, battered violin, took it, restored it with more trash from the landfill, and gave it to a student, teaching her to play it. As God is able to do, more and more instruments were made from this huge dump, allowing more and more of his children to develop a love for music and play for his glory. The message here from this community is that nothing is really trash; nothing should ever be considered of no value, especially people, especially children. The message for us is that God, our Father, has done the same with us. He has taken us sinners and redeemed us through his Son, Jesus Christ, recycling us for his glory. It's just that simple. We have been transformed by the Redeemer himself to make beautiful music for him with our lives. The description for this movie is "transforming trash into music; about love, courage, and creativity." This too is the perfect description for our lives. The Lord has transformed us to make a life of music for his glory through love, courage, and creativity. This is a story that you will never forget. It is the story of each and every life redeemed by our Father. It is the story of the indomitable human spirit!

June 23. Spiders and Snakes, Oh My!

A righteous man may have many troubles, but the Lord
delivers him from them all.

—Psalm 34:19

Walking out in the country is so delightful, but this time of year it brings a special set of circumstances with it. It is during the summer months that snakes are out and about, free from hibernating all winter, enjoying the warm summer sun. Spiders are busy building their incredible webs, some the likes of which cannot be believed. Last month I was doing just this, walking on a country road, enjoying the summer sun. At first, I accidentally walked through an enormous spider's web that he had probably been working on for eons. It covered quite a large area and was magnificent in its structure. Yet breaking through it creeped me out. Then, about ten feet in front of me I saw a long, gray snake covering my path with his body. I stopped and slowly began to step backward in order not to alarm him in any way. So, these unpleasant sightings in nature lead us to think on the times in our lives when the "spiders and snakes" of life have crossed our paths, causing alarm and worry. We have been given the perfect tool with which to deal with these trials in life: Jesus Christ. He calls us to "let go and let God." These are scary times that we will all experience at one time or another. But thanks to the mercy and grace of our Lord and Savior, we can find assurance and peace by placing them in his perfect hands, resting in the certain knowledge that he has all of the tools necessary to handle any of these troublesome "spiders and snakes" that we will cross over as we journey along through our days.

June 24. Missing the Cacti

> I always thank God for you because of his grace given
> you in Christ Jesus. For in him you have been enriched
> in every way—in all your speaking and in all your
> knowledge—because our testimony about
> Christ was confirmed in you.
>
> —1 Corinthians 1:4–7

While on a quick visit to some property in southwest Texas, my dog, Mojo, and I went walking on the property, which is filled with cacti. These cacti were everywhere, in full bloom and so beautiful with bright yellow and orange blooms just bursting forth in a summer array of color. Mojo loves to walk off leash. He sprints through the terrain, weaving his way through these cacti seemingly without any problem. I find this fascinating, for he is moving quite quickly through fields of them problem-free. Somehow, someway, he manages to miss stepping on them every time. We have this same gift given to us by Jesus. As we move through the cacti of life, we can be prepared to miss stepping on them by relying on the presence of our Lord, our Savior. He is here with us in life, showing us how to miss all these prickly situations that would make us very uncomfortable. When we start our day, if we begin in prayer asking Jesus to provide us with his grace, our days will be better. That's it. Our days will be better, and who of us does not want a cactus-free day? Let us remember, like Mojo who is able to skirt through those potentially pain-producing plants, how we will be able to miss many of the painful situations that life could present by relying on the Lord.

June 25. The Whole Thing!

When he had received the drink,
Jesus said, "It is finished."

—John 19:30

Summertime, and the livin' is easy. I seem to eat more in the summer than in the wintertime. In the summer, meals are so much more fun; the food is light, the daylight lasts longer. This is my time of year! I cannot actually pinpoint when I started eating everything that I see rather than just a portion of it, but I am so enjoying this summer fare. I am reminded of our Savior who took our sins, not in part but in whole! He took all of it, every undesirable part, so that we might be justified and washed as white as snow. To really get our minds around that, we must think of the alternative. What if he had decided to just take a part of our sins? What if he had decided that there was some of it that he didn't want to take as his own and gave us the leftovers? What if we were left living with the sinful parts of life forever that he couldn't quite stomach? That is why we call him Savior, the Finisher of our Faith, because he did finish the job, once and for all, and we are now complete! Now we can sing with great joy, as in this hymn by H. G. Spafford: "My sin, not in part but the whole, / Is nailed to the cross and I bear it no more. / It is well, it is well with my soul."

June 26. Flying Free

> For this reason I kneel before the Father, from whom his
> whole family in heaven and on earth derives its name. I
> pray that out of his glorious riches he may strengthen you
> with power through his Spirit in your inner being, so that
> Christ may dwell in your hearts through faith. And I pray
> that you, being rooted and established in love, may have
> power, together with all the saints, to grasp how wide and
> long and high and deep is the love of Christ, and to know
> this love that surpasses knowledge—that you may be
> filled to the measure of all the fullness of God.
>
> —Ephesians 3:14–19

Butterflies—is there anything more beautiful than a butterfly in flight with its gossamer wings spread out and floating through the air as it flutters by, its magnificent colors reflecting the sun's light? They seem to move about with a freedom that is enviable to all who see them. In the same way, let us think of God's wrapping up our troubles, removing them from our thoughts and lives, replacing them with his freedom, freeing us from the worry and pain. He and only he is truly able to take them ever so gently away, as if on the wings of a butterfly. Through the power of the cross, we can release them into the world carried on the shoulders of the one who loves us. He replaces our difficulties with his never-ending love, filling that now-empty place with the fullness of God. Just to think that, like these lovely creatures who fly freely in this wonderful world, we too can do this if only we allow ourselves to release our troubles to Jesus, removing the weight often too much for us to handle. He is here, always here, just waiting to set us free if we will just call on his name.

June 27. Pairing Mode

The Lord is near to all who call on him,
to all who call on him in truth.

—Psalm 145:18

I just love all this new technology that has come to us in the last year or so. I have a Jawbone, which is a wireless Bluetooth box that connects to my phone and plays music through it. So much music! So much fun! When I connect my Jawbone box, after turning it on a voice says, "Jawbone is in pairing mode." Pairing mode—waiting to pair up to the phone and receive the music that will come from there. The thought crossed my mind this morning as I heard it say those words, "pairing mode," that this is exactly what the Lord does each and every day, waiting patiently for us to connect to him. He is always there, in pairing mode, immediately connecting with us when we choose. Not once will he not sense our signal if we send it. Not once will he not be available to connect to us. As hard as it is for us to understand how these technical devices work, it is just that easy for us to understand that the Lord is always there, talking with us clearly and lovingly. He never disappoints. We have an instant connection to the one we need to hear from the most—our encourager, our healer, our protector, our counselor, our light of the world. Amen!

June 28. Clear the Way!

Then Job replied to the Lord:
"I know that you can do all things;
no plan of yours can be thwarted."

—Job 42:2

Walking along for exercise, just minding my own business today, I kept stepping on some unusual-looking, fairly large green thingamajigs that had come from some tree. Not recognizing what they were, yet stepping lightly on one, I realized right away that they were hard, unyielding, and could potentially cause me to slip, possibly breaking something or another. So I kept my eyes to the ground, dodging them as if they were hazards on the road. I kept kicking them away, out of my path, to provide a clear way for myself. Isn't this what our Father does for us? He goes before us in life, kicking away the unseen difficulties so that we will have a smoother way to walk. We will never truly know how many thingamajigs he has removed from our path of life. He longs to make the way safe and hazard-free for all of us, his children. Yet there are times when we do come across a burr that trips us up. We stumble, we may even fall, but we can know with his complete assurance that, no matter how rough the fall, he will always upright us, put a bandage on our scrape, and send us on our way. How mighty is our Father to straighten out our paths and place us exactly where he wants us to be!

June 29. But the Lord Said No!

"For I know the plans that I have for you," declares
the Lord, "plans to prosper you and not to harm you,
plans to give you hope and a future."

—Jeremiah 29:11

About six or eight years ago, I was walking and thinking on some sad news that I had just received. While praying I heard the words in my mind, several verses to be exact, to write as a song about the situation about which I was praying. I ran home and wrote down these verses to my song, thinking that this was the start of my long-desired career in songwriting. I even got a young musician friend to put music to it. But the Lord said no. No songwriting career for me. So my song sits in my bookcase, unheard, and not making me a songwriter for the Lord. Are we happy when the Lord says no to something that we really long to do? Probably not. Do we sort of wish for a yes, yet not knowing what else he has in store for us? Probably so. In my case, my Father knew that one day he needed me and my mind to be free of all else so that I could hear his voice for these writings. He has a mighty plan for each of us, one that we cannot possibly know until he reveals it to us. Would I love to have been a songwriter? Absolutely! Do I know that his plan for me is the perfect one? For sure! All we can ever know is that he has our best interests at heart, and when he is ready we will know it. Beyond a shadow of a doubt, we will hear his plan for our lives. So let's keep reaching for that apple called our dreams, and at that perfect time allowed by God it will drop into our hands, ripe and ready to eat, fulfilling our greatest desires!

June 30. Oh, Joy!

> May the God of hope fill you with all joy
> and peace as you trust in him...
>
> —Romans 15:13

My husband and I attended a wedding last Saturday night that celebrated the union of a couple that is so precious and dear to us. At the end of the minister's chat with the adorable couple getting married, he said this: "Find joy in your life and do not let your life take your joy." Find joy in your life. Sometimes we get so caught up in the act of living that joy does become hard to find. Either we are moving so fast that we lose sight of the joy in our lives or we let ourselves get towed under by our work, our meetings, our to-do list, our whatever, and that leaves little time for true joy. The minister's call to not let your life take your joy away reminds us to focus on the one truth that we all know as believers—we belong to Jesus. Even in the darkest of times we can know his ray of light in this very thought—Jesus loves us, has redeemed us, and will never leave us. Joy is defined in the dictionary as "a lively emotion of happiness; anything which causes delight." Our being children of the most high God brings great delight to us. But adding to this delight is the contentment, peace, and reassurance we have in Jesus. Knowing these feelings can enhance our joy and take it to its deepest level. So may we know pure joy each and every day by thinking on the joy found in Jesus, no matter what each day may bring. Oh, joy!

July 1. The One Less Traveled

> By faith, Abraham, when called to go to a place he would
> later receive as his inheritance, obeyed and went,
> even though he did not know where he was going.
>
> —Hebrews 11:8

A well-known and loved poem "The Road Not Taken" by Robert
Frost says:

> Two roads diverged in a yellow wood,
> And sorry I could not travel both
> And be one traveler, long I stood
> And looked down one as far as I could
> To where it bent in the undergrowth;
> Then took the other, as just as fair,…
> Two roads diverged in a wood, and I—
> I took the one less traveled by,
> And that has made all of the difference.

I have always been fascinated by this poem, for it seems to hold
some sort of mystery. Yet we as believers know that whatever
road one takes does not matter one little bit. What does matter
is that we put our faith in the absolute knowledge that the Lord
is guiding our steps and traveling the road we are on with us.
The good news is that although, like Abraham, none of us really
knows where the road will take us, we can be certain that all
we need to do is trust and obey. The road, whether rocky or
smooth, steep or downhill, will be paved by our glorious God.
Just as Abraham trusted that his steps were being directed by the
Lord, so shall we too rely not on the road but on the road keeper!
Enjoy your travels, no matter where they lead. Whatever road you
find yourself walking down, Jesus is there, and that has made all
the difference.

July 2. You Light up My Life

I have come into the world as a light, so that no one
who believes in me should stay in darkness.

—John 12:46

While vacationing in Florida, our younger son had to return home from the trip early for work, so my husband and I drove him to the airport at nightfall. Just as we started out, the clouds erupted with this driving rain, the likes of which I cannot remember in quite some time. I was driving, and I could hardly see an inch in front of me because the rain was coming down so hard. The only way that I could stay the course was to follow this long line of very bright yellow lights that lined the road on which we were traveling. They were the brightest yellow that you have ever seen, making a perfect line of sorts for your eye to follow. I decided right away that the only way I could get us to the airport safely was to keep my eyes on this string of glowing yellow lights, for everything else was completely covered in rain—pouring, beating down, driving rain! Thanks to Jesus and this string of beautiful lights, we managed to arrive at our destination safely without a scratch. Just as my eyes were drawn to these lifesaving lights that night, so are our eyes to be focused on the Lord, whose light will always show us the way. These lights that night were a lifesaver, and so is he! He is the only one whose light will never grow dim, even in the downpours of life. By his guidance, we will always arrive safely, even if we hit a curb or two along the way.

July 3. Let Freedom Ring!

Now the Lord is the Spirit, and where the
Spirit of the Lord is, there is freedom.

—2 Corinthians 3:17

On July 4, 1776, our forefathers gathered to sign the Declaration of Independence: "We hold these truths to be self-evident, that all men are created equal, that they are endowed by their Creator with certain unalienable Rights, that among these are Life, Liberty, and the pursuit of Happiness." Our forefathers must have written these words with the scripture above in mind, for they set up the laws of our country with the certainty that where the Spirit of the Lord is, there is freedom. And freedom is exactly what they fought for and won for our nation. Thanks be to God for his leading these men to such victory! So now, today, how does this impact us? What we as Christians know is that we can always stand on this verse, no matter what our circumstances, no matter where we are in life. Whatever our imprisonment looks like to us, we have freedom! We have freedom through our faith in Jesus Christ, for he has given us his Spirit to secure our freedom in all circumstances. So we have much to celebrate today, freedom that continues to be a gracious gift by those who serve in our military. Just as the rockets' red glare gave proof through the night that our flag was still there, so will we know, as we see the exciting bursts of color from the fireworks this July 4, that our freedom still rings! Step out with joy and shout with excitement that we are free. Free to be you and me!

July 4. Independence Day

> Find rest, O my soul, in God alone; my hope comes from
> him. He alone is my rock and my salvation; he is my
> fortress, I will not be shaken. My salvation and my honor
> depend on God; he is my mighty rock, my refuge.
>
> —Psalm 62:5–7

Last week, I was talking with the lovely woman who helps me in my home, reminding her that Independence Day falls this week, a national holiday. She looked confused, and I could readily tell that she was not familiar with this holiday as she is from Costa Rica. So I gave her the update on what this day is to Americans. It helped me redefine for myself what this holiday really does mean to all of us blessed to be called Americans. America, land of the free and home of the brave; freedom from the rule of others, including the freedom to worship as we please. This independence allows us to be dependent on God, dependent on his leading, dependent on his guidance, dependent to hear his voice in the wilderness of life, a dependence that we must cherish always. Now most of us, I am sure, like to think that we are independent. But the reality is that we are called by our Father to be dependent, dependent on him for everything in life. There is some irony to the fact that as we celebrate our Independence Day, we must also be thankful that we are now able to depend on Christ for all things as we worship him freely. Let's celebrate with great joy that through our independence we have been given the freedom of dependence, dependence on our one true God who delivered us then and still delivers us today!

July 5. Move Over, Please

> He replied, "Because you have so little faith, I tell you
> the truth. If you have faith as small as a mustard seed,
> you can say to this mountain, 'Move from here to there,'
> and it will move. Nothing will be impossible for you."
>
> —Matthew 17:20

I am not a great cook. Actually, I can cook, but it isn't one of my favorite things to do anymore. Now, with a lot of time and no children at home, I still do not cook. But I do know what a mustard seed looks like. Those little things are really small, so small you cannot hold one in your hand. And if you drop it, it is gone forever, for you cannot see it anywhere. So to hear the Lord say that all it takes to move a mountain is to have the faith of a mustard seed is such a gift, truly. I am sure that most of us think that surely our faith is at least as big as that teeny, tiny mustard seed. To know that this small amount of faith can move mountains is such big news! A blanket of comfort and assurance washes over us to know that this is true. Faith means everything to God, for he will make mountains move for his faithful. He can take the teeniest bit of faith and use it to move mountains. Now that's impressive, wouldn't you say? And that is exactly who the Lord is! Move over, please. A little faith comin' through!

July 6. Those Fab Fans

> I will lie down and sleep in peace, for you alone,
> O Lord, make me dwell in safety.
>
> —Psalm 4:8

While on a family trip to Florida, one of our sons wanted to go buy a fan because the room in which he was staying was mighty hot. So we went to the store and purchased three fans on the outside chance that someone else would need one. The funny thing about this is that everyone wanted a fan once they saw how fans make life so much better. Not only did the fans cool the room, they also provided a humming sound that blocked out other noises and brought a sense of peace to the room. It got to be hysterical because someone in one room would snatch the fan out of another's. Then that person would come in later and snatch his fan back for the rest of the night. When I went to bed that last night, my fan was missing. It was as if we had all reverted to being babies, needing that soothing humming of a fan to lull us to sleep. In much the same way, the Lord is the perfect sound machine by which to go to sleep, listening to his voice as he talks with us before we close our eyes. At the end of the day, whether it has been a super-duper day of joy or a day of difficulty, the Lord's voice is the last sound that we should hear before we close our eyes. How glorious to know that he is ready and willing to hum away the time before sleep, comforting, assuring, and sharing his love with us until we awaken, his mercies new every morning.

July 7. Closed for Repairs

> He makes me lie down in green pastures; he leads me
> beside quiet waters, he restores my soul. He guides me in
> paths of righteousness for his name's sake.
>
> —Psalm 23:2–3

The Statue of Liberty reopened on July 4th, a few days ago, after having been closed for just under a year. At first it was in need of maintenance from just daily wear, but then it was hit by Hurricane Sandy and, once again, it had to be closed eight long months for repairs. The Statue of Liberty is a monument to freedom offered to all who enter our shores that draws thousands upon thousands of visitors to it year after year. Without those repairs, this monument would not be able to withstand the onslaught of those cold and fierce New York winters, the pounding of the waves against her base, and the harsh glare of the summer sun beating down upon her head. Sometimes life causes cracks in her façade that need repair. So it goes for all of us! There are times in our lives that the Lord says to us, "In need of repairs." So he gently takes us to a place where he can fill in our cracks, wash down the rust and icky things of life that get stuck to our souls, and repaint us with his glory, ready to face life again. When our Father sees that we need to be healed from a break of some kind, he gently removes us for a time to get us back to our original beauty. He truly is the Restorer of our souls. Let this be a sweet time of drawing close to the Lord, spending time in his presence. No matter where we are in life, when we have to be closed for repairs, we can know with complete assurance that our Maker is working mightily to restore us to a place where we can once again welcome all who long to be with us, reflecting his glory for everyone to see.

July 8. Catch as Catch Can?

Be still, and know that I am God.

—Psalm 46:10

I am not sure what I do all day every day, but somehow each day gets filled up with errands of all kinds. I noticed the other day that I am constantly grabbing lunch on the run, never really sitting down to eat and thinking about what I am eating. Most days I cannot even remember what I ate nor where I ate it. I did begin to think that this might be the way I am handling my spiritual life, a bite here and a bite there. Just giving my Father bits and pieces of myself on the run but never really sitting down and sharing time with the one who means the most. Am I throwing out a quick prayer here and a little thanks there, moving at a blistering pace with no quality time to spend with my Lord? We are called to slow down and spend special, quiet time with our Maker, giving him the best fruits of our life rather than just a piece here and there. Let's carve out that special time daily when we just sit and chat with God, listening for his voice and letting him know that he is the most important part of our day. Those errands and phone calls will get done, and when we have spent time in his presence, the world is right-side up and we can find him in all things throughout our day.

July 9. A Simple Thank You

> ...I have come that they may have life,
> and have it to the full.
>
> —John 10:10

Having celebrated my birthday today, now it is time for me to start writing my thank-yous. It means so much to me to sit down and think of all the sweet and lovely things that family and friends have done to celebrate my life, and I can't wait to thank them for this. I was thinking about taking the time to do it tonight, and the thought crossed my mind. The first person whom I need to thank is my Jesus. He is the one who gave me life. He is the one who gave me family. He is the one who gave me friends, dogs, sunshine, cool breezes, delicious Popsicles, and all things that make life so lovely. But because he gave us life to the fullest, not only will we share time with him here on earth but forever in eternity, and that is truly the abundant life. It is because he loves us so that we can share these special times in life and know that we will all share life forever with Jesus. Without his love and caring so deeply for us, life would be *life-less*, so much less than the glory we know in Jesus. As we all know, just a simple thank you will do. He just loves to hear from us. Isn't it just so grand to think on the absolute truth that Jesus, who gave us life and all of the precious, countless things that make it beautiful, loves us no matter what? That is the gift that just keeps on giving!

July 10. Thy Will Be Done

> He said to them, "When you pray, say:
> 'Father, hallowed be your name, your kingdom come.
> Give us each day our daily bread. Forgive us our sins,
> for we also forgive everyone who sins against us.
> And lead us not into temptation.'"
>
> —Luke 11:2–4

I just celebrated my birthday. The good news is that life only gets more interesting, and the longer I live, the more I know that I have so much left to learn. And I love that! Some of my teaching moments, well, trials that is, sputtered at the start because I was a little slow to realize that this was God, my Father, teaching me something that was really important. Then with the help of the Holy Spirit, I began to understand what this teachable moment was. I had to learn to embrace it, and let go and let God. We all come to a place eventually where we know that it is time for God's will to be done, not ours. Let go and let God. When we are able to do this, it's like carrying a ten-pound weight on the top of your shoulders and then putting it down. Wow! What a difference that makes! So if you feel the press of some odd weight around your shoulders or hanging like a cannonball around your neck, give that thing to the Lord. If he can make the world, he can certainly run it! And that, my friends, is the best birthday present that anyone could hope for!

July 11. Living in the Shadows

> Jesus looked at them and said, "With man this is
> impossible, but with God all things are possible."
>
> —Matthew 19:26

Last week, I struck out walking, walking quite a while in the shadows formed by the beautiful trees that line the streets in my neighborhood. I kept my eyes to the ground for some odd reason, never bothering to look up. But near the end of my walk, I looked above into the bluest, most beautiful sky backlit by the most gorgeous sun yet to be seen this summer. Now this sky with its bright rays of summer sun had been there the whole time, but I had never had the thought to look upward. The glory of this blue sky empowered me with such joy and assurance that the Lord is here, always here, to be enjoyed each and every day. Do we live life stuck walking in the shadows here on earth, never looking up to our power known as Jesus? Do we just continue to plow through the earthly darkness and never look to the Lord whose perfect power is always here? Here is where our joy lies. From here comes our strength. The next time you venture outside, look to the heavens and find that beautiful blue sky streaked with golden rays of sunshine reflecting the face of the Lord, our Savior, in whom all things are possible. As you look upward to the skies, you will feel his power, you will see his face. Let him illuminate our hearts, our minds, our lives so that we, in turn, can reflect his glorious love. He is the light of the world whose welcoming face always reveals his glory.

July 12. Broken Blessings

> But blessed is the man who trusts in the Lord, whose
> confidence is in him. He will be like a tree planted by the
> water that sends its roots by the stream. It does not fear
> when the heat comes; its leaves are always green. It has no
> worries in a year of drought and never fails to bear fruit.
>
> —Jeremiah 17:7–8

Years ago, I was walking along, talking with the Lord, and the hair band holding my hair back that hot July day broke. So I said, "Lord, if you would just provide a rubber band for my hair, I could get it out of my face and we could continue on with our conversation." Not three steps ahead I stepped across a rubber band, and this was the beginning of my calling these rubber bands that I find *rubber band blessings*. Over the years, I have found so many, and I always stop to pick them up no matter where they are. Although I usually find whole ones, ones that are not broken, occasionally I do find one that is broken. But I always pick these up too, and it causes me to pause and think, *This rubber band blessing has been broken by man but will be restored by the Lord.* His blessings come in so many ways, often in ways that we do not recognize and sometimes would not choose. He uses the broken things of life, restoring them and using them for his glory. He even uses the things that break our hearts as blessings to draw us closer to him, calling his name out of pain and despair. He takes these times and turns them into blessings, for it is from these times of greatest pain that we know him in the most powerful way. So as we travel through this life, let us not fear the broken road ahead, as the Lord is waiting along the way to take these broken bends in the road and turn them into blessings—beautiful, meaningful blessings that point us to the very heart of the Lord.

July 13. Proceed with Confidence

The fruit of righteousness will be peace; the effect of
righteousness will be quietness and confidence forever.

—Isaiah 32:17

All the time that I walk my dog, Mojo, I pass over alleys where
often cars come blazing down them. I always tell myself to be
careful and look before I step into the alley. The other day, I
passed across an alley, and right before me was one of those terrific
mirrors on a pole that reflect the activity in the alley. I could
see clearly if anyone was coming, passing with all confidence in
knowing that the coast was clear. It reminded me of looking to
Jesus each day before we step out to begin. I thought of how
blessed we all are to give each day to the Lord, knowing that
he goes before us and prepares the way. Jesus is our mirror who
reflects his protection and strength, giving us the way to walk
as the days unfold. When we look clearly into his face, he will
show us how to proceed for he knows the paths that we will go
down and longs to clear them for us. What confidence we find
in looking to Jesus on how to pass through the unknown days
to come. He provides a quietness and confidence with which to
trust him with all of our days. He freely gives to us not only the
safest way to live, but also the best place to step, safely guiding us
no matter what may come down our alleys of life.

July 14. Feelin' Good

> This is the day that the Lord has made.
> Let us rejoice and be glad in it.
>
> —Psalm 118:24

A website that highlights a clothing line on the Internet is upbeat and colorful, and it has a clever tagline at the end of the page: "Every day should be this good." This is exactly how we, as believers, should feel each and every day. Now that probably sounds like a reach to feel this way some days. Yet knowing that we have been saved from sin by our Savior, that he has removed our sin as far as the east is from the west, that he has promised to be with us each and every day that we live, should cause us to say each day that we awake that this will be a good day, someway, somehow, because we are loved by the Lord of the universe. Let us wake up and say to ourselves, "This is the day that the Lord has made. Let us rejoice and be glad in it." His goodness will follow somehow. Is this a tall order? Yes, yes, yes. Would it possibly take some practice? Yes, yes, yes. Are we called by our Maker to think on these things? Yes, yes, yes! It means waking up each day knowing with all certainty that God has gone before us, no matter where we are in life. When we think on his goodness, somewhere, someway, we will find joy!

July 15. Room without a View

> For God, who said, "Let light shine out of the darkness,"
> made his light shine in our hearts to give us the light of
> the knowledge of the glory of God in the face of Christ.
>
> —2 Corinthians 4:6

At our property in south Texas, the middle bedroom of the house has no windows. We call it The Cave. I am pretty sure that most people want a room with a view wherever they are. But the funniest thing happens when someone does sleep in our interior room. Although I am certain that they are thinking that they are getting the worst bedroom in the house, in all actuality it is the best bedroom that we have because it is just like a cave in there: no light, no noise, sound sleeping! So this is exactly how life works. We sometimes feel as if we are living in a room without a view, for we cannot see our way and we feel as if we have been swallowed up by a cave of life. But nothing is further from the truth. Jesus knows when we are in one of those caves, with no view and no light to see our way out, that we are being renewed and strengthened by him all along the way. It is in these times of life with no view that we are becoming stronger, resting comfortably and letting Jesus work on our behalf. This imposed rest is actually restoring us and getting us ready to face life another day. We can remember that the light of our world is still there. Just because we have no view does not mean that we have been left in the dark all alone. After a time of restoration, we will once again come out full of the "light of the knowledge of the glory of God in the face of Christ." This allows time for him to handle our trials while we are in the cave, thereby proving that sometimes a room without a view is just the best room in the house!

July 16. Risky Business

> The wicked man flees though no one pursues,
> but the righteous are as bold as a lion.
>
> —Proverbs 28:1

I was watching *60 Minutes* last week, and the featured story was on the Metropolitan Opera and, in particular, the opera *Rigoletto*. The director has taken a radical approach to getting more exposure for opera in general by showing selected operas at movie theaters around the world. This allows many more folks to be exposed to opera than was possible before. He claims that opera has become a losing proposition. In order to keep it around, he says that he needs to be creative. He says, "The risk of doing nothing is the greatest risk of all." As we believers hear these words, it is challenging to apply them to our faith. For those of us who love the Lord, doing nothing could be the greatest risk of all. If we know of a time when we can really make a difference in someone's life and we choose to do nothing, then we risk living with the knowledge that what we could have done would have made a difference. If we hear from the Lord as to one of our own circumstances and we choose to do nothing, then we may have consequences that are not what we would want, and on and on it goes. For those who are not believers yet have the opportunity to know him and do nothing, they will have set up the greatest risk of all. Let us remember that there is no risk involved when we follow Jesus. Let us act as bold as a lion when we hear his call!

July 17. Drawn to the Light

> When Jesus spoke again to the people, he said,
> "I am the light of the world. Whoever follows me will
> never walk in darkness, but will have the light of life."
>
> —John 8:12

At our property just outside of Dallas, we have a parking area with lights that we turn on at night so everyone can see as they walk about after the sun goes down. The only problem with this is that it not only provides light for us to see, but the bugs swarm to the lights and hover around them like crazy. It creates somewhat of a challenge when we go outside or try to open the door. When the door opens, here come the bugs, wanting to join us inside. So we are constantly turning on and off the lights, needing to shoo the bugs away yet use the light to see outdoors. Being drawn to the light is the same for us as believers. We are drawn to the light of the Lord Jesus, wanting to be near his warmth and his presence to provide protection and guidance for us as we live. Just like these bugs, we long to hover in his presence, for it is here that we feel safe and can rest in the certain knowledge that he is our guiding light. The good news for us is that we never have to turn on the light in order to move about. It is just the opposite. Because of his light, we now have all that we need to see, where to go and how to live, relying on the glowing warmth given off through his love for us. He is the light of the world, our light, our Savior. And as we continue to draw close to him, we can know that no matter what door may open, he will always show us the way through his never-ending love and care, and we will never walk in darkness again!

July 18. Happy Birthday!

> In reply Jesus declared, "I tell you the truth, no one can
> see the kingdom of God unless he is born again."
>
> —John 3:3

Summer birthdays are sort of different from birthdays during the school year, for so often those with whom you would like to celebrate are off on vacations. The good thing about a summer birthday is that when these friends or family return, you still get to celebrate. I took our five-year-old grandson to our property near Waco, Texas, with our nine-year-old granddaughter and her friend. They asked him when he was born, for he has a summer birthday. When they asked this, it made me think of when I was born—born again in Jesus! I was reminded of when I became a new person in Christ, the birthday of my renewal through accepting Jesus as my Lord and Savior. All of us, as believers, have had this unique and precious experience, and how wonderful to celebrate it with the Lord each and every day. It truly is the most important day of our lives. It is because of this day, time, or experience that we now know the hope found in loving Jesus. Just as we know joy in celebrating our birthday, we also know the true joy of being born again in Christ. Now that is something to celebrate!

July 19. The Forecast: Unexpected Rain

> God is our refuge and strength,
> an ever-present help in trouble.
>
> —Psalm 46:1

I was walking on Thursday last week. My dog and I were just clicking along when, all of sudden, we were in a shower—a sprinkler shower! We both had taken several steps into it because I was not watching where I was going. We were so surprised! He started shaking the water off him, and I looked up to see how quickly we could get out of the sprinklers! I thought to myself, *This is life. One day we are cruisin' along enjoying a sunny day, when out of the blue we are getting wet, not sure where that rain is coming from nor how to stop it.* When the rains of life come down unexpectedly, how do we exit this rain shower and return our lives to sunny days? Follow the lead of the Lord. We can know with every assurance that our Father, our Lord and Savior, is there in the midst of that rain, ready with his umbrella of grace to cover our heads and stop the rain from pouring down—our ever-present help in time of trouble.

July 20. The Fragrance of Christ

> But thanks be to God, who always leads us in triumphal
> procession in Christ and through us spreads everywhere
> the fragrance of the knowledge of him.
>
> —2 Corinthians 2:14

Last week, I was searching for an appropriate Bible verse to use for one of my devotional entries and looked up this one above from 2 Corinthians. It caught my attention, for I have never really thought of us as being the fragrance of Christ. For my birthday, I received the most beautiful candle and, boy, was I excited. This one is particularly special because I could smell its fragrance while it was still wrapped in paper. In the verse above, it says that we are the fragrance of the knowledge of him (Christ). So what does this mean for us as believers? We have a special calling as we go about our lives to reveal the glory of Christ to others just by their being in our presence. We may not even have to speak a word. But then when we do interact with others, our love for Christ should become even more obvious and reveal to them the glory that we know by his love for us. This is a great calling and one that bears great responsibility. Not only will others know Christ from sharing time with us, but, like my candle, his presence will be even more impactful as they see his meaning in our lives. How exciting for us to remember that we are empowered with the fragrance of the knowledge of him and have every opportunity each and every day to point someone to the love of Christ.

July 21. Save the Worms!

And the God of all grace, who called you to his eternal
glory of Christ, after you suffered a little while, will
himself restore you and make you strong, firm and
steadfast. To him be the power forever and ever. Amen.

—Peter 5:10–11

I have something to confess. I save worms. Well, actually, I do
not pick them up and put them in a jar for safekeeping. No, as
I walk daily, I see these little worms stuck in the middle of the
very hot sidewalk, wiggling and looking like they are suffering,
trying their best to get to the other side of the sidewalk to no
avail. I look around and see so very many of them, dried up and
dead in the middle of that sidewalk. I actually love picking up
these wiggling worms and placing them in the cool grass to live
another day. It always reminds me of the undeserved but glorious
redemptive act of our Lord who, because he loves us so, keeps us
from the depths of hell, here and when we die. Not only will he
keep us from that place when we die, but he keeps us from there
now. For through the trials and storms of life, we have someone
who assures us that he will comfort us, that he will restore our
souls, that he will keep us from being consumed with fear, even
in the presence of life's toughest trials. He is there, making sure
that our cup overflows with peace and grace. It's funny, isn't it?
How the glory of our Lord is revealed even in something as lowly
as a worm!

July 22. The Gift Giver

> But each man has his own gift from God;
> one has this gift, another has that.
>
> —1 Corinthians 7:7

Ryan Wang is unbelievable! He is a five-year-old prodigy who plays the piano. He doesn't just play the piano, he is a master of it. To see and hear him in action is something that we may never see again in our lifetimes. Not only can he play, but he has the most adorable way about him—charming, clever, sweet, and humble. He has already wowed them at Carnegie Hall. I started thinking about the gifts that God gives to each of us and how unbelievable some of these gifts are: the intellect of Steve Jobs, the vision of Thomas Jefferson, the dedication of Michelangelo, the love of Mother Teresa, and on and on. But God has given gifts to all of us—special, special gifts that he longs for us to use to magnify his glory. God's gifts are freely given, not costing us a thing. Let's not put the glorious gifts that we have from our Father in a gift closet somewhere, unused and unappreciated. What gifts have you been given by our Father? Get your special gifts out and use them so that our Father can know that his perfect and gracious gifts that we have each been given will not go to waste. Let's use his good gifts to bless his name, for our gift giver is the most generous one we know!

July 23. First Things First

> May the words of my mouth and the meditation
> of my heart be pleasing in your sight,
> O Lord, my Rock and my Redeemer.
>
> —Psalm 19:14

England's Prince William and his wife, Duchess Kate, have had their first child, a boy who will be the third in line to the throne of the British monarchy. Out of respect for the crown and Prince William's grandmother, Queen Elizabeth, no one was to know the baby's gender until she was told. Once the news was revealed to her, all in the United Kingdom and the rest of the world could know. As believers, here is a message that we can take away from their protocol. Just as their monarch must be the first to be in the know, so should ours. We should reveal all things to him, God, our King, before we go forward with life. How many times has a life-impacting event happened and we have not even talked to our King about it? How many times have minutes, hours, even days passed, and we have not even thought about discussing the latest event with our Maker? He longs to be first in our lives, for we are first in his. If his eye is always on the sparrow, he certainly never takes his eye off us. Whether we are having the best day of our lives or the worst or even something in between, more joy and more peace can be had by going to God our King with the news. Whether it be celebratory news or a difficult situation, he should be our first call. For who will be more excited or more comforting to talk with than the one who loves us most?

July 24. "More Cost, More Worship"

> Praise be to the God and Father of our Lord Jesus Christ.
> In his great mercy he has given us new birth into a living
> hope through the resurrection of Jesus Christ from the
> dead, and into an inheritance that can never perish, spoil,
> or fade—kept in heaven for you, who through faith are
> shielded by God's power until the coming of the salvation
> that is ready to be revealed in the last time.
>
> —1 Peter 1:3–5

"More Cost, More Worship." I ran across this phrase while reading and found it thought provoking. We can all relate to this, for it seems that the more something costs, the better we as a nation like it and want it. This is obvious if we just go shopping. Many of the stores sell similar items, but the ones with a higher price tag are usually the items that people would most love to own. People often seem to believe that the more something costs, the more we should worship or desire it. It's not always true that everyone wants the most expensive thing that they can buy. But generally if asked, many would probably rather have that more expensive thing than a less pricey one. This rule, however, always applies in relation to Jesus. He is the perfect example of "more cost, more worship" than any other example we know. He paid the highest cost that anyone could by laying down his life for us. Because he went to the cross for us, we now have a new birth, an inheritance that can never perish, spoil, or fade. In thinking on this, because he paid the greatest cost for our salvation, he and only he deserves the greatest worship, and the only one that we are called to worship, actually. Let us worship him with everything that we have, putting no others before him, giving him and only him the glory.

July 25. America the Beautiful

I will lie down and sleep in peace, for You alone,
O Lord, make me dwell in safety.

—Psalm 4:8

America—our homeland, the country where our forefathers came, settled, and began a new world so that we, today, this very day, can worship freely, live freely, and know opportunity like no other place in the world. The widely accepted view of how our country became known as America is that the name originated from cartographer, explorer, and navigator Amerigo Vespuci, who was the first person to recognize North and South America as distinct continents previously unknown to Europeans, Asians, and Africans. We cannot help but see God's hand in all this. It is no accident that our country was established, that our forefathers endured horrific hardship to set up the colonies, and that they were led by the one true God whose plan is mighty and reaches from generation to generation. Here we sit today, in our America, still being led by God whose plan will not be thwarted, not by another country, not by any person around the world, not by anyone nor anything known to man. Much is going on in the world to make us feel unsettled. But as we go to sleep tonight and lift our prayers to our Father for our America, we can rest peacefully knowing that, just as the new land named America came into being by the hand of the Almighty, America today will continue to go forward under the plan of God, the one who designed it and made it all happen. Praise be to God for this beautiful America, our home and our great gift from our Father who loves us so.

July 26. Seeing Is Believing

> Holy, holy, holy is the Lord Almighty;
> the whole earth is full of his glory.
>
> —Isaiah 6:3

I pulled a page out of a magazine yesterday with a swirl of colors on it and this quote from Henry David Thoreau: "It's not what you look at that matters, it's what you see." So often we go through life, but because we are distracted, some things that should make an impact don't even register with us. I thought of looking at other people we see and yet not really seeing them. I thought of passing by someone who could use a word of encouragement yet not really seizing this opportunity. I thought of the times that I looked at our world, our beautiful gift from our Father who designed it all, and I don't always see him as I go about my day. If we are just looking at things and not really seeing them, then we have missed a million opportunities to know the Lord each day. Looking and seeing, as Thoreau so wisely wrote, are really two different things. Let us learn to actually see our world as the Lord has made it and all his gifts within it. This will not only give us unlimited opportunity to find joy after joy in just seeing God every day, but we will also have chance after chance to see an opportunity to bring him to someone or to a situation where his presence will make a difference. Seeing with the eyes of Jesus is exciting, for it opens up a whole new way of looking at our world, knowing and sharing Jesus at every opportunity.

July 27. Picking Low-Hanging Fruit

> I urge you, brothers, to watch out for those who cause
> divisions and put obstacles in your way that are contrary
> to the teaching you have learned...I want you to be wise
> about what is good and innocent about what is evil.
> The God of peace will soon crush Satan under your feet.
>
> —Romans 16:17–20

Low-hanging fruit! The obvious explanation for this phrase is that this is a fruit that hangs so low off the tree that anyone, human or animal, can pick it right off without any effort—easy to reach and easy to harvest! Another definition sometimes used is selecting the easiest targets with the least amount of effort. In business, this term is often used by those in sales who are seeking out their easiest customers first to get a sale in the bag, so to speak. What this term brings to mind for us as believers is that we need to be mindful to not be a low-hanging fruit for Satan to pick easily. He scours the land looking for this low-hanging fruit, easy pickin's to bring into his fold, easing us away from focusing on our Lord and Savior. Satan is not that picky, more concerned with quantity than quality, and to get both in one picking makes it even more satisfying. So he knows when we are ripe for the pickin', hanging low for the taking. So how do we keep from being this low-hanging fruit? Keep our eyes upon Jesus. Set our hearts on him. Then we will be so very high up on the tree that there is no way that Satan could ever reach us. We will have a web of protection provided by our Maker who keeps all prey away from our hearts and our minds, even Satan, who thinks that he is the master picker. But truth be known that God, our Lord, our Father who made us all, picked us before the beginning of time and has placed us where no prey can ever touch us—in his loving arms!

July 28. Are We Listening?

And I will ask the Father, and he will give you another
Counselor to be with you forever—the Spirit of truth.

—John 14:16

So many times these days I find that either I am not hearing what someone is saying or they cannot hear me, and one of us ends up saying, "Are you listening?" It reminds me of the times when our children were growing up, and I was probably droning on and on about something that they did not want to hear. I would say, "Are you listening to me?" Most of us have heard that being a good listener is a gift that we give to others. All throughout my school days, my teachers called all of us in class to be good listeners. Now I understand why. Listening can make a huge difference in how circumstances evolve. It also reveals a heart for others in that we are willing to give them one-on-one attention, realizing that we value them. As we listen to what the Holy Spirit reveals to us, this will directly impact every part of our spiritual lives. If we are not being attentive to his call, we will instead let life's stuff overtake our emotions, thus becoming the focus of what is directing us. How much better to let the Spirit of the Lord be the one to whom we listen rather than the cacophony of life. We can bet that with his direction, we will always be in a better place. May our ears be attuned to the calling of the Lord where we will find the right way to go, no matter where we are headed or to what we are listening.

July 29. Jenga

> See, I lay a stone in Zion, a tested stone,
> a precious cornerstone for a sure foundation;
> the one who trusts will never be dismayed.
>
> —Isaiah 28:16

Our grandson came over recently and used Jenga blocks of wood to build a fort for his superhero characters. He figured out rather quickly that the best technique for building his tower was to start with a cornerstone, to set up the best block of wood on the first corner so that there would be more stability as the building continued. This cornerstone theory is one that has been used for centuries by builders throughout the ages. The cornerstone is the first stone set in the construction of a masonry foundation. All the stones will be set in reference to this stone, and it determines the position of the entire structure. So, too, did our Maker know that we needed a cornerstone on which to build our lives. He sent Jesus as our cornerstone so that we could set a firm foundation on him. Jesus establishes the perfect positioning for life as we know it by his presence. He is the one who keeps our lives from falling apart. He is the one around whom we build our lives day after day so that when someone or something comes along and tries to pull a piece out from under us, we will still be left standing. We are forever centered on the Lord, our cornerstone. May we remain solidly grounded by our stabilizer, Jesus, the cornerstone of our lives.

July 30. Walk by Faith, Not by Sight

Jesus answered, "I am the way and the truth and the life.
No one comes to the Father except through me."

—John 14:6

As I started on my walk the other day, it was so bright that I had to close my eyes for a minute before continuing on my way. I started thinking about being able to walk without seeing what was ahead of me every day of my life. If you try closing your eyes and maneuvering your way, you learn two things: your senses are sharpened to a point that they wouldn't be otherwise, and you must rely on something other than your sight to find your way. This is exactly what we are called to do all throughout our lives. Jesus came as a carpenter so that we must have faith that God's word is true rather than seeing Jesus as how an earthly king would look. That would be so easy to accept, a Lord who came as a king, riding on a magnificent steed, welding a sword and exuding great power. But to know that the Lord, our King, was born in a stable to a common man, causes us to accept him as our King on faith. It is so much richer and deeper to not see the truth with our eyes but to know it in our hearts. If we rely on the world for our knowledge, we are on shaky ground. The world speaks to us according to man's desires; God speaks to us with his wisdom and what he longs for us to live by—his word. So when we are blinded by the bright lights of the world, let us close our eyes and take the Lord's hand to steady the way, for he and only he is the way, the truth, and the life.

July 31. Never Misses a Call

> What other nation is so great as to have their gods near
> them the way the Lord our God is near to us whenever
> we pray to him?
>
> —Deuteronomy 4:7

The other day, I was walking my dog, Mojo, and passed a telephone repairman working on the box that holds all the wires connecting the phones in a large area. He was fiddling with them, and I was amazed. I have never in my life seen so many wires connected to so many wires and who knows what. I could not believe that he could pick out the very wire that he needed to fix. He seemed quite confident that he was fixing the problem, and he was not confused looking for a minute—that look was on my face. In this box of telephone wires is the solution to enable thousands and thousands of people to communicate with each other. I thought of the thousands and thousands and millions and millions and kabillions of prayers and conversations that go up to our Father minute by minute, day and night. These conversations and these prayers mean so much to those who are talking with God, and he never misses one. Isn't that mind-boggling? But not really, for we know the character of the Lord. He is all-knowing and all-powerful. If he can move mountains, he will certainly never miss a prayer nor a chat with any of us. So the next time we see that box of never-ending wires connecting our lives together via the phone, we can get the big picture that God is even more amazing than that, for he never drops a call nor needs repair!

August 1. "Motto: Let Your Pillow Be Your Counselor"

> And he will be called Wonderful Counselor,
> Mighty God, Everlasting Father, Prince of Peace.
>
> —Isaiah 9:6

I love magazines. Magazines of all kinds, and I spend an inordinate amount of time reading through them. I wish that I could say that I read two or three books a week, but, alas, it's actually magazines that I whip through with ease. The other day I saw a headline, "Let your pillow be your counselor." Such great advice! Although this refers to our getting sleep to ease our burdens, we, as believers, can lay our burdens down at the end of the day with Jesus. There is no better time than when our heads hit our pillows to chat with Jesus about all sorts of things. I so look forward to settling in and laying my head on my pillow so that I have this quiet and precious time with my Jesus. It is exactly at this time that I lay all my troubles down; that I talk to him about prayer requests, lifting those in need of prayer to him for care; that I thank him for each little bit of goodness that this day has given me. All of us, I am sure, know this moment in time when we get to come into his presence and talk, talk, talk until we fall asleep. This may actually be the sweetest time of the day. As we go to sleep tonight, let our pillows guide us to the perfect counselor who knows us inside out and is waiting patiently to share the day with us. Sweet dreams tonight as you spend these golden moments with Jesus.

August 2. The Majesty of God

Glorious and majestic are his deeds,
and his righteousness endures forever.
He has caused his wonders to be remembered;
the Lord is gracious and compassionate.

—Psalm 111:3–4

I just returned from an amazing trip with precious friends to Montana. Having never been there, the dear friend that we were visiting took us to see all the sights, and it is here that the majesty of God is so evident. We went on a half-day tour of Glacier National Park, and our tour guide was most knowledgeable about the entire park that covers just over one million acres. There are still some glaciers there that we could see high up in the mountains, yet many have melted, creating the stunning mountains with valleys below. To be there and experience all these wonders of nature is so impressive, yet it brings into sharp focus the glory provided by God and his work here upon the earth. Mountain goats, bighorn rams, gorgeous waterfalls coming down from high in the mountains, bridges with windows cutting into the sides of the mountains, the wild flowers, the trees. There is so much of God's handiwork that it might take many visits to really take it all in. But one fact that really impressed me was when our guide started talking about the avalanches, and he pointed out areas where an avalanche came down the mountain and crushed everything in its path. There you see acres and acres of broken trees. Yet the wondrous part of this area is that growing underneath and all around the brokenness are the most verdant and beautiful plants. The dragging of the avalanche over the terrain caused great damage, yet after the damage great beauty arises, bringing foliage more beautiful than anywhere in the park. So it is with us. All of us in one way or another have been through a trial. We have all experienced some sort of challenge that has impacted our lives dramatically. Yet here is the beauty of these experiences. God takes these journeys and uses them for good in our lives. He takes the brokenness and the crushed terrain of our days and restores us in a beautiful and meaningful way, just as he has done in the forests of Glacier National Park. There is no experience that he cannot use for his blessing. So we can rest in this promise that no matter what trials we may go through, God is there and will bring blessing upon blessing, just like the gorgeous flowers and new growth that he has restored in his park. It is then that we will see and know the majesty of God in our lives, just as we can see and know it here in nature at Glacier National Park.

August 3. In the Queue

> And my God will meet all your needs according
> to his glorious riches in Christ Jesus.
>
> —Philippians 4:19

Often I begin writing devotional entries a few days before the actual day that I send them. I try to do this so I don't get caught in a tight bind without one of them in the queue. When I began to write these postings, it wasn't always this way. In the beginning, I would go to bed at night and talk to the Lord about the fact that I didn't have any message to write the next day. He always reassured me that he would provide. Isn't that just like our Father to always provide? He hasn't failed yet to send along a little idea here or there for me to muse upon each day. He never fails, not me, not you, not one of us who takes him at his word that he will provide. His provision covers all aspects of our lives, not just my writing, not just turning night into day, not just putting food on our table. He provides for every need that we have. Even when we ask for something and we don't get an answer right away, he is there. He is always there, waiting for his perfect timing to provide the answer. So as we put our requests in the queue, we can know for certain that he knows what we need and when we need it, for he is the keeper of the queue, our perfect provider!

August 4. Cloud Cover

> But let all who take refuge in you be glad; let them ever
> sing for joy. Spread your protection over them, that those
> who love your name may rejoice in you. For surely,
> O Lord, you bless the righteous; you surround them
> with your favor as with a shield.
>
> —Psalms 5:11–12

Last week, I was going in and out watering these sad-looking hydrangea plants, and I kept thinking to myself, *Today is going to be really, really hot. Yet it doesn't feel that hot out here yet.* As I came in and out, I realized that the Lord was providing cloud cover so that the sun wasn't able to beat down upon those of us here in Big D. These beautifully formed clouds held back the hot summer sun, and I could be outside and not feel that rough Texas heat. Our Father provides beautiful, billowy clouds of protection so many times to protect us from life's harmful rays. These are the clouds that keep the searing heat of life's trials from getting through. These are the clouds of beauty that bring so much comfort and pleasure to our lives. These are the clouds that remind us of Jesus, our perfect cloud cover, who provides his precious relief from the blistering *dog days* of life. Just to be able to look up and see these glorious, white clouds that fill our beautiful, blue summer sky can always bring to mind what a gift we have in Jesus, the best protection from the hot times of life that there is. As the psalmist writes above, let us sing for joy, for the Lord, our precious Savior, protects us day and night, surrounding us with his favor! We are his *favor-ites*. Now that is definitely a reason for rejoicing!

August 5. Flat Worn Out

> To him who is able to keep you from falling and to
> present you before his glorious presence without fault
> and with great joy—to the only God our Savior be glory,
> majesty, power and authority, through Jesus Christ our
> Lord, before all ages, now and forevermore! Amen.
>
> —Jude 24–25

Walking, walking, walking, and so much to see! Today I saw one of the worms that I love to save way out in the middle of the street. All alone there, I realized that he would never make it back to safety. So I picked him up and gently placed him smack-dab in the middle of a protective grassy area, safe once again. The thing is, unlike every other time that I have saved a worm from the heat of the concrete, this one did not wiggle at all. He just let me pick him up, providing no resistance whatsoever. I'm pretty sure that he was just flat worn-out. We have all been there. We find ourselves in the middle of a trial, and after much struggling to free ourselves from it, we become just flat worn-out. But the good news is that our Savior comes right alongside of us and knows that we need reviving. We need his protective and saving hand to lift us up out of this struggle, setting us in his secure and peaceful spot where we can regain our strength. Life mimics nature. Just as this worm, we can get worn-out but revived again in the fresh, grassy places of life. Thanks be to our Savior who does exactly as his name implies, saves us over and over and over again.

August 6. "Feeding in Progress"

Just as the living Father sent me, and I live because of the
Father, so the one who feeds on me will live because of
me. This is the bread that came down from heaven.

—John 6:57–58

I walk the Katy Trail here in Dallas several times a week, enjoying the glory of the Lord found there in the beautiful trees and foliage. A new sign there says, "Organic Feeding in the Air: Plant Feeding in Progress." Reading this sign, I now know that all the plants there are helped along by this service of being fed and nurtured by organic supplements. The plant feeding isn't obvious, but yet it is going on, stimulating the plants and giving them just what they need to be the best that they can be. Isn't that just how the Lord feeds us? His love is always in the air, feeding us even when we don't know it. No one around us can tell by just looking that we are being fed by our Father, but we can rest assured that we won't go hungry. He is right here with us, day in, day out, feeding us in so many ways. His love is all around us, everywhere that we are, surrounding us with his protection from the pollutants in the world. He feeds us by surrounding us with other believers whose faith walks are mighty and show us his way. As we awaken each morning and close our eyes at night, we are fed through prayer, rest, and restoration. He feeds us as we attend worship service, singing and praising him for his grace and mercy. He feeds us until we are full up, able to share our feedings with others who are hungry and long to be fed because we are being fed by the best one possible, our Father, whose nourishment is perfect in every way!

August 7. Halcyon Days

> Praise the Lord, O my soul...who satisfies your
> desires with good things so that your youth
> is renewed like the eagle's.
>
> —Psalm 103:1–5

Years ago, at least when I was as young as forty, I collected enamel boxes that are produced by a company called Halcyon Days. I never have given a thought to the name of this company until yesterday, when I saw that term used again in a different way. It occurred to me that this name must have a special meaning, so I looked it up. I discovered that the halcyon is a bird of Greek legend, the name commonly given now to the European kingfisher. The ancient Greeks believed that this bird had the power to calm the waves while laying her eggs. Through the ages, this reference to the nesting bird was lost and the figurative meaning became *calm days*. The current use of the term *halcyon days* tends to be nostalgic, recalling the seemingly endless sunny days of youth. We may long for the halcyon days of our youth. But all our days are halcyon days, for no matter what the weather— real or emotional—looks like each day, our Father brings to us his calming presence. He has provided us with the opportunity to know that every day that we live is a halcyon day because we have Jesus who makes all things new. Calm days were ours since the first day that we believed. Live today with the energized excitement of youth and the calmness that can only be found by trusting in Jesus.

August 8. "Freedom Is in Peril! Defend It with All Your Might!"

Now the Lord is the Spirit, and where the
Spirit of the Lord is, there is freedom.

—2 Corinthians 3:17

Watching the Olympics reveals the strength of the human spirit. Held in London, one of the commentators talked about the British slogan "Keep Calm and Carry On." The background on this slogan is that it was actually the final one in a series of three that the British government produced as a rallying war cry to bring out the best in everyone before their becoming part of World War II. It was an encouragement for their people to stay on the offensive mentally. The first slogan written was the one above, "Freedom is in peril! Defend it with all your might!" That just makes us want to jump up, pump our fists, and scream, "Yay!" especially when we remember that our freedom in worshipping God is safe and secure here in our country. The good news is found in the verse above: "Where the Spirit of the Lord is, there is freedom." As believers, we can access the freedom of lifesaving grace. That makes us all winners without running a race, flying on the parallel bars, or returning even one high-flying volleyball. We are all victorious through the love of Christ, and freedom was given to us at a great price. Although we don't have any gold metals to wear to show the world that we have won, we are the victors. Our lives reveal the love of God reflected in us as he refines us like gold. So shine on! Ours is the victory!

August 9. "Your Courage, Your Cheerfulness, Your Resolution Will Bring Us Victory"

> I have told you these things, so that in me you may have peace. In this world you will have trouble. But take heart!
> I have overcome the world.
>
> —John 16:33

Slogan 2 for the British as they faced certain war with the Germans in World War II: "Your courage, your cheerfulness, your resolution will bring us victory." With the author of these slogans unknown, whoever it was had a passion for his country, a determination to win, and the desire to win with a positive attitude. These slogans are inspirational. They inspire in us the hope that winning is possible, no matter the trial that we are facing. In the same way, the verse from John is filled with hope, for it assures all of us that, yes, we will have trials in this life. But to live through them in light of the fact that Christ has overcome the world and that he will provide the peace and fortitude that we need to make it through these trials is reason to cheer and cheer loudly. We can rest in his promise that this too will pass away, and what sweet victory will await us at the end of our journeys. The Lord has provided assurance that no matter what we face or how long it lasts, his peace and his victory over sin and sorrow will provide us sweet comfort during times of our own personal wars. So even when being cheerful does not come easy, even when our feeling peaceful is not on our radar, let us remember this slogan and the words of the Lord, that through him we will find that peace and that ability to walk through our trials with an inner joy. Who better to put our hope in than the one who has already saved the day? It's always smart to bet on a sure winner!

August 10. "Keep Calm and Carry On!"

> I heard and my heart pounded, my lips quivered at the
> sound; decay crept into my bones and my legs trembled.
> Yet I will wait patiently for the day of calamity to come
> to the nation invading us. Though the fig tree does not
> bud and there are no grapes on the vines, though the olive
> crop fails and the fields produce no food, though there are
> no sheep in the pen and no cattle in the stalls, yet I will
> rejoice in the Lord. I will be joyful in God my Savior.
>
> —Habakkuk 3:16–19

"Keep Calm and Carry On." This was the third and final slogan for Britain facing certain war with Germany in World War II. The author of this slogan most surely understood that in stressful and unsure situations, one of two behaviors will occur: you can choose crazy or you can choose calm. The thing is, whether you go nuts or whether you remain calm, the minutes continue to pass, the night turns into day, and God's mercies are new every morning. Calm is the better choice. Calm places our minds on the bigger picture. Calm helps us sift through what we can fix and what we cannot. Calm brings us to a place of reason, knowing that this too will pass. Calm brings us to a quicker resolution and helps others to remain calm also. Calm gives us that ability to focus on Jesus, the ultimate Restorer of our souls. Calm enables us to carry on in the certain knowledge that Christ has gone before and will carry us through to a better place. Just as Habakkuk writes in the verses above, we will respond with humanness at times. Our hearts will pound and our lips will quiver. But if we can set our minds on our Redeemer, we can know calm, and we can carry on. After all, bringing calm to the party is like putting a balm on a wound: apply freely and with love!

August 11. Too Hot to Handle

Cry out, "Save us, O God our Savior; gather us and
deliver us from the nations, that we may give thanks to
your holy name, that we may glory in your praise."

—1 Chronicles 16:35

There is an old metaphor that says if you put a frog into a pot of cold water and slowly turn up the heat bit by bit until the water boils, the frog will stay in the pot, not realizing that he should jump out to save his life. Although scientists have proven this untrue, it is an interesting metaphor for our day-to-day living. Is this how we live sometimes? We start out a journey in a pot of cold water, and life is good. But then, as life tends to do, the heat slowly begins to crank up, getting our water of life a little bit warmer and a little bit warmer until here we sit in a pot of boiling water. Like this frog who doesn't realize that he should jump out of that pot before it's too late, we do exactly the same thing. We continue to let life keep us stuck in our pot as the pressure builds greater and greater and greater, and then we are simply cooked! How much better if we would remember that the Lord is there to pluck us out of this pot if we would just call on him for assistance. No need to be boiled in hot water because we didn't think to ask our Father to turn down the heat. As we know deep in our hearts, there isn't any pot of boiling water too hot for the Lord to handle!

August 12. Eyes on the Prize...

> Not that I have already obtained all this, or have already
> been made perfect, but I press on to take hold of that for
> which Christ Jesus took hold of me...forgetting what lies
> behind and straining forward to what lies ahead, I press
> on toward the goal for the prize of the upward call of
> God in Christ Jesus.
>
> —Philippians 3:12–14

When I was a teenager, my family owned a '57 Thunderbird that they gave to me to drive at the ripe old age of fourteen. You see, we could get our driver's license at fourteen back then. I was at my best friend's house, and while backing out of her driveway, I was honking and waving at a friend driving by and *boom!* Yep, I hit something, and that something was the tree that was growing next to her driveway. I can't count how many times I had backed out of her driveway without hitting that tree. But this day, I took my eyes off the prize, so to speak. The prize being to back out without an accident. Isn't that the way life is? We are cruising along missing that tree day in and day out. Then we take our eyes off what we are doing for a split second, and that's when we lose sight of the prize. We miss the chance to obtain the upward call of God in Christ Jesus, for we have taken our eyes off him. But the good news of Christ is that we can get right back on the road by refocusing on him. Praise be to God for his grace and redemptive spirit. The prize is never lost. There is no fender bender too much for the Lord to straighten out.

August 13. "Lost: Pet Rock"

For this reason I kneel before the Father, from whom his
whole family in heaven and earth derives its name.
I pray that out of his glorious riches he may strengthen
you with power through his spirit in your inner being,
so that Christ may dwell in your hearts through faith.

—Ephesians 3:14–17

"Lost: Pet Rock. Please call Tammy." This is the flyer that I found today as I was walking outside. It had a picture of a female pet rock on it with a face, eyelashes, and pretty pink lips. Now I don't know if this flyer was a joke or if some precious child actually lost her pet rock and was hoping to find it. In the same way, people sometimes think that they have lost their Jesus, that he is gone forever, and would love to post a flyer so that someone would find him for them and bring him back. There is no need to post a flyer saying "Lost: My Jesus" when we are feeling separated from the Lord and have forgotten that he knows exactly where we are. All we need to do is to go into our hearts where he is kept. He is never truly lost. He is always there, always with us, just waiting for us to return to the love that he has for us and find him right where we left him, in the center of our hearts. He is and will always be with us, no flyer needed!

August 14. Gifts Galore

> If anyone serves, he should do it with the strength
> God provides, so that in all things God may be praised
> through Jesus Christ.
>
> —1 Peter 4:11

Dogs, dogs, dogs—what a precious gift from the Lord. How wonderful that he gives us dogs, cats, and animals to love. I have noticed lately that many of the dogs that I see are adorned with brightly colored bandannas, beautiful collars with their names on them, some with stones, all revealing how much their owners love them. In this same way, our Father has adorned us beautifully with special gifts. Gifts we are to use to reflect his glory. He has adorned us with hands to give his love, hearts to care for others, and bodies to serve his people. He has covered us with so many special gifts that we can use to show how much he loves us by using them to serve his people. We are called to share our gifts with others. Just as these pet owners love to shower their pets with colorful and beautiful additions, our Father gave us these special tools to use so that we can use them to beautify the lives of those we meet. Let our gracious gifts given to us by the one who made us be seen by everyone who passes by, showing to the world that only a Father who loves his children beyond measure would give them these good and priceless gifts.

August 15. Saved My Pain

> The Lord is my helper; I will not be afraid.
>
> —Hebrews 13:6

After my internist so intuitively sent me to a neurologist who specializes in headaches and he found that I suffer from migraines, I told his PA on my second visit, "Tell my doctor that he saved my pain!" I could not believe how much better I was feeling, not going to bed with a crushing headache and not waking up with the same each day. On my way home, I was thinking on this, and I realized that this is exactly what our Jesus does for each of us as we walk through the pains of life: He "saves our pain." Through his mercy and grace he leads us to a place of restoration and peace so that no matter what we are facing, or have faced, or will be facing, Jesus is able to take the pain of life's struggles away and replace it with his peace. Now that we know his promise to do this and now that we can remember it as we awaken each day, we have a halo of care under which we walk, knowing with all certainty that our Jesus is with us, providing a way out of our pain as we struggle against the trials of life. Such peace can be found in this simple truth: He saves our pain!

August 16. Buggers That Bite!

> Praise be to the God and Father of our Lord Jesus Christ,
> the Father of compassion and the God of all comfort, who
> comforts us in all our troubles, so that we can comfort those
> in any trouble with the comfort we ourselves have received
> from God. For just as the sufferings of Christ flow over
> into our lives, so also through Christ our comfort overflows.
>
> —2 Corinthians 1:3–5

I am one of those fortunate people who rarely gets bitten by a mosquito. It is uncanny. I can be outside with friends, and almost everyone there is getting bitten by them, yet I still don't have a bite. However, the other day I decided to walk next door and see how the pool being built by our neighbors was coming. I didn't even notice that my ankles were surrounded by dozens of mosquitoes. Suddenly, my ankles began to itch and itch, and big whelps popped up on them. I had a packet of a special bug-biting formula that saved the day. The minute I rubbed it on my multiple bites, they began to disappear, and the insane itching went away. This made me realize that until you experience something yourself, it is hard to relate to it. So it is with life. As the Lord leads us through trials, we now have the opportunity to reach out and let others know that we understand. We now have the experience to relate to what people we know and love may be going through themselves. Although our experience is not exactly the same as theirs, we can better understand what they are facing by having lived through our own challenges. The Lord walks us through our journey, giving us a caring heart and a deep understanding for the pain of others so that we can then go forth and give them love, care, comfort, and peace, the same love, care, comfort, and peace that he has poured over us. Once we are washed over with it, we are then able to share it with those who desperately need someone to just know, to just get it, to just be there in prayer for them. We can share the soothing and precious love of Christ with them. What greater gift do we have to give than sharing the love of Christ with others?

August 17. Engraved with His Name

"The virgin will be with Child and will give birth to a
son, and they will call him Immanuel"—which means,
"God with us."

—Matthew 1:23

Walking at Southern Methodist University a few weeks ago, I
noticed the lovely bricks carved with the names of supporters of
the school scattered around. This idea is such a great one, used
to raise funds for hospitals, schools, and parks—lots of places.
But these bricks also allow those who walk by the opportunity
to see the love and support that is felt there. I started thinking
about how we have been stacked with the bricks of the Lord as
he continues to build us day by day. He takes the days of our
lives and inscribes his name on each one, growing us in his love
and grace. If we could unstack ourselves as if we were made of
actual bricks, each and every one would have the name of Jesus
inscribed on it, for it is he who keeps us strong; it is he who made
us and continues to grow us; and it is he who builds us up each
day and guides us in his ways. It is because he first loved us that
we have his name emblazoned on the bricks of our lives forever,
and as we build each day, one on another, we can know with all
certainty that written on each and every brick is the name of
Jesus, "God with us," bringing to our lives his perfection provided
in all things. No other name needs to be inscribed there, for his is
all we will ever need, now and eternally: Jesus!

August 18. Taken for Granted

Show me your ways, O Lord, teach me your paths; guide
me in your truth and teach me, for you are God my
Savior, and my hope is in you all day long.

—Psalm 25:4–5

There are so many things in this life that we all take for granted, and this was evident the other night when we got a call from our son saying that his air conditioner had gone out. Best guess is that their house was topping out at probably ninety-eight degrees. Whatever the case, it was too hot for sleeping, so they packed up their twin boys and headed over to try to recoup some of the lost sleep. Air conditioning—I know for sure that I have taken this for granted, day in and day out. It made me think of what else I take for granted, and the thought crossed my mind that there are probably too many gifts to count. The one thing that none of us wants to take for granted is the unconditional and precious love of our Savior. We should spend time each and every day coming into his chamber and dancing at his feet, thanking him for life, our abundant and graciously given life. As we pray this day and in the days to come, let us add somewhere in our prayers one thing each day that we take for granted: air conditioning, electricity, health, friends, family, food to eat. And let's always end our prayer with the biggest thanks of all. Thank you, God, for our Savior. Never wanting him to feel taken for granted!

August 19. Covered by the Vines of Love

> The Lord will restore the splendor of Jacob like the
> splendor of Israel, though destroyers have laid them
> waste and ruined their vines.
>
> —Nahum 2:2

On my way to an appointment today, I passed an old chain-link fence, rusted and falling down. It was in need of repair to restore it to its original and best-working condition. Yet growing along the top of it and spilling down on the sides was the most beautiful vine covered with electric-blue flowers that took my breath away. It was particularly stunning because the contrast between the fence and the vine was so obvious and most unusual to see right now. We are in the middle of a drought. Yet here is this vine, blooming profusely in all its glory. So it made me remember that no matter what our lives look like, worn down with worry, broken by trials, rusted from the pulls of life, caught in the heat of the moment, Jesus can and will always bring back into our lives the beauty of living because each and every day he continues to create us in his glory. He takes us where we are and waters us with his love so that we will begin to bloom again. Just as this broken-down fence is covered with the beautiful vine of startling blue flowers, we also are covered daily by the glorious vine of Christ's love. Looking at the fence yet seeing this spectacular vine helps us to know with certainty that no matter how badly in need of repair we may be, Jesus is restoring us day by day, moment by moment. This allows us and others to see his splendor in the same way that this vine could not be missed. Let us bloom in his perfect care, restored to our original beauty so that others may know the glory of his majesty.

August 20. In the Neighborhood

...love your neighbor as yourself.

—Leviticus 19:18

One of our children's very favorite television shows was *Mr. Rogers*. He was such a gentle soul and talked sweetly about people and places in life that mean so much. I couldn't help but think of him today as one of our dearest neighbors drove by and waved. She moved off our street last week, but it is so good to know that she is still in the neighborhood, living a few blocks over. Our neighborhood, our street, actually, is turning over. Many sweet people moving out and new ones moving in. But no matter who moves in or who moves out, we, as believers, are all joined together in the neighborhood of Christ, living and loving through his grace and mercy. So this connection forms a tie that binds us all together, no matter where our actual neighborhood is. We know without a doubt that we have each other and can lean on one another because he first loved us. Mr. Rogers talked day after day about our postman, our milkman, our yardman, and so on, and how important each of these kind people is in our lives. Let us also remember each other, you and you and you and me, and thank our Father for everyone who makes such a difference to us, whether they are working around us or lifting us in prayer. We all matter. We matter to each other and we really matter to God. Just like Mr. Rogers always said, "It's a beautiful day in the neighborhood," where our Father is loving us all day long!

August 21. Letters from Camp

> You yourselves are our letter, written on our hearts,
> known and read by everybody. You show that you are a
> letter from Christ, the result of our ministry, written not
> with ink but with the Spirit of the living God, not on
> tablets of stone but on tablets of human hearts.
>
> —2 Corinthians 3:2–3

As the Apostle Paul wrote in 2 Corinthians above, our lives are living letters from Christ to be read by everyone, whose author is the Spirit of the Living God. I love that. It makes me realize that what we do, what we say, and how we live must reflect our love for the Lord. I recently got a letter written by our eight-year-old granddaughter who had gone to camp for the first time. It was one of those fill-in-the-blank letters, where the beginning of the sentence is printed, and then she fills in the rest of it with her own thoughts. So it went something like this.

Dear _____ (Nana),
Camp is _____ (good).
The food is _____ (delicious).
My friends are _____ (sweet).
My counselors are _____ (fun)!
My activities are _____ (blob, swimming, tumbling).
I _____ (miss) _____ you.
Love, _____ (Jenny)

So, I was thinking about a letter that we would write to our Father from camp. It would go like this.

Dear _____ (Father),
Life is _____ (precious).
Your food is _____ (always nourishing)!
My Friend is _____ (always by my side)!
My Counselor is _____ (faithful and true)

My activities are _____ (finding you in all things, loving
the life that you gave me, knowing your unconditional
love).
I _____ (need) you!
Thanks for everything! You're the best!
Love, All of Us

Why don't we write our Father a letter today, whether it is an
actual letter or a mental one, revealing our love for him? The
postage is free, and there's nothing quite like getting a letter from
someone you love!

August 22. Finding Your Footing

> But when you pray, go into your room, close the door and
> pray to your Father, who is unseen. Then your Father,
> who sees what is done in secret, will reward you.
>
> —Matthew 6:6

Find your footing. In light of the recent tragedies, I was thinking and praying to the Lord, *Father, how do we process our feelings of helplessness among the pain and heartbreak of the recent events, nationally and in our own community?* The phrase that the Holy Spirit kept putting on my heart was "find your footing." Thinking deeply about how this was to happen, it came to me that the way for us to find our footing amidst all these tragedies was to pray, but not a quick prayer of help, although that is always good. We should go to a place of quiet, away from the world as we know it, and commune with our Father in prayer, heartfelt, crying-out prayer, for comfort and peace for these families near and far who are suffering so greatly. In the time of Jesus, the Jewish households had a room or a secret place for private devotion, where a private communion with God could be held, unseen by others. It was here that they could truly come into his presence. And so can we. Unable to find our footing, slipping and struggling to get our feet back on the ground, is a scary and unsettling state in which to be. But the promise above in Matthew 6:6 is that when we pray in secret, our Father will reward us. The rewards cannot be bought, and the rewards cannot come from any other but the searcher of our hearts. The rewards are his ever-present gift to us, delivered through the birth of his Son, our Lord and our Redeemer, Jesus Christ. It is here in silence that we will be reminded of his promise to walk beside all of us through life—the good and the bad, the easy and the difficult—and provide comfort and strength for those who are suffering so greatly. So as the days and weeks continue on, let us find our footing by going quietly and often into a private place of prayer with our Father who knows us best, and let him wash his peace and strength over us. It is here that we will be reminded over and over again that he will bind up the brokenhearted. It is here that we can know with all certainty that he is with those who are suffering, carrying them in his mighty arms. Praise be to God that he always has the answer, for he is the answer for all people everywhere.

August 23. Finding Value

I will bless them and the places surrounding my hill.
I will send down showers in season.

—Ezekiel 34:26

Our Father speaks to me when I need a little pick me up, and even when I don't. My prayer for each of you is that something in this world speaks of our Father's love to you. He has blessed me with finding rubber bands. Simple, little rubber bands that I find along the way. Our minister this past weekend was speaking on regrets. The unfortunate part about regrets is that there is nothing, absolutely nothing, that we can do about them. But, as God reminded me, there is everything that he can do about them, and already has, for his love covers all. I was reviewing a few of these with the Lord, not feeling too great about them. Then, and right then, I found one of my rubber band blessings. Was this a coincidence? To some, maybe, but not to me. My father's peace washed over me like cleansing water as he called me to hand him my regrets. I realized that I no longer needed to suffer over them, having carried them with me for too long. That is what finding that little, valueless rubber band did for me, and that is what I long for you to know also. There is nothing like finding the Lord's love along life's journey. So may each of you seek his face and, when you find something that speaks to your heart of his presence, there will never again be anything in this life of more value than this one special thing, even if it is made out of rubber!

August 24. "It's Yours for Keeps"

> The Lord bless you and keep you; the Lord make his face
> to shine upon you and be gracious unto you; the Lord
> turn his face toward you and give you peace.
>
> —Numbers 6:24–26

I am starting to remind myself of my mother, for no one liked a sale better than she did. If we just wait thirty minutes or so, something that we want will be on sale. So as I search Internet shops for my new favorite thing, I always go to the sale option first just to see what has recently been discounted. I went to a website that sells workout clothes, and there they do not list the things that they have on sale as "sale" items. They list them under the category "We made too much"—a clever marketing tool. Then if you decide to purchase something on sale, it says, "It's yours for keeps." Again, a clever way of saying no returns—final sale. So when I read this post, I immediately thought of Jesus. It brought to mind that he is ours to keep! Isn't that just the best? Once we have been called to his side, he is ours to keep forever. He is great and precious, something that we can and will keep for now and all eternity. No returns allowed, and what a blessing that is for all of us who believe in him. So as you start to do your fall shopping or look for summer sales that will be a great value, think on Jesus. How wonderful to know that from now until beyond infinity, we have a Savior that not only is ours to keep but keeps us right in the palm of his precious hand.

August 25. Carrying the Load

> Then he called the crowd to him along with his disciples
> and said: "If anyone would come after me, he must deny
> himself and take up his cross and follow me."
>
> —Mark 8:34

These days, I try not to pick up anything too heavy. I strained my back a while back and the thought crossed my mind that it couldn't be worth it to keep picking up stuff that I shouldn't. Not only did Jesus, our Lord and Savior, literally pick up and carry his heavy, heavy wooden cross, he also carried the sins of the world on his back, a heavy load for sure. Not one word of complaint came from his lips as he walked ever so slowly to Calvary. He did what he knew his Father was calling him to do, regardless of the consequence. Now it's our turn to carry his cross for his glory. This is one thing that we can certainly pick up as he lightens our load while we go through trials. In picking up the cross of Christ, we are called to love more, judge less, seek justice, and care for others. Let us remember that we are following Christ's call to deny ourselves and follow him. Let us suffer for Christ, let us sacrifice for Christ. Paul, Christ's disciple, says that the cross was everything to him. So shall it be for us, his believers. Let us find comfort in carrying the cross of the Lord. We have a golden opportunity to pick up this load and remain Christ-centered, no matter what comes our way. He bought our freedom from sin with the greatest price that anyone can pay. What a joy for us to be able to join in his walk of faith and lift high his cross while suffering so that others may see the absolute and infinite mercy and grace found there.

August 26. Going It Alone

My sheep listen to my voice; I know them, and they
follow me.

—John 10:27

I just took a little trip by myself to California to meet a dear friend for a few days. Now this isn't something that I do often— like almost never. The only other time that I can remember traveling alone was on my return trip from taking our son to college his freshman year out of state—14 years ago. I really don't like being alone too much. So this makes me think about our Jesus and his promises to us. He has said that we will never be alone. As we take his words to heart, here's the important part of this reflection. We, through the grace of our Savior, Jesus Christ, are never alone. He has said it; we must believe it. Afraid and alone? Jesus is there. Lonely and in need of company? Jesus is there. Longing to share good news with someone yet standing alone? Jesus is there. All we need to do is speak to him from our hearts, and we will instantly realize that we were and never will be truly alone.

August 27. "Going to Life!"

His divine power has given us everything we need for life.
—2 Peter 1:3

In watching the news recently and seeing all of the people pouring into Austria and Germany fleeing their countries to safety, one of the men interviewed was asked why all of these people would think about taking their families and walking the long and treacherous miles with their children. He said, "We are going to life." It's a simple yet powerful statement that explains why a father would risk the lives of his family to get to safety. We are all going to life if we have belief in Jesus Christ. He is life to us, for without him, our lives are not secure. Without him our lives are not protected. Without him our lives are empty, empty of the mercy and grace found in him each and every day that we live. So, just as these people are "going to life," so may we know that we are "going to life" every day through the power of our Savior, Jesus Christ.

August 28. Walking with Jesus

> When Jesus again spoke to the people, he said,
> "I am the light of the world. Whoever follows me will
> never walk in darkness, but will have the light of life."
>
> —John 8:12

Here at home, I tape a few shows to watch when I need to walk inside on the treadmill, and one of them is *Meet The Press*. The tagline of *Meet The Press* is "If It's Sunday, It's Meet The Press." This helps their viewers think of this show when Sunday rolls around, linking the day Sunday to that program and remembering to turn it on. Upon hearing this catchphrase, it made me think of what catchphrase comes to our minds with each day of the week—Sunday, Monday, Tuesday, and so on, in the same way as this one. The words, "If it's Monday, it's walk with Jesus," "If it's Tuesday, it's walk with Jesus," and so on popped into my head. Most of us would associate this idea of walking with Jesus on Sundays. But every bit as important is for us to link the reality that Jesus is walking with us each and every day of the week, no matter what month, what year, or what century. He never leaves us to walk alone. He has promised to be with us always, and that means always. So as we step out today and start walking to wherever life takes us, we have Jesus right beside us, guiding our footsteps and sharing time with us as we move about and go through the day. Is there anyone better that we would want to join us more than he, the one who made us and knows us inside out? He is our perfect companion, and he never walks out of step, no matter how quickly nor how slowly we may go!

August 29. Colorado High

> We proclaim him, admonishing and teaching everyone
> with all wisdom, so that we may present everyone perfect
> in Christ. To this end I labor, struggling with all his
> energy, which so powerfully works in me.
>
> —Colossians 1:28–29

Our family just got back from Colorado fly-fishing in the Fryingpan River. To watch that bright green fishing line float through the Colorado blue sky then land on the swirling blue river and gently float downstream is a peaceful and joyful experience. I had great fun when a rainbow trout hit my line. I watched as it began to fight against this thing that had caught it and was keeping it from going where it wanted to go. The trout began to swim back and forth, trying to stay in the deeper current to be safe. What it didn't realize was that when I finally reeled him in, I would gently release him back to the river, happy for him to be going on his way again. In the same way in life, when we realize that we have gotten ourselves into a trap, we do the exact same thing as these beautiful fishes. We fight and struggle against the current, yet when we are finally out of gas, we come to know that at the end of every struggle is a gentle release given to us by our Lord and Savior. He has been waiting in the bend of the river for us to give up the battle and let him unhook us from our fishing line, letting us go free from this trial. He longs to return us to a life of easy river livin', and so we must surrender to be set free. So here is the dichotomy: As we are caught struggling against whatever has captured us, we need to stop our struggling as we let go and let God. The Lord calls us to stop, rest, and place our lives in his perfect hands so that he can lead us to freedom. As it says in Colossians above, he calls us to use his energy in our struggles, which so powerfully works in us. Just as I gently placed my beautiful fish back into his comfort zone, so will the Lord return us to a place of peace and safety as we leave our struggles up to him.

August 30. Wrong Passcode

Therefore, since we have been justified through faith,
we have peace with God through our Lord Jesus Christ,
through whom we have gained access by faith into this
grace in which we now stand.

—Romans 5:1–2

Thinking recently that I had lost my phone and someone had erased all of the information held on it, they suggested at the phone store that I put a four-number passcode on it. If someone does actually find my phone, they cannot get into my pertinent information and change or erase anything. However, now every time I want to use my phone, I have to type in these four numbers to get to my screen. I quite often type in the wrong four numbers. Up pops these bright red words in all caps: WRONG PASSCODE! We all have a passcode to our Father by calling on his Son, Jesus. There are limitless passcodes to reach him, some as simple as the word "help!" Just call on him in any way with any passcode you choose, and we have instant access to his throne of grace. We will never be denied access, for he is readily available at all times. He never shuts us out with the words, "wrong passcode." What good news to know that he always answers when we are calling, even if we hit the wrong number time after time after time!

August 31. That's My Boy!

> And a voice from heaven said, "This is my Son,
> whom I love; with him I am well-pleased."
>
> —Matthew 3:17

Football season will soon be here. Now, Texas football is something to behold. Tackle football starts in the fourth grade. Watching the dads on the sidelines is fascinating, for they are so proud when their sons make a great play or throw a great pass. If you don't hear them say, "That's my boy!" you can sense it in their facial expressions and the way they clap and get so excited. When we read the verse above where God reveals that Jesus is truly his Son, speaking his love for his Son and telling all that he is "well-pleased," we can almost hear God proclaim, "That's my Son!" There is just something about the way this phrase is said by those who say it that reveals a depth of love that only a parent can have for a child, speaking out boldly his love for this child who is a part of him. Knowing that we are grafted into the Lord's family when we accepted Christ as our Savior, wouldn't it be so great to know that our Father is speaking those words about us as we move through our lives, reflecting his glory and scoring for the Lord daily? Let's prepare our plays in life, loving the unlovely, caring for those in need, offering a hand up to someone, listening with a caring ear to those who need support, and smiling as we go about our day; that will cause our Father to be filled with joy as he calls us his own. Down, Set, Hut. It's game time!

September 1. Reality

> Strengthen the feeble hands, steady the knees
> that give way; say to those with fearful hearts,
> "Be strong, do not fear, your God will come."
>
> —Isaiah 35:3

Reality—we can be certain that for all the presidential candidates, they each have big and bold ideas. Yet often when they get elected, reality sets in. They realize that some of their ideas will have to shift, keeping them from accomplishing all that they had intended to do. So it is the same for everyone, don't we think? No matter what age we are, we all awaken some days with a wonderful, profound agenda. Then we step out into life and we come face to face with the reality that it might not come to fruition as we have planned or hoped or dreamed. But for us who believe in Jesus Christ, the one true reality that we can always count on—that will never change, that was true way long ago, is true today, and will hold true forever—is that Jesus, as our Lord and Savior, has now and forever redeemed us from sin and will always and forever be by our side, no matter what of life's realities we face. Our promises that we know in loving him will never have to shift. He will always accomplish what he came to do. His wonderful, profound agenda has been accomplished. What joy to be found in the assurance that whenever and however our reality changes to a different hue, the bright and perfect light of Jesus will restore us to that place where we feel confident and prepared to greet another day.

September 2. Find Another Way

Jesus answered, "I am the way, the truth and the life."

—John 14:6

We have a yard service take care of our yard every week. They are such nice guys, but they continually leave the front gate open as they leave. This is problematic because our dog, Mojo, whom we adore, could get out if I fail to see that the gate has been left open. I have chatted with the owner of the service time and time again to no avail. So I decided to stop beating my head against the gate, so to speak, and find another way. I called our fence company and had them come out and put a self-closing spring on the gate. Now it cannot be left open. Find another way. So many times in life we come up against a problem and try as hard as we can to find the answer. But not until we find another way, putting it in the hands of our Jesus, do we finally see results. As we come up against a problem that seems to have no solution, we always have a solution: Jesus Christ, our Lord and Savior. Jesus tells us that he is the way, the one means through which we will all spend eternity in heaven praising and worshiping God. But he is also our way here on earth, providing us with his truth and guidance through all things: He's our way, the only way! He is the answer. He is the solution. He is the way!

September 3. Handle with Care

O Lord, what is man, that you care for him,
the son of man that you think of him?

—Psalm 144:3

Last week I was reading about a man who bought some old, antique speakers, speakers that are used to hook up to stereos to amplify the sound. In having them shipped, this man didn't buy insurance to cover the cost of damage in case something happened to his prized speakers in transit. As bad luck would have it, they arrived all busted up, splintered into many pieces. Brokenhearted, the man not only lost the cost of his speakers, but he was not able to find any more like these. In just the same way as this man with his speakers, our Father sees us as valuable and irreplaceable in his eyes. Yet we have insurance—we all have insurance—and we are covered by the greatest and best policy out there, insured by our Father's love. He provides not only the best care as we travel through life, but he also provides a replacement policy just in case we get damaged on our journey. Arriving at our destination from one of life's journeys, we will still be intact. We will arrive wrapped in the arms of Jesus, whose insulation from the bang-ups of life will insure that we are delivered just like we left our original location, perfectly! He assures us that, even if we get a dent here or there or something breaks along the way, he will fix us back to our original condition, perfectly restored by his grace.

September 4. The Scars of Life

Go back and tell Hezekiah, the leader of my people,
"This is what the Lord, the God of your father David,
says: 'I have heard your prayer and seen your tears;
I will heal you.'"

—2 Kings 20:5

When I was fifty-three years old, my internist found a rare carcinoid tumor in the mouth of my pancreas. By finding this cancer through a preventive CT scan, my surgeon was able to save my life by performing a surgical procedure called the Whipple. In order to remove this encapsulated tumor surgically, he had to create an eight-inch scar that would run vertically down the middle of my body. Smiling at me, my surgeon said, "I guess that this is the end of your bikini days!" I have a pretty good idea that he knew those days had been gone for quite some time. But the strangest thing about this whole experience is that I love that scar. I look at that scar, and I see the victory of Christ who, through the prompting of the Holy Spirit, saved my life by not letting me forget to get that CT scan. If I were twenty-four instead of sixty-four, you can be sure that you would be seeing me in some cute, brightly colored bikini, not being bothered a bit by a scar that reminds me each and every day that I was blessed by the Lord. We all have scars, and this isn't my only scar. But whether our scars are ones we can see or whether they are hidden deep within us, the beauty is found in the fact that all scars are healed by the love of Christ. We must choose to trust in him. No matter how our scars get there, he will heal them so that our bikini days are never really over!

September 5. Words Cannot Express

The same Lord is Lord of all and richly blesses all who call
on him.

—Romans 10:12

Have you ever been thanking the Lord for his blessings and felt like you could not find enough words to reveal just how thankful you truly were? Yesterday, I was praying a prayer of thanks to our Lord for his blessings for someone whom I love dearly, going over how blessing upon blessing has been poured out on this person so dear to me. I became overwhelmed as I realized that my words could not begin to express the gratitude that I felt to our Lord for his covering of grace on this person who has come through a difficult time into this place of blessing. I just couldn't find enough words to reveal all that I was feeling in my heart. All of us at one time or another have felt this deep and sincere thankfulness to our Lord during our lives for something that he has done for us or someone that we love. Feeling inadequate, I then realized that God knows our hearts; he knows what we are trying to say. He even knows when we cannot even utter a single word about how we are feeling. So as we live out each day and thank our Savior for all that he has done, let us rest in his assurance that even when we are speechless at how he has loved, he can hear our shouts of love and thanks.

September 6. Slow on the Uptake

> And pray in the Spirit on all occasions with
> all kinds of prayers and requests. With this in mind,
> be alert and always keep on praying for all the saints.
>
> —Ephesians 6:18

During my walk this week, I came upon a sharp, rusted piece of metal in the street. Not wanting to leave it there to create the possibility of a flat tire for someone, I picked it up, looked at it, and then thought to myself, *Now what do I do with this thing?* I continued to carry it until I arrived home. I carefully wrapped it up and carried it outside to our trash can. All of this reminds us of prayer requests, crying out to the Lord for others for his protection, peace, and love. Many times we are called to pray for someone, and what an honor, for prayer is powerful and complete. In the same way that this rusted piece of iron had really needed careful attention, so does each prayer request. We are called to pray earnestly and with devotion, laying our prayers at the foot of the very throne of God, where he will care for them. He will carefully wrap each one in his arms tightly, answering these cries in his own timing and with his perfect and holy touch. What a treasure for each of us to know that we can place all the cries of his children at his feet. He's the best caretaker we know. Oh, what a relief it is to know that he can handle any of our needs, no matter how sharp and painful they may be!

September 7. Striving for Perfection

> Love never fails. But where there are prophecies, they will
> cease; where there are tongues, they will be stilled; where
> there is knowledge, it will pass away. For we know in part,
> and we prophesy in part, but when perfection comes,
> the imperfect disappears.
>
> —1 Corinthians 13:8–10

Perfection. Often we set out on a project or in a relationship and expect or hope to accomplish perfection. We want things in life to be perfect. Yet is that a goal that we should set for ourselves? Perfection from imperfect people? I read recently that the monks in the Czech Republic have this to say about perfection: Perfection is not for man, only for God. Isn't that such a great response from the monks? Isn't that a response that makes us realize that, although we try to do our very best, only God is perfection, and we will always fall short? That's why we need him, we call on him, we cherish him. If we could live perfectly, in a perfection state of being, why would we need our perfect and holy God? We can be certain that the Lord calls us to do our best, to look to him for the perfect way, but to know that as we strive for perfection, true perfection is the Lord's, just as the monks so wisely explained. As we start each day, end each day, and live each moment in between, may we trust that we are always on a journey toward reaching that perfect state, following our perfect example, Jesus Christ. Yet when we fall short, and we will, he will redirect our paths and set us straight again to doing better through his perfect power. Then as it says in 1 Corinthians above, "When perfection comes, the imperfect disappears." Perfection coming—now that's something to look forward to each and every day!

September 8. The Game of Life

> Therefore, prepare your minds for action;
> be self-controlled; set your hope fully on the grace
> given you when Jesus Christ is revealed.
>
> —1 Peter 1:13

Last week I read an article written by a man about his dad who was a tennis coach at a high school in Cambridge, Massachusetts. He was reflecting on what he had learned from his dad's coaching that was applicable to life. His dad's message to his tennis players was always, "Run with your racket back. Be ready for anything." Our two older children played tennis in high school, so I have seen a lot of tennis over the years. Run with your racket back seems like sound advice. With your racket already back, when you reach the ball you will be ready to hit it. This coaching idea is easily applied to our lives. We can approach life each day with our racket back, prepared for anything that might come our way, because we have Jesus. He provides us with the necessary tools with which to hit any ball that life lobs at us. In tennis you need a strong follow-through, and with Jesus we have one. We are then prepared at all times to strike at what life whizzes by us. Keeping Jesus gripped strongly in our hands, we will have him at the ready, for life will throw something at us that will have us running, trying desperately to return its volley. We will be ready with Jesus on our side, making certain that each time a fast-moving ball approaches, we return it with strength and accuracy. Jesus is our answer to becoming winners in the game of life, preparing our minds for action through the power of Christ.

September 9. Rainy Day People

I love the Lord, for he heard my voice; he heard my
cry for mercy. Because he turned his ear to me,
I will call on him as long as I live.

—Psalm 116:1

A song came on my headset yesterday that I remember from the seventies. I realized that I knew the first line of the song but not many of the others. This piqued my interest, so I decided to look up the words. The song is entitled "Rainy Day People." It talks about those people in our lives who are there for us when the rains of life begin to fall. They know how to listen, they know what to say, they know how to comfort, and they know how to love. We all know rainy-day people. Those people who just know what to say when the times are tough; those people who know when not to say anything when the times are tough; and those people who are good listeners and feel our pain. They have been there, and they get it. Heading the top of our list of rainy-day people is Jesus. He is always there to listen. He feels our pain. In the sunshiny days or days of rain, he is there. He knows that there is no sorrow that he cannot help us to rise above. He sweeps the rain out of our lives with his love, never withholding his love from us. He just passes it on!

September 10. A Pinch of This and That

When Jesus spoke again to the people, he said,
"I am the light of the world. Whoever follows me will
never walk in darkness, but will have the light of life."

—John 8:12

Recipes—now where exactly do these come from? I want to say thanks to the dedicated people who spend untold hours working on getting a certain recipe just right. This is one gift that I for sure don't have. The time spent putting in a pinch of this and a dash of that to get a recipe tasting just right boggles my mind. I feel certain that it takes many, many, many times over and over again making the same recipe to get just the taste, texture, and right amount of everything in it so that others can take this recipe and have great success. The Lord has given us a recipe for life, providing just the right batter we need to get life right. He didn't have to try over and over again to give us the perfect recipe for living. His recipe isn't hard to understand nor is it confusing in any way. It is simply two words for us to use as we stir together the days of our lives. Our Lord, Jesus, said, "Follow me." That's it—follow me. He spoke this to his disciples back then, and the recipe is still the same for us today. Follow me, and if we follow him the results will always be the same, no lopsided cupcakes or deflated soufflés of life. We will live a life whose recipe for success has come from the perfect baker himself!

September 11. Remember, Pray, and Know Hope

Find rest, O my soul, in God alone; my hope comes
from him. He alone is my rock and my salvation;
he is my fortress, I will not be shaken.

—Psalm 62:5

September 11, 2001—this is a day that none of us will ever forget. I know for certain that each of us remembers where we were at that awful moment in time when we knew what this day would become, forever and ever. The pain and searing loss felt by so many on this day makes our hearts ache terribly for the families touched by this immense tragedy and for our nation forever changed. Wanting to provide comfort and strength to those who lost someone they loved, these are my thoughts. Let us remember those lost on this day and remember them with deep love and honor, for they are the ones who paid the greatest price for this evil. Let us remember and pray mightily for their loved ones and friends who lost them in a moment of time, with absolutely no warning. Let us pray for our nation and our leaders that they may know the course to take to keep such evil from reaching our shores ever again. And let us pray with a heart filled with thanks that we know our Lord and Savior, Jesus Christ, who still sits on his throne and will provide peace and comfort to these families. Let us be filled completely with the certain knowledge that he reigns and will reign forever and ever, with his promise that the best is yet to come. As with all tragedies, hope is the one thing left standing at the end of the day. He has promised to rescue us from our trials, he has promised to be there when no one else is, he has promised that he can bind up all our wounds and return us to a place of peace. He has promised hope. As Psalms 62:5–9 say, "Find rest, O my soul, in God alone; my hope comes from him...I will not be shaken."

September 12. A Legacy of Love

Store up for yourselves treasures in heaven,
where moth and rust do not destroy, and where thieves
do not break in and steal. For where your treasure is,
there your heart will be also.

—Matthew 6:20–21

I was walking on the Southern Methodist University campus today, and I saw the handsome statue of Doak Walker, a football star who played for the Mustangs in the forties. Written there under his statue was a wonderful paragraph about who he was, and part of it said that he had "unfailing good humor." What a precious description to be remembered by those who knew you as always bringing happiness to any situation. Unfailing—that just says it all. He never failed to bring humor wherever he went, and we all know that humor can soften every day with smiles. There are so many special words that can define each of us as how we lived: loving, kind, generous, nurturing, friendly, and the list goes on. The one that defines Doak Walker tells the reader a very exact and likable characteristic about him. However, the one phrase that I am certain each of us would most want said about us is "loved Jesus." We loved Jesus. Matthew says above that "where your treasure is, there will be your heart also." Let us greet each and every day with that thought in mind, revealing to the world that our greatest treasure is Jesus. Let us love the Lord, and let it show!

September 13. The Earthly Café

> Rejoice in the Lord always. I will say it again: Rejoice!
> Let your gentleness be evident to all. The Lord is near.
> Do not be anxious about anything, but in everything,
> by prayer and petition, with thanksgiving, present your
> requests to God. And the peace of God which transcends
> all understanding, will guard your hearts and your minds
> in Christ Jesus.
>
> —Philippians 4:4–7

"Welcome to the Earthly Café. May I take your order?"

"We will have some grace, please, with a serving of mercy on the side."

"Oh, my, we don't serve that here."

"Really? What do you offer?"

"We have conflicts, trials, confusion, and exhaustion. Would you like any of these?"

"No thanks, I eat all of those things at home, at the office, in my relationships. Are you certain that you don't have any grace and mercy sprinkled with a little peace? That is what I am really hungry for today."

"Well, we don't have that on our menu unless you know our owner."

"How can we meet him? Please!"

"You must meet him and then love him, the one who made us and cares for all things here."

"His name, please?"

"His name is Jesus. He longs for you to know him and call on him to serve you the things that make life good: his grace, his mercy, his peace, and his love. Accept him through faith, and he will serve these items daily for your comfort and joy. Come back soon when you can call on his name. The meals here on earth become much better, so much better, when he is the one making them."

September 14. Locked Out

Let us approach the throne of grace with confidence so
that we may receive mercy and find grace to help us in
our time of need.

—Hebrews 4:16

I work out at a gym where you need one of those magnetic cards
to get into the building. When you want to gain access, you hold
your magnetic card up to the handle on the door, then the red
light turns to green and you can go in. Last week, my card would
not open the door. I tried, and I tried, and I tried again, yet no
entry. My card had accidentally been cut off, stopping me from
getting in. This was all just a glitch that life sometimes brings
our way. It made me realize how blessed we are to always have
entry to Jesus. There is never a time that we try to open up a
conversation with him or need to be able to know his grace and
mercy that he is not there. He never cuts us off, no matter what
we do nor what we need. His door is always open, welcoming
us to come right through, gaining instant access to him. Joseph
Scriven said it so beautifully in his poem and hymn, "What a
friend we have in Jesus, / All our sins and griefs to bear! / What
a privilege to carry / Everything to God in prayer!"

September 15. Listening for Thunder

"Peace, peace, to those far and near," says the Lord.

—Isaiah 57:19

So many times in life we are living our lives "listening for the thunder." We wake up each day wondering what unpleasant or painful thing will happen that day. Many people call this the glass-half-empty approach to living. Sometimes during a storm those huge claps of thunder scare us right out of our chairs. So it is with life. Listening for thunder, we are living on the edge, uptight and anxious about what is to come. We will not be able to hear the precious calling by our Savior, whose words bring peace and calm to our lives. He is calling to us softly. It will be hard to hear the precious and tender words whispered by our Savior if our minds are focused on thunder, those loud, unexpected claps that make us shudder. Let us hear his voice as the day begins and unfolds, so that when the thunder does come, his tender words will have already prepared us, covering us with his peace rather than life's chaos. Let the rains come and the thunder with it, for we have the voice of the Lord to filter the noise.

September 16. God of Wonders

> ...the Lord God formed the man from the dust of the
> ground and breathed into his nostrils the breath of life,
> and the man became a living being.
>
> —Genesis 2:7

Fall is coming. Although it is still hot, we can feel fall in the air. There are so many things that we can trust to happen: The sun will come up; fall will arrive soon; as good as today is, there will be trials. And Jesus is here. We cannot always wrap our minds around a lot of things: the fax, the iPad, electricity, and how in the world we dispose of all that trash. But we can know with all certainty that we live each and every day wrapped in our faith. Faith in the Lord that this world and everything in it was called into being by our most holy God. No mortal man nor any coincidence in nature could make a baby nor teach us what love truly is. God alone has that power. We live and we love because he first loved us. True love? We couldn't know true love without knowing first how our Father loves us unconditionally. God is a God of wonders, and it is through his love for us that we live, breathe, and find joy, even in the simplest of things. We are here by his grace, and we will be forever with him by his mercy, plain and simple. That's who he is, that's how he works, and that's our God of wonders!

September 17. Fashionably Dressed!

> But since we belong to the day, let us be self-controlled,
> putting on faith and love as a breastplate,
> and the hope of salvation as a helmet.
>
> —1 Thessalonians 5:8

Last week, the start of the big push for fall fashions by the retailers of the world began. Designers, cosmetics companies, and anyone involved in the fashion industry participate in a big way. Fashion, and what we wear, has become a big thing in this society, where people of all ages talk about what they are going to wear, what someone else is wearing, and what looks best each season on what people. Billions of dollars trade hands over fashion. In processing this, the thought crossed my mind, *Are believers in fashion? Is it fashionable now to love Jesus? What does that look like to the rest of the world? Are we, who do accept Christ as our Savior, reflecting his look, putting on faith and love as a breastplate and helmet? When others look at us, do they see how much we love them as Christ loves us?* Although the retailers are smart in constantly changing what is in to encourage us to spend more money on new stuff, let's keep our old garments on, those of faith and love, that represent the Lord. Rather than taking these most treasured garments to the resale shop to sell in order to buy new ones, let's continue to wear these old ones that we know so well and bring so much joy to us and to others. No way can we replace these with anything better. So as we get dressed today, let's remember our most important fashion accessory, our breastplate and helmet of faith and love. Don't be surprised when someone comes up to you and wants to know where you bought them—the perfect entree into sharing the love of the Lord!

September 18. A Friendly Reminder

Therefore, encourage one another and build
each other up just as in fact you are doing.

—1 Thessalonians 5:11

A few weeks ago in church, our minister was preaching, and I saw the pencils and pens flying as congregants were writing down his words: "You show me your friends, and I will show you your future." This statement is so impactful, personally and worldwide. The encouraging and supportive words of friends are what edifies us as they make us just feel good. I thought of our children and how extremely important their friends became as they grew older. Many a time, our children would receive letters of encouragement from their friends or ours, lifting them up and giving them a solid ground on which to stand through kind and precious words as life wavered around them. For us, as believers, the impact is beyond powerful, for Jesus is the one friend and encourager who changes everything. It is through the promise of his words to us that we can know that we are loved and loved dearly. We become emboldened to love and encourage others. Being an encourager just feels good, it feels right, and it sends a wave of warmth and love throughout the world that is contagious. So let's start that wave of uplifting words that will swell like the rising seas as we pass along encouraging words, leading others to do the same.

September 19. Heaven's Silence

> Now to him who is able to establish you by my gospel
> and the proclamation of Jesus Christ, according to the
> revelation of the mystery hidden for long ages past, but
> now revealed and made known through the prophetic
> writings by the command of the eternal God, so that all
> nations might believe and obey him—to the only wise
> God be glory forever through Jesus Christ! Amen.
>
> —Romans 16:25–27

I am sure that all of us at times have felt that the Lord, our Father who is in heaven, has not heard our prayer for something that we have asked. We go day after day, month after month thinking that we are not hearing from our Father, waiting for his answer to our request. We also often experience silence here on earth. Silence from those we know and communicate with daily. Although so many people are carrying a cell phone, there are countless times throughout a week that we call or text someone and hear nothing. Just as sometimes people take their time to respond, so it is with God. He has definitely heard our prayer, he definitely has an answer, and he definitely will get back to us but in his own timing. He knows just when the right time is for that answer and how it needs to be *styled* for our best interest. He isn't delaying on purpose. He has a mighty plan that he is unfolding, just as it should unfold. This plan of answering our prayers was revealed when he broke heaven's silence and sent us Jesus. Jesus was the answer to generations of people needing to know their Savior. Jesus was the answer to God's people crying out for him to reveal himself on earth. Jesus is the answer for us today. We know him as our Savior, and we know that he is working mightily on our behalf to draw us closer to him and bring peace and balance and joy to our lives each and every day. Thank the Lord that he sent the only one who could show us the way. Thank the Lord that he gave us Jesus, in his own timing and in his perfect way.

September 20. He Runs to You

> But while he [the prodigal son] was a long way off,
> his father saw him and was filled with compassion
> for him; he ran to his son, threw his arms around
> him and kissed him.
>
> —Luke 15:20

Prodigal sons and daughters—who doesn't feel something deep inside when we read of the prodigal son who had turned from his father, having only wanted the material things that his dad could give to him? Yet when he repents and longs to give and receive the love of his father, his father never hesitates to run for him. Have you ever had someone running, running just for you? Recently our youngest child got engaged out of town on the top of a hill. After he asked and she said yes, they rode down the hill on a golf cart. She didn't know that twenty-seven of us would be waiting at the bottom to celebrate and share this special time with her. As she rounded the turn of the hill and saw all of us there, she started jumping up and down with her hands high in the air, smiling, shouting, and filled with joy. Seeing her dad and me waiting for her, she jumped out of the cart and ran straight into our arms. Now, I have to tell you, there is nothing that can match this feeling. Knowing that you are the very one being sought out by someone you love fills your heart with pure joy. So this is how it is for us to know the love of our Father. The story of the prodigal son is a parable that tells us the story of our Father's love for us. Just as we come to our Father, repenting and seeking his love, he runs to us! He doesn't wait for us to seek him out; he doesn't wait until we reach him and fall to our knees. He knows that we are coming, even when we are so far down the road that he can hardly see us. He starts to run to us, calling our name. This is how he loves, and this is how we should love. This is perfect love given by our perfect Father.

September 21. Treasure Chest

> My purpose is that they may be encouraged in heart and
> united in love, so that they may have the full riches of
> complete understanding, in order that they may know the
> mystery of God, namely, Christ, in whom are hidden all
> of the treasures of wisdom and knowledge.
>
> —Colossians 2:2–3

I remember so vividly dragging our four children to the orthodontist for years, over and over and over again. At each visit, they were able to select a treasure from the treasure chest there, filled with all sorts of things. These little treasures were not valuable as far as true worth goes, but it made the trip bearable. Our real treasures are held in the hands of our Savior who supplies our lives with treasures that cannot be bought: mercy, grace, love, peace, joy, restoration, forgiveness, and hope—all the things in life that really matter and only can come from our holy Lord. Each of us considers different things as treasures in our lives, but the greatest ones are given unconditionally by our treasure found in Jesus. He gives us each and every day his perfect love—a treasure that is truly priceless!

September 22. It Was Scary!

> Lord my God, I take refuge in you.
>
> —Psalm 7:1

Last week we attended our local high school's varsity football game. Our oldest grandson, who is a senior, is on the team. The final score was 28-26, and it all came down to one play at the end of the game. In talking with one of the players afterward, he said, "It was fun and it was scary." This guy is 6'2" and 275 pounds of football player. So, to hear him say that it was scary caught my attention. It was an honest assessment from an honest young man, to be sure. He didn't look scared, but yet, the situation was scary to him. Most of us would not think that anyone of that size and age would find life scary, at least not yet. Here is the reality for all of us: life is scary at times, whether we are eighteen years old, or ninety-eight years old, or anything in between. We may not look scared, but inside we are so scared. Life will be difficult at times. It will cause us to feel panicked, not sure of where to turn or what to do. But for us as believers, when life turns scary, we have the answer. It is Jesus. Jesus is the one, when we are "scared," to whom we can turn over our "scaredness" and let him lead the way. What a gift we have in Jesus, who can always take our fears and replace them with his strength and mercy and grace. "It was scary" can forevermore be placed in the hands of our powerful Savior who will always turn scary into peace, his perfect peace.

September 23. A Mind of Its Own

> You, however, are controlled not by the sinful nature but
> by the Spirit, if the Spirit of God lives in you...But if
> Christ is in you, your body is dead because of sin, yet your
> spirit is alive because of righteousness. And if the Spirit
> of him who raised Jesus from the dead is living in you, he
> who raised Christ from the dead will also give life to your
> mortal bodies through his Spirit, who lives in you.
>
> —Romans 8:9–11

The newspaper last week had a terrific article on research into bacteria and how good bacteria is really so important for our systems to function properly. It discusses at length the benefits of taking probiotics that provide good bacteria in our systems, saying, "There's no question that the composition of our microbial communities determines our health." One researcher goes on to say, "I found out we're actually more bacteria than we are human. We've got one hundred trillion bacteria in our gut. That's ten to one hundred times more bacteria than cells in your body. It's almost as if we have another organ inside us with a mind of its own." While this scientific statement may be true, we have something living within us that is much more important than even the good bacteria found there—the Holy Spirit. Yes, Jesus sent us the Holy Spirit to live within us to guide us and show us his way. We see the results of the indwelling Holy Spirit throughout each and every day. If we attune ourselves to listening to his voice, we can follow his lead and respond to his perfect guidance or requests for us. As much as we want to rely on our good bacteria to keep our systems functioning at peak performance, more so do we want to rely on the Holy Spirit to keep our lives functioning as God wants. Our Holy Spirit gives us strength, peace, and guidance for each day we live, making us healthy so that we can approach life well and live it to its fullest! So here's to the scientists of the world and the amazing new discoveries that they are finding. But our greatest thanks goes to the Lord for our indwelling Holy Spirit, for without him, nothing else would feel quite right!

September 24. "Save Up for the Long Run"

> My son, if you accept my words and store up my
> commands within you, turning your ear to wisdom and
> applying your heart to understanding, and if you call
> out for insight and cry aloud for understanding, and if
> you look for it as for silver and search for it as hidden
> treasure, then you will understand the fear of the Lord
> and find the knowledge of God.
>
> —Proverbs 2:1–6

I read an article recently entitled "Save Up for the Long Run." It addressed the issue of financial security in retirement and how people today are worrying that their savings or Social Security benefits will not be enough to provide for them. This is a sobering thought, for people are living longer, much longer, and the focus needs to shift to this reality. But the title of this article also brought to mind the more important reality for us as believers that we are saving up for the long run, and that long run not only includes our life here on earth but all eternity. We have a faith in the One, Jesus, who will take us through the longest run of our lives into an eternal time spent worshipping him. When the long run arrives and we reach heaven's gates, we will be covered with his goodness because we started here on earth saving up. The added bonus to making preparation for the future is that we will live a life that brings him the glory because we have studied and absorbed the truth that he calls us to know and live out. Jesus is our Savior, the one who has given us life and everything in it, and to him will always go the glory.

September 25. Deeper Water

> As the deer pants for streams of water, so my soul pants
> for you, O God. My soul thirsts for God, for the living
> God. When can I go and meet with God?
>
> —Psalm 42:1–2

Texas is in a drought—a serious drought—and it is so disheartening to see the beautiful lakes in our state drying up and revealing sandy shores filled with stumps, preventing anyone from enjoying time on them. The lake on our property has dried up like the other lakes in Texas. We have a lot of fish in the lake that are now struggling to survive. Our lake is actually divided in two parts by a ridge of land. One side has more water than the other, so we are having someone catch the fish with a net in the drier part of the lake and move them into the other side where there is more water. The fish in the drier lake are exposed to the buzzards that can easily swoop down and grab a tasty meal as they please. Just like these fish, often along life's road we are exposed to buzzards that will eat us up if we are allowed to stay in this area of drought, needing the Lord's protection. Moving the fish to a safer place reflects exactly what the Lord does for us. When he finds us exposed to danger, he fishes us out of the shallow water and gently places us in the fresh water of a deeper lake, giving us new life away from the trials we were facing. We can continue on in the midst of our trial, struggling to surface and catch our breath, or we can call on our holy God. He is the only one who can provide more oxygen. He is the one who longs to revive us as we move through difficulty, our safety net from life's dried-up streams!

September 26. "Pray without Ceasing"

Be joyful always; pray continually;
give thanks in all circumstances,
for this is God's will for you in Christ Jesus.
—1 Thessalonians 5:16–18

I recently found this quote: "If you only pray when you're in trouble, then you're in trouble." These words are so simple and so true. We who believe in the Risen Lord do turn to him in prayer when trouble comes knocking on our door, praying his name and asking for his help. Yet here's the thing. Jesus longs to hear our prayers all the time. Not just when we are desperate, not just when we are in crisis, not just when we have nowhere else to turn. He wants us to be praying with him all throughout the day, every day of every year, not just at Christmas and not just at Easter. Prayer is the way that we have an open line of communication with the Lord, our Maker and the one who loves to hear from us all the time. Communication is key to staying connected. Communication is how we tightly weave our lives with those we love. Loving Jesus is our number-one priority, and the best way that he can know our love and that we can know his is through talking with him. He has called us to pray without ceasing, so let's do just that. Let's begin today to pray prayers of thanks, prayers of hello, prayers of help, so that our line of communication with Jesus remains open 24/7. "This is God's will for you in Christ Jesus."

September 27. Permanent Marker

> ...but because Jesus lives forever, he has a permanent
> priesthood. Therefore he is able to save completely those
> who come to God through him, because he always lives
> to intercede for them.
>
> —Hebrews 7:24–25

I recently ran across this phrase, and it has really set me to thinking: *a permanent solution to a temporary problem.* Problems are a part of life. We all experience problems of differing magnitude. Some of our problems are tiny, easily solved. Then we move on to bigger and bigger problems. We are knee-deep in a trial, broken, confused, and needing a permanent solution to a temporary problem! The reason that we long for a permanent solution to our problem is that we don't ever—no, never—want to go down this road again, for traveling that road named trial is a rough and unpleasant one at best. The only permanent solution to any problem is the Lord and Savior Jesus Christ. If we choose to leave our problem and all of its challenges with him, we will be done once and for all with it. Although we may still have to travel along its path in the future, we have forever tucked the rough spots into his loving arms, permanently. You see, Jesus is like a permanent marker. Once he is applied to something, he never comes out. He is written on its surface, his mark covering it with love. It is his to take care of, relieving us from this burden. If by chance we meet this situation again, we will find that he is already there, having marked it out, highlighting us with his grace.

September 28. World Changers Shaped Here

"Come, follow me," Jesus said,
"and I will make you fishers of men."

—Matthew 4:19

Here in our wonderful city of Dallas, we share a fantastic university, Southern Methodist University. So many alumni and people everywhere have helped to build this world-class university where students can excel, becoming the leaders of tomorrow. Not only is the campus stunningly beautiful with gorgeous fountains, handsome buildings, and immaculate grounds, the quality of teaching that goes on here is superb. Yesterday I saw one of the SMU shuttles drive by, and on the side was their logo: World Changers Shaped Here. What a great introduction to this superior university knowing that the students are becoming the leaders of tomorrow by being shaped by all that they will learn here. We, as believers, are also world changers, as we have been chosen and shaped by the one who does it best, Jesus. We have the precious opportunity to make a difference in his world, knowing his goodness and his grace. This phrase encourages us too to go out there and shape the world made by the Lord in a myriad of ways—the opportunities are truly limitless. We have been given the perfect tool to shape others for Christ, our belief in him. Just as the students at SMU will be encouraged to reach high and go forth to shape the world that they will know after graduation, we also have this encouragement through the love and power of Jesus. Let's not waste one more day, using it to shape the world as we know it for the better, for his glory.

September 29. Safe Water

> On the last and greatest day of the Feast,
> Jesus stood and said in a loud voice, "If anyone is thirsty,
> let him come to me and drink. Whoever believes in me,
> as the Scripture has said, streams of living water
> will flow from within him."
>
> —John 7:37–38

Tucked in the back of the morning paper was a small article with this title: "Underground water supply found in Kenya." Then a paragraph followed about Kenyan officials, along with the help of the United Nations, who had discovered a potentially enormous underground water supply, a find that could improve the lives of people in northern Kenya for years to come. The next and final sentence says, "Out of Kenya's population of forty-one million people, seventeen million lack access to safe drinking water." Now on reading this and seeing its lack of importance in the paper, we have this thought: If we were able to provide this same technology to the areas of the world that do not have safe water, couldn't there possibly be many more of these undiscovered water supplies, just waiting to save the lives of millions of people? Thanks be to God that we have safe drinking water right at our fingertips. But more importantly our living water is readily available to us just by turning on his tap. We can access his wisdom and drink from his well of goodness any time, any place, all day and night, without wasting a drop. His well is deep and has no end. Let us strive to reveal this precious water of life to all with whom we come in contact, for not only can it save lives here on earth, but he can and will save lives for all eternity, and that is a discovery worth searching for by all who do not know him.

September 30. Welcome to the State Fair of Texas!

May the nations be glad and sing for joy, for you rule the
peoples justly and guide the nations of the earth.

—Psalms 67:4

The State Fair of Texas—always such a welcoming experience. For to most of us, it represents the beginning of fall and all of the changes it brings with it: cooler weather; beautiful leaves; and crisp, sunny days. My friend and I took our grandsons to the fair. Wisely, as we walked in past Big Tex, my friend said to them, "If you guys get lost, here is Big Tex. Look for him and go to where he is. There you will find this police station with this nice policeman, and he will help you find us." Big Tex is a great guide to use to find our way around at the fair. I have never been lost at the fair, but I have certainly been lost in life, more times than I care to remember. Praise God that we have the perfect guide to look for in these tumultuous times of life, Jesus. So many times, life has brought us to our knees, and we cannot find our way until we looked to Jesus to guide us to a place of peace and security. Jesus guides the nations of the earth, as it says in Psalms 67:4 above, and we can be glad and sing for joy. Amen to that! But we also know that Jesus guides each and every one of us as we are faced with life's challenges when we don't know which way to turn; when we cannot find our way out of the maze of confusion; when we really, really need to rest in his peace until he clears the way and answers are known. So just as we can rely on Big Tex to guide the way in case we get lost at the fair, more importantly, we can rely on Jesus to guide us through those tough times when we have lost our way and cannot see through the foggy days of life. Jesus is ever available to lead the way to sunny days, always prepared to guide us where he wants us to go.

October 1. What a Difference!

She will give birth to a son, and you are to give him the
name Jesus because he will save his people from their sins.

—Matthew 1:21

I have horrific allergies. But lately, like everyone else, mine have
been ratcheted up a thousand times worse than usual. I went
to a new allergist who needed a CT scan of my sinuses. I have
had many CT scans due to my pancreatic surgery twelve years
ago, so when I went in I told the cute girl doing the scan that
I would be keeping my eyes closed as this is what I have always
done. It makes it so much easier to not see the machine closing
right in over your head and making one feel claustrophobic. I lay
down and got ready, keeping my eyes tightly shut, waiting on the
machine to pass over my head very near my nose. When the scan
was finished, and when I got up, I realized that the new machine
was at least twelve inches and maybe more above my head. I
couldn't believe it. I started thinking, "Wow! What a difference
twelve years makes!" In the same way, what a difference one life
has made. The life of Jesus Christ. Our lives are totally different
from what they would have been had our Father, God, not sent
his only son to die on the cross for our sins. We would probably be
living each and every day with our eyes shut tightly, not wanting
to live in a world without Jesus. But because he lived, everything
changed for the better. We do not have to fear the future because
he has it in his grip, caring for us each step of the way. We can
live out each day knowing that Jesus has it all under control. We
can trust, giving it all up to him. What a difference a day makes
in more ways than one!

October 2. He Is Enough

> He is before all things,
> and in him all things hold together.
>
> —Colossians 1:17

Change is coming. Can't you just feel it in the air? Schools are beginning to start, and even though it is still officially summer outside, we can all begin to sense the change that sets our minds to shift from summer mode into fall and all that it brings. We are starting to move in the direction of fall—darker colors, more of a shoe. Fall flowers begin to be seen around the neighborhood and then we know. We all know that fall is here. This sense that things are changing is exactly what happens when we are in the midst of a trial. We may do many things to try to fix it, but then when we rest on his promise that he is enough, things change. We settle in and know, we just know, he is enough. I was praying last night for a couple who is in the midst of a difficult and painful trial. As I lifted them up in prayer, these words kept reoccurring in my head: He is enough. He is enough, for them and for all of us. So just as we can sense that change is on the way as fall comes over us, we can know with complete assurance that when we cry out "Jesus," he will answer our every need. We can sense the difference in what is happening. Change will come over us as we find strength and comfort in these three most important and encouraging words: He is enough. For in him, all things hold together.

October 3. Knowing Who You Are

You have been given fullness in Christ, who is the head over every power and authority.

—Colossians 2:10

In walking the mall last week, I read this sign on the window of a store there: "Beauty comes from knowing who you are." That thought made an impression on me, and what a great message for the youth of today. Beauty comes from within. It is not your outward appearance that makes the difference but the beauty that shines from a heart that loves. Beauty cannot be found in what we wear, in how much we have, in the things of the world. Beauty is what is seen by others when each of us knows who we are, how we love, and how we meet each day with kindness and gratitude. More importantly, knowing who we are, that we belong to Jesus, brings that inner glow that reveals the love with which we are showered from our Lord and Savior. Because he first loved us, and now we know love and give love, we are surrounded each day with his beauty, living in the certainty that we are loved by the Lord of the universe. And that is exactly what makes each one of us beautiful inside and out!

October 4. Is It Still Raining?

Since you are my rock and my fortress,
for the sake of your name lead and guide me.

—Psalm 31:3

Walking last week with my dog, Mojo, it started to mist just slightly. I was very ready to return home in hopes of missing a downpour that would drench us rather than the mist that was just gently falling over us. As I pulled on his leash, he really wasn't ready to return home. He kept walking away from my lead, ignoring me and doing his best to stay there in the misty rain. His tugging on the leash reminded me of how we sometimes go against the grain of where the Lord longs to lead us. We are walking in the middle of the rains of life, and we don't even realize that he wants to take us to a place of safety, of calm and restoration. We just keep plugging along, not paying attention to his leading us, and all of a sudden we have moved from the mist of a trial to a torrential downpour. We think that we are handling things pretty well, without calling on his help, and suddenly we find ourselves in a deluge of life. How much better if we had felt the gentle tug of the Lord in the beginning, keeping us from this soaking. Yet even if we find that we have been completely soaked, he will always find a way to lead us back to a place where it is safe and dry. When we find ourselves walking in the rain, he will lead us out of the storm and into his loving arms if we just remember to call on him to lead the way.

October 5. What's in Your Storehouse?

> My son, keep my words and store up my commands
> within you. Keep my commands and you will live; guard
> my teachings as the apple of your eye. Bind them on your
> fingers; write them on the tablet of your heart.
>
> —Proverbs 7:1–3

Last week, I was walking on one of our glorious fall days, and I happened to look down as I passed a very large oak tree in a neighbor's yard. Much to my surprise, there were all of these holes in the dirt surrounding this tree. I surmised that those cute squirrels that inhabit our neighborhood had taken their little paws and buried their treasure for future use. They have stored those nuts that they so love deep in the ground to reclaim during the upcoming winter months when no nuts will be available. Seeing these holes reminds us that we also need to store up nuts for the winter, for not only will our actual Dallas winter be coming soon, but another winter of life will be on its way. The question that we need to ask ourselves is this: *Are we prepared just as these squirrels are to face one of life's winters? Are we prepared with God's promises to dig up out of the recesses of our hearts and minds when another winter of life knocks at the door?* There is nothing more reassuring than to know that we are prepared for whatever may come our way. So let's create within our hearts and minds a treasure trove of God's promises to rely on once that winter comes. Then we can open up that door, armed with the promises of God and wrapped in the blanket of his love, and that wintry chill of life will not be able to touch our souls. Let's get to storin', winter's on the way!

October 6. Between the Hedges

Have you not put a hedge of protection around him and
his household and everything that he has?

—Job 1:10

Saturday college football—welcome fall! There is nothing quite like the start of fall and college football to those of us who are football fans. There is an excitement in the air that is almost palpable. Our younger daughter attended the University of Georgia in Athens, where football is played "between the hedges." This phrase refers to the hedges that were planted in 1929 around the football field to resemble the rose bushes found around the Rose Bowl. They provide crowd control, hemming in the swarms of people who want to rush the field after a big victory. Between the hedges—that is a term that I use often in my prayers, for I want God to hem me in, in between his hedges of care and protection where I will be held safely. I also pray this protection for my family and for those whom I love. What could be more comforting than to know that our Father, our protector, has hemmed us in between his hedges, where we can find security and strength? So as we fire up the television for game day today, when the score for Georgia comes across our screen, let us think of that glorious, comforting hedge of protection provided by our Savior and be thankful. Let's water his hedge with our prayers, keeping it strong and healthy, for who knows when the next drought will come?

October 7. Twirling with Joy

> Sing to the Lord, for he has done glorious things; let this
> be known to all the world. Shout aloud and sing for joy,
> people of Zion, for great is the Holy One of Israel.
>
> —Isaiah 12:5–6

We have an SPCA dog named Mojo, who is a mix between an Irish setter and a chow. Beautiful, right? But more beautiful than his appearance is his spirit. When we adopted him, he had been dropped off and left at the SPCA for over a month. He was in a funk, as they say. He would only face the wall of his cage, depressed at losing his family. So the sweet and caring people there took him out his cage and put him in his own room, trying to cheer him up. After having been adopted, he now is filled with joy, and today when he saw that I was going to take him walking, he started twirling and hopping for joy. This makes us wonder, *Is that how we greet the Lord daily as he prepares to walk us through the day? Does he know that we are jumping for joy at this beautiful day he has provided, knowing that, no matter what the day brings, he is at our side?* He can know our thankfulness by knowing our hearts. How thankful we all are that we have been adopted by God. So shall we reveal this joy by waking each day, smiling and twirling with joy, showing the Lord that his blessing has not been overlooked and we are joyful at being a part of his precious family.

October 8. Face to a Name

> Then God said, "Let us make man in our image,
> in our likeness…"
>
> —Genesis 1:26

Don't you just love it when you hear stories about your friend's friends, people that they know and love yet you have never met? When we meet them sometime later, the stories seem complete. I often say, "It's so nice to put a face to a name." I love meeting these people that I have heard so much about, and as life moves forward I can picture them as their stories unfold. A face to a name. Don't we think that the people in this world who don't know Jesus would love to be able to see Jesus in the here and now, putting a face to his name? There are so many who have no idea of who Jesus really is. Truth be told, we don't really know what he looked like either, having not seen him ourselves here on earth. But we do know him, and we have a pretty good shot at picturing who he is in our mind's eye. Kind? Yes. Loving? Yes. Accepting? Yes. Gave his life for us? Yes. And so the lines in the drawing go on and on as we know and experience who he is. How are we to help those who don't know Jesus put his face to his name? By living our lives so that he is glorified in all that we do. Let us live our lives in order that others can see Jesus through us, so that when they do meet him face-to-face, they will say, "It's so nice to put a face to your name, Jesus!"

October 9. Sitting in the Teepee

You are my hiding place; you will protect me from trouble
and surround me with songs of deliverance.

—Psalm 32:7

I recently purchased a teepee made out of this fun cloth fabric from a store here in Dallas for our grandchildren to play in when they come over. The sales person suggested that I also get a large and comfy pillow to put inside so that they will have a cushiony place to sit. Well, as these things go, Mojo, our rescue dog, thinks that this cozy teepee is his. I was looking for him the other day, and there, sticking out of the door of the teepee were two furry paws and a beautiful tail. Yep, Mojo had gone into that teepee headfirst to go to sleep. Ever since, I find him sleeping there, where he feels protected and safe and away from the bright lights and noise of our lives. Jesus provides us with his teepee of comfort, one that lets us escape for a time, getting away from the chaos of life, providing sweet rest and protection from life's craziness. He is our hiding place, where we will be protected from trouble and surrounded with songs of deliverance. Enter in and find sweet restoration there.

October 10. Poster Children of the Most High God

As water reflects a face, so a man's heart reflects the man.

—Proverbs 27:19

Seeing all of the school posters in our community showing photos of students and their respective high school activities is so enjoyable. Through these, we have the opportunity to see a little glimpse of these outstanding young people representing what they love. Just as these students reflect a love and passion for what they are involved in, we too have the opportunity to reflect the love and passion that we have for Jesus. We are able to show others his attributes through our lives, revealing his love, his compassion, his strength—all the priceless gifts that he provides to us in boundless love. We will not need to have posters of ourselves placed around the town, for we are living, breathing posters for Jesus as we live our lives according to his purpose. As it says in Proverbs above, may our hearts be a reflection of the love of Jesus that we have sealed there. How grand and glorious to be called his children and be given every chance to reflect his glory as poster children of our Almighty God.

October 11. Noah and the Flood

> Noah was as righteous man, blameless among the people
> of his time, and he walked with God.
>
> —Genesis 6:9

Having recently reread the story of Noah, we have the opportunity to reflect on God's purpose for him and God's purpose for each of us. I am sure that most of us have wondered what he has in mind for us to do to further his kingdom. In reviewing Noah's purpose, we realize that the Lord had a mighty plan for this one man, and accomplish it he did. Noah was faithful to God's plan against all odds, facing ridicule and scorn for believing and following his God. Yet God called him a "righteous man, blameless among the people of his time, and he walked with God." Here is the essence of the story: He walked with God. We, as believers, are all called to walk with God, for this will keep us on the right path, the path of righteousness. We are being called by our Father to walk in his ways, revealing his love for man and calling them to his side. How shall each of us respond to this call of the Lord? We have to decide through thoughtful prayer how the Lord can best use us to shepherd his flock and fulfill his purpose in our lives. Let us use each day to honor him as we listen to his voice, giving us direction on how to live for his glory, walking with him through all eternity.

October 12. The Chosen

> When morning came, he called his disciples to him and
> chose twelve of them, whom he also designated apostles:
> Simon (whom he named Peter), his brother Andrew, James,
> John, Phillip, Bartholomew, Matthew, Thomas, James son
> of Alphaeus, Simon who was called the Zealot, Judas son
> of James, and Judas Iscariot, who became a traitor.
>
> —Luke 6:13–16

Last week, we had the pleasure of attending our home church's plant church. It is the most beautiful old church with magnificent stained-glass windows depicting the twelve disciples. To sit there and gaze upon them is almost as if we are sitting in the room with them, and it warms our heart to experience their presence in the house of the Lord. In thinking on them and soaking in their beautiful faces so expertly done in that gorgeous stained glass, I wanted to learn more about these men that Jesus handpicked, calling them to leave everything that they knew and loved to follow him. To think of being asked to leave all that you know, all that you love, and all of your security in life to follow a simple man would change one's life forever. These twelve disciples had to step out in faith, being led by a love so strong that they could not turn from it. It is the same for us. God had a mighty plan for us before he formed the earth. He knows us by name, just as he knew these men of God whom he called to change the world through the knowledge of him. The names of the twelve disciples are found in the Scripture above. The first disciple he called was Simon, whom he named Peter. Now Peter was so human. We just have to love him, for we can see so much of ourselves in him. How thoughtful of the Lord to call Peter first, for Peter is the one disciple with whom most people can best relate. First walking on water by faith, then sinking in doubt the next. Yet Jesus adored Peter, and he loves us in the same way. Going forward, we can continue to reflect on Peter's life and how it reveals so much to us about how to live.

October 13. Regular People

> When the disciples saw him walking on the lake, they
> were terrified. "It's a ghost," they said, and cried out in
> fear. But Jesus immediately said to them: "Take courage!
> It is I. Don't be afraid." "Lord, if it's you," Peter replied,
> "tell me to come to you on the water." "Come," he said.
> Then Peter got down out of the boat, walked on the water
> and came toward Jesus. But when he saw the wind, he was
> afraid and, beginning to sink, cried out, "Lord, save me!"
> Immediately Jesus reached out his hand and caught him.
> "You of little faith," he said, "why did you doubt?"
>
> —Matthew 14:26–31

Twelve men that the Lord selected from his early followers to become his closest disciples have the same traits that the Lord has given us, traits belonging to ordinary people. It is easy for us to relate to their humanness, reading stories that enable us to know the Lord through his interaction with them. So now about Peter. What a character—what a lovable character—and so like us. Impulsive? Yes. Emotional? Yes. Spokesman for the twelve? Yes. Even though Peter denies Jesus when things get difficult, he is the one that Jesus had selected all along to become a bold evangelist and missionary for his work in the world. Peter became one of the greatest leaders of the early church, fulfilling his calling given to him by his Lord. Peter was one of the four disciples whom Jesus chose to witness the transfiguration as well as Jesus's agony in the garden of Gethsemane. Most of us remember Peter for denying knowing Jesus three times during the night of his trial. Peter, emotionally devastated we can be sure, was assured by the Lord that he was forgiven, just as we can be sure today. The other memorable story about Peter is the one that tells us about that one day at predawn when Peter was in a boat with his fellow disciples and saw Jesus walking on water toward him. Peter calls out to our Savior, asking him to call Peter to walk to him on the water. Jesus says, "Come." Peter gets out of the boat and begins to walk on the water, but, becoming afraid, starts to sink, crying out, "Lord, save me." Jesus immediately reaches out his hand and catches Peter. Now if this is the only story that we ever heard about Peter, what a takeaway we have for our own lives. We love the Lord, just as Peter did. We long to walk in faith, just as Peter did. But then our faith slips and we are afraid, just as Peter was. We are fearful, and we call out to the Lord "save me!" and he does. There are two things we can learn about Peter's relationship with Christ: Jesus redeems and Jesus saves. Peter knew it and we do too. We just have to cling to these truths each and every day that we live.

October 14. Brotherly Love

> Andrew, Simon Peter's brother, was one of the two who
> had heard what John [the Baptist] had said and who
> followed Jesus. The first thing Andrew did was to find his
> brother Simon and tell him, "We have found the Messiah"
> (that is, the Christ). And he brought him to Jesus.
>
> —John 1:40-42

Now here is the kind of brother that everyone longs to have. Andrew, the brother of Simon Peter, has been listening to John the Baptist, clinging to his words. While in John the Baptist's presence, Andrew hears him call out that Jesus, the Lamb of God, was passing by. One of the very first things that Andrew does upon knowing that he had encountered the Living Christ was to go find Simon Peter. He could not wait to share this life-changing news with him. Andrew didn't want to hog Jesus to himself, and he didn't hide this fact from his brother so that he could become Jesus's favorite. Andrew rushed to Simon Peter's side, bringing this joyous revelation to him. Peter, being the more outgoing of the two, steps out in front to become one of the leaders among the apostles and in the early church. Andrew, on the other hand, steps back into the shadow of his brother, happy for him to take the lead. Andrew didn't mind being in the background, for he knew the call of the Lord and that his plan would be revealed in so many different ways through each of the disciples. It takes a wise and compassionate man to let his brother be in the forefront, supporting and encouraging him along the way. After Andrew leads Simon Peter to Christ, not much more is known about him, but we can know him well by his unselfish and loving actions, sharing the most important thing that anyone will ever know with his brother whom he loved so. Andrew thirsted for the truth, found it in his Lord and Savior, and willingly stepped aside to let his brother become the spokesman for Christ's disciples. That, dear friends, is the epitome of unselfishness, not always found among the people of this world. What an amazing quality to have, and one that we should all emulate from knowing this lover of Christ, his disciple, Andrew.

October 15. The Inner Circle

> After six days Jesus took with him Peter, James and
> John the brother of James, and led them high up a high
> mountain by themselves. There he was transfigured
> before them. His face shone like the sun, and his clothes
> became as white as the light.
>
> —Matthew 17:1–2

James was one of the three disciples who were honored with a favored position by their Lord to be in his inner circle. James was fishing with his brother John when Jesus called them to follow him. They immediately left their fishing business that they ran with their father to follow the young rabbi. Because James is always mentioned first in the Bible, it is assumed that he was the older brother. James, along with John and Peter, bore witness to three events of great magnitude: Jesus's raising of the daughter of Jairus from the dead, the transfiguration, and Jesus's agony in the garden of Gethsemane. Passionate about his Savior, James spoke out in anger when a Samaritan village rejected his Lord, wanting to call fire down upon that place. James always revealed a tremendous zeal for Christ. This is one characteristic that we can admire and take as our own, for James was honored by his Lord for his outward and obvious overwhelming love for his Savior. To be passionate for Christ calls us to live each day with him on our minds, revealing our love for him in all that we do. Think on the times that you have been completely over the top for something, the outpouring of joy, the excitement and eagerness that you felt and revealed. That is what we need to let the world see. How very much we love Jesus. Just as James was part of Christ's inner circle, so too the Lord pulls us close to his side as we eagerly live large in love for the Lord.

October 16. Impassioned One

> Jesus said to her, "I am the resurrection and the life.
> He who believes in me will live, even though he dies;
> and whoever lives and believes in me will never die.
> Do you believe this?"
>
> —John 11:25–26

It was likely known by those of that day that John was the brother of James for they had many similar characteristics. We most likely know John well for having authored three very powerful books of the Bible: the Gospel of John; the letters of 1, 2, 3 John; and possibly Revelation. John had James's zeal for life, and he was especially loyal to Jesus. John was thought to be that lone disciple at the cross when Jesus died. On the cross, Jesus entrusts the care of Mary, his mother, to an unnamed disciple that many believe was John. John then took Mary into his own home to care for her. John's writings all point to one very important message: that Jesus was the Christ, the Son of God. John emphasized throughout his writings that Jesus had come to take away the sins of the world, and it is through his messages that many of our names for Jesus are first used, such as the Lamb of God, the Son of God, the Great I Am, and the Vine. Thanks to John and his vivid names for the Lord, we can know Jesus like the lights spinning off a kaleidoscope, revealing his many glorious and colorful names that he brings to our lives. Interestingly, John asks Jesus for a favored position in Jesus's kingdom. What we must love about this is that John is just like all of us, wanting to be the closest and most loved by the Lord. But the beautiful answer to this longing is that we are all loved equally, each and every one, by the Lord of the universe. John refers to himself throughout his writings as "the one Jesus loved." John knew firsthand the powerful and irreplaceable love of Jesus, and through his gift to us, his writings, we too can know this love. There is so much certainty for us in the opening of his book, John: "In the beginning was the Word, and the Word was with God, and the Word was God. He was with God in the beginning." These words set the stage for us to know unequivocally that Jesus has always been. John goes on to tell us that the Word became flesh and made his dwelling among us, assuring us that Jesus is in the now and will be with us forever. There are so many life-empowering thoughts revealed by John in his writings. We could cling to just these and know Jesus for who he is—our Savior, our Lord. The impassioned John and the knowledge that he leaves for us, centuries later, are gifts to be cherished, absorbed, and tucked away, assuring us that Jesus is God's Son, the Great I Am, who calls us all, as he did John, to go out and be fishers of men.

October 17. Seekers of the Messiah

> Philip found Nathanael [also called Bartholomew] and
> told him, "We have found the one Moses wrote about in
> the law, and about whom the prophets also wrote—Jesus
> of Nazareth, the son of Joseph."
>
> —John 1:45

Philip was a Galilean, and it is believed that he was one of the very first followers of Jesus, having lived in the region where John the Baptist preached. Philip, being a disciple of John the Baptist, was looking for the Messiah, as John the Baptist had said that "one greater than he was coming." Philip, as seen above in the book of John, is thought to have been a friend of Nathanael who was also known as Bartholomew. Having received a personal call from Jesus, Philip recruits the skeptical Bartholomew. Yet Bartholomew doesn't buy into following Jesus quite as quickly as Philip had. When he hears that Jesus, the Lord of Lords, was from Nazareth, Bartholomew scoffs, "Nazareth! Can anything good come from there?" Here, in this simple question, we can know that, in being human, often we all wonder if anything good can come from here or there. Yet God chose to have the Lord, our Savior, our King of Kings, come from "there." Bartholomew quickly realizes that since his Savior came from a place that he would least expect, so should we remember that it doesn't matter where we are from but where we are going and with whom that makes the difference. Whether we are like Philip who immediately recognized the Lord for who he is or like Bartholomew who first questioned how the Savior of the world could come from Nazareth, the important thing that matters is that we know him as Lord and will follow him anywhere. These two men had two different approaches yet both became disciples of Christ. What better journey to have than to walk with the Lord, not caring from where he came. In the same way, let us embrace everyone we meet, not caring from where they come but loving them for who they are—children of our Almighty God!

October 18. A Changed Man

> As Jesus went on from there, he saw a man named
> Matthew sitting at the tax collector's booth. "Follow me,"
> he told him, and Matthew got up and followed him.
>
> —Matthew 9:9

Matthew wrote one of the four Gospels that opens the New Testament, and he was the perfect one to do this, for his attention to detail was impeccable. The fact that the Lord chose Matthew to be one of his disciples reveals to anyone who might question whether they are worthy to follow the Lord that all are worthy. Even though Matthew was a dishonest tax collector, greedy and all up in himself, Jesus knew that Matthew would be one of the most faithful to him, never wavering from the moment that he committed to follow the Lord. Matthew was an accurate record keeper, so he was the right choice to write down his thoughts as the book of Matthew, including the smallest of details about the coming of Jesus, his birth, his baptism, his life, and his instructions on many important topics. One reason that Matthew was such a good choice as a disciple is that he knew the human heart and the longings of the Jewish people. He could be influential to the Jews of that day by showing them that their long-awaited King of Kings had come, not on a black steed but on the back of a donkey. Greedy, driven by material success, smart, and well-written, Matthew is a great example of the saying: "What you have is less important than what you do with what you have." Well, Matthew fits this bill perfectly. Before he met Jesus he had it all—wealth, control over the people, backing by the entire Roman army. What could be better than that? Jesus, that's what. When Matthew met Jesus, he never hesitated when Jesus called him, saying, "Follow me." Matthew, who had it all, gave it all up to do something better. Oh, so much better. Knowing the Jews so well, Matthew perfectly presented Jesus to them as their Lord and Savior, accurately writing his book to answer their questions about this

Messiah. In reading and knowing about Matthew, we can see that by Jesus selecting this man despised by the citizens and travelers of that day, he can use anyone to further his kingdom. Whether we think that we have it all, like Matthew, or we feel inadequate in some way—education, money, an unpleasant past—nothing must keep us from following our Lord and Savior. He calls us all to the highest calling that any of us will ever know—serving God. We just need to remember that it's not what we have or don't have that matters, it's what we do with it that will make all the difference in the world.

October 19. Doubting Thomas

Then he said to Thomas, "Put your finger here; see my
hands. Reach out your hand and put it into my side.
Stop doubting and believe."

—John 20:27

Doubting Thomas. Has anyone ever said that to you over the years? This phrase has been used time and time again when someone expresses doubt over a situation. The reference comes from Jesus's disciple, Thomas, who was not present when the risen Christ appeared. Thomas said that he would not believe that Jesus had risen from the dead unless he could actually touch Jesus's wound. How comforting that the Lord would select this man as a disciple to reassure all of us that, even though we may doubt at times, Jesus will always find a way to remove our doubts and answer our questions of life. Jesus did not reprimand Thomas for doubting. He allowed him the opportunity to actually touch his wounds, giving Thomas the proof that he sought. The reality is that millions of people in today's world doubt that Jesus was a true man and the Son of God, for they are not able to see him and prove to themselves his existence. But how great, so very great, that we have to take this truth on faith. This is the one thing that we must love about faith. God could show us Jesus. He could return Jesus to the earth so that all would believe, offering physical proof like he did for Thomas. How much greater that we know Jesus and believe in him without seeing him. That is the true test that we are called to pass, believing without seeing. What glory there is to be found in accepting Jesus Christ as Lord on faith, and faith alone. We do see his wonders and know him as he blesses us each and every day that we live. It's really not that hard to believe when all of us who have called his name have had prayers answered time and time again! That very fact alone leads us to know the Lord for who he is, removing all doubts that he is our Savior, the Savior of the world!

October 20. Moving in the Shadows

Then he appeared to James, then to all the disciples.

—1 Corinthians 15:7

Three James are listed in the Bible: two are disciples and the other is the brother of the Lord. The James known as James the Less is described this way only to distinguish him from the other two James. Speculation says that James the Less could possibly have been the first disciple to be in the presence of the Risen Christ. Other than this, nothing else is known about him. Simon the Zealot, another disciple, was either a member of the radical zealot party or he was full of zeal in his faith for the Lord. Thaddeus, also a disciple of the Lord, does not have much written about him. He wrote the book of Jude and finished it with a doxology, expressing glorious praise to God. This is considered the finest doxology in the New Testament. So here we have three disciples about whom little is known. But the one thing that we can know for certain, and the most important thing that anyone can know about anyone, is that they loved their Lord, dropped everything to follow him, and gave up all that they had for their Savior. If that is all that anyone will ever know about any of us, it is enough. Let Jesus find this complete and utter devotion for him in our hearts, just as he knew it in the hearts of his special men, even those who moved in the shadows.

October 21. Never Too Late

> While he was still speaking, Judas, one of the Twelve,
> arrived. With him was a large crowd armed with swords
> and clubs, sent from the chief priests and the elders of the
> people. Now the betrayer [Judas] had arranged a signal
> with them: "The one I kiss is the man; arrest him."
>
> —Matthew 26:47–48

Oh my! It's just hard to wrap our minds around this whole experience written above in Matthew. On one hand, some feel hatred for this Judas, the twelfth disciple of the Lord. Others could possibly pity him, for who would ever want to walk in those shoes? Whatever the feelings are that we have for him, one thing is certain: our Lord, his Savior, was just waiting to forgive Judas, yet he never asked. Here is a man, one of only twelve in the entire world, who was asked to become a disciple of the Son of God, traveling and studying with Christ for over three years. Yet Judas still wanted more, more than what he could get from the Lord. But is there more? What could be more to someone than the love of Jesus Christ? The lure of the world and its momentary pleasures drove Judas away from the most important man to ever walk our earth and then led him to do the unthinkable—betray Jesus. Although Judas felt remorse for his actions, he never asked his Lord for his forgiveness. That was all it would have taken for Jesus to forgive him. Just two simple words: forgive me. Yet Judas, overwrought with grief, took his own life, unable to live as a result of what he had done. But here's the most important takeaway from the life of Judas—forgiveness is free. Forgiveness is always available. Forgiveness is ours. Just ask me, says the Lord. What more could all of us want from our Savior than his forgiveness so freely given? When we think that all hope is lost and we are overwhelmed by our actions, he just longs for us to call out his name, accepting his forgiveness and restoration. It's never too late! It would have made all the difference to Judas, and it will make all the difference to us!

October 22. Twelve Simple Truths

> Then the eleven disciples went to Galilee, to the
> mountain where Jesus had told them to go. When they
> saw him, they worshipped him; but some doubted.
> Then Jesus came to them and said, "All authority in
> heaven and on earth has been given to me. Therefore
> go and make disciples of all nations, baptizing them in
> the name of the Father and of the Son and of the Holy
> Spirit, and teaching them to obey everything that I have
> commanded you. And surely I am with you always, to the
> very end of the age."
>
> Matthew 28:16–20

Twelve disciples of the Lord, Jesus Christ. Twelve men who
answered his call yet responded in many different ways to what
they had been called to do. Each has given us one particular lesson
to think on as we remember their following our Lord and Savior.

1. Peter: Trust and obey, for Jesus redeems, and Jesus saves.

2. Andrew: Jesus is the most important thing you will ever
   share with anyone.

3. James: Be passionate for the Lord.

4. John: Jesus is the Christ, the Great I Am.

5. Philip: Recognize the Lord for who he is, the Savior of
   the world, God's precious Son.

6. Bartholomew: No matter where someone is from, it's where
   he is going and who he is following that really matters.

7. Matthew: It doesn't matter what we have or don't have.
   What really matters is what we do with what we have to
   further the kingdom of the Lord.

8. Thomas: Stop doubting and believe.

9. James the Less: Love the Lord with all your heart, with all your soul, and with all your might.

10. Simon: You can't ever be too zealous for the Lord.

11. Thaddeus: Give God the glory.

12. Judas: It's yours for the asking: Forgiveness.

And so it is unto us, also. Amen!

October 23. "Quit Fooling Around"

> But be sure to fear the Lord and serve him faithfully
> with all your heart; consider what great things
> he has done for you.
>
> —1 Samuel 12:24

How many times have we heard these words or used them ourselves, either growing up or with children we know? I was walking my dog, Mojo, yesterday, and he kept stopping, starting, changing directions, and being silly. So out of my mouth came, "Mojo, quit fooling around." Quit fooling around implies that whoever is being addressed needs to rechannel their energy and go forward doing what they are supposed to be doing. As we apply this to our faith, should we quit fooling around? Should we all redirect our energies toward the one who deserves our time and focus? There are so many minutes in the day that would be time better spent sharing sweetness with the Lord. Hearing his call to go out and serve him. What joy lies ahead when we focus some of the time given to us in each day doing what Jesus calls us to do. "Be still, and know that I am God" (Psalm 46:10); "Come, follow me…and I will make you fishers of men." (Matthew 4:19); "God is not unjust; he will not forget your work and the love you have shown him as you have helped his people" (Hebrews 6:10). It's exciting to think of his words and know that he will be well pleased as we stop fooling around and go out to serve those he loves so well.

October 24. Up, Up, and Away

This is what the Lord says: "Heaven is my throne,
and the earth is my footstool."

—Isaiah 66:1

Have you ever wondered why the Lord chose heaven to be above us rather than beside us or below us? Last week, I was looking up into his wonderful clouds, seeing his face among them. The brilliant blue sky above as the day was breaking into its full glory made me think, *This is exactly where the Lord wants our focus to be.* If we were looking ahead instead of up, we would have to look through the world and all of its distractions before we could focus on the Lord and the Lord only. Distraction after distraction would keep us from quickly and easily knowing his presence in an instant. If we had to look down to find the Lord, we would become disoriented and confused, for it is hard to move about and focus at the same time when one is faced downward, not able to see what's ahead. The Lord knows that to have to look through the world to find him would keep us seconds, minutes, or even hours away from feeling his presence, knowing his love. Isn't it just grand to have a Father who always knows what is best for us and makes it happen? So as we set out on our day, let us keep our eyes upon Jesus, looking up toward the heavens from where our help comes. No matter what your day brings, give it up to the Lord, for he is there, longing to share the joys and the pain with us. Let us know that the Lord, the powerful and loving provider of all that we need, is here, there, and everywhere, loving us all the day long.

October 25. No-Brainer

> And we know that in all things God works for the
> good of those who love him, who have been called
> according to his purpose.
>
> —Romans 8:28

No-brainer! This funny term is one that I used to hear a lot growing up, referring to a decision that could be made pretty quickly by just knowing a few facts. Often in life, we need to take time to mull over a decision, giving it the thought and attention it warrants. Other times the choice is pretty clear due to an obvious fact. These are the decisions we call no-brainers! And so it is with our faith and whom we shall have take the lead in life. A no-brainer for sure! As believers, we have learned that the times when we took the lead, not consulting the Lord and making decisions on our own, usually didn't end up as well as the times that we turned things over to him for guidance. Time and again, when we try to fix a problem by ourselves, without trusting in the Lord to make a way, it just hasn't worked out as well as letting him be in charge. We know in our hearts that we should first turn to the Lord for his guidance, knowing that all things work together for the good of those who love him. Should we be in charge or should he be in charge? Now that's a no-brainer if we've ever heard one!

October 26. Light and Shadows

You, O Lord, keep my lamp burning; my God turns
my darkness into light. With your help I can advance
against a troop; with my God I can scale a wall.

—Psalm 18:28–29

Light and shadows. For any of us who have painted or watched someone paint, it is amazing to see how the blending of paints can create light and shadows, forming such beautiful paintings of various subjects. My sweet, precious daddy had a heart attack at the age of fifty, so he took up oil painting to fill the void of community and church work. I used to sit and watch him oil paint, using various colors to create a sunset or a sunrise, a duck's wing or a foggy marsh. His ability to play the light against the shadows was fascinating. Today, I also use light and shadows when I walk. In the summer, I walk in the shadows to dodge the scorching heat of the sun. In the winter, I seek the sunshine to keep myself warm, and I never fail to notice how God sprinkles the sunshine through the trees to cast a play of shadow dancing as I walk. Life is also full of sunshine and shadows. We awaken one day to a beautiful day of sunshine, but by nightfall the shadows have rolled in, literally or figuratively. We must not fear nor let ourselves worry about our tomorrow. The Lord is still with us. He wants us to learn that whether we are basking in the sunshine of life or quivering in its shadows, he is here. God is with us. He is always here, working mightily in our lives to return us to the days of sunshine as he has promised. He never fails. All we have to do is seek his face and know his love, and each day will reveal a bit of his sunshine, no matter how our day unfolds, for he is our light among the shadows.

October 27. Such a Gift as This!

"For I know the plans I have for you," declares the Lord,
"plans to prosper you and not to harm you,
plans to give you hope and a future."

—Jeremiah 29:11

Working steadily on writings for this devotional, my NIV Study Bible that I have had for thirty-plus years finally fell apart—it literally split into several parts and fell onto the table in pieces. I guess that the back and forth of looking up verses did it in. So now what? I went to the Internet to see about ordering another. When I put this selection in the Amazon toolbar, many options popped up, one of which was a used NIV Study Bible available from a third party, that being the Detroit Salvation Army store. It was defined as being in "good" condition with tabs, and the cost was $6. A new one costs $50 plus tax, so being the sale shopper that I have become, I decided to order the one from Detroit, mainly because my old one has tabs, and I actually had put those in about thirty years ago. Now if you haven't put tabs in a Bible lately, let me say that, although it is quite worth it, be sure that you are a detail-oriented person, which I am not. It is a laborious task at best. So, a few days later, here comes my "new" Bible. I was beside myself with joy! It is absolutely like brand new, cover and all! It has beautiful new tabs perfectly aligned in it, helping me find the appropriate books of the Bible that I am needing. I could not be happier. I started wondering about how it got to the Salvation Army store, and in whose hands it had been before mine. No marks anywhere inside, until I finally found, marked in brackets in the palest pencil ever, was the verse from Jeremiah 29:11 which says, "For I know the plans I have for you," declares the Lord, "plans to prosper you and not to harm you, plans to give you hope and a future." Immediately I thought to myself, *If this is the only take-away that this person took from owning this Bible, he received the hope of God to carry him on, and that is good—that is very good.* And this same hope is ours for the having, thanks to the love of our faithful and loving Savior.

October 28. Thought Be Gone

O Lord, you have searched me and you know me.
You know when I sit and when I rise; you perceive my
thoughts from afar. You discern my going out and my
lying down; you are familiar with all my ways.

—Psalm 139:1–3

In writing these devotional entries, I often begin them days ahead so that when I sit down to write, I already have some thoughts on paper to kick-start the process. The reality is that I have no recollection of any that I have written in the past. Oh, I might be able to call up one or two that have a more memorable theme, but for the most part, no can do. I call this problem "thought be gone." I was discussing this with a friend. With sweet and encouraging words, she assured me that even if I repeat a thought or subject, it was put there by the Holy Spirit as someone needed to hear it again. Isn't that just the best friend ever? So I try not to worry about whether I have written on the same topic in the past or whether I use the same phrase over and over again. The correlation with our Father, the one who made us, is that he never has us out of his thoughts. He always has us on his mind. We need never worry that he doesn't have time for us when we talk to him or that he won't know our voices when we call. He holds us close to his heart, and there is never a time that he has to wonder, "Who is this calling to me?" He knows us inside and out, for he has known us since before the beginning of time. There are no thoughts be gone to the Lord. Isn't that the best news that you have heard today? Let it make our hearts sing with joy just knowing that we are always on his mind.

October 29. We Are Family!

You are all sons of the light and sons of the day.

—1 Thessalonians 5:5

In reading the paper today, I came across an article about a homeless man, Charles "Chucky" Alexander, who helped pull an attacker off a police officer. Chucky lives on the street with a group of eight people, and he considers them his family. They "stick together to stay out of trouble," Chucky says. In appreciation for his bravery, the Dallas Police Department awarded him with the Citizens Certificate of Merit. To accept his honor, Chucky brought with him a homeless woman, one of his adopted family members. This article touched me on so many levels because lives were changed for the good. But the part of the article that literally brought me to tears was to hear what the woman had to say about Chucky. She praised his heroism and talent. She remained his cheerleader through the ceremony. When Chucky was called forward to receive his certificate, she called after him, reminding him to shake the officer's hand. I love that! Her reminder to shake the officer's hand is what we do when we want our family to be the best that they can be. And it is what our Father, our perfect and all-loving Father, does for us as we go about our lives. In those times when he could just burst with pride over something that we have done, something as large as saving a man's life or something as small as speaking kindly to someone we don't know, he applauds, and then he reminds us to shake the officer's hand— to take that extra step, do just a little extra, to reveal his power within us. Add a smile as we speak to someone we don't know. Praise God as we "save someone's life." The article today ends with these words, "A handshake from the officer presenting the award wasn't enough. Alexander pulled him into a hug." And so will our Father in heaven pull us into a hug, whose hugs make life worth living! We are family. Hugs all around!

October 30. Hardwired

Teach me knowledge and good judgment,
for I believe in your commands.

—Psalm 119:66

Halloween—it's almost here. I am sure that each of us has a different take on Halloween, and the world has sure ratcheted up the celebration of this holiday! In yards everywhere I see big blow-up Halloween decorations—black cats and jack-o'-lanterns and ghosts dancing in the air. I was walking Mojo, my dog, last week, and the most interesting thing happened. Mojo really doesn't like cats. Every time we see a cat, he goes nuts, jerking at his leash and wanting so badly to get a hold of that cat. Here we are, walking along, enjoying the morning, and all of a sudden we come upon a big, black blow-up cat in a yard. I didn't think a thing about it, but he sure did. He started going nuts, just as if he had seen a real cat. Yet this one was enormous and made out of plastic! How in the world he could possibly know that this thing represented a cat? Mojo must be hardwired to know a cat when he sees one. We, as believers, are just as hardwired to know the Lord when we see him. From that moment that we believed, we became hardwired to know him in all things, to know his love no matter what the circumstance. Being hardwired to the presence of the Lord is a gift beyond all gifts. This precious knowledge enables us to always seek his face, find him at all times, and come into his presence no matter what the situation. We are now hardwired to long to draw close to our Savior, resting in his presence and receiving his peace and comfort. All this came for free, accepting him through faith as the priceless gift that he is—the Savior of the world!

October 31. Boo to You!

And for you, the anointing you received from him
remains in you, and you do not need anyone to teach you.
But as his anointing teaches you about all things and
as that anointing is real, not counterfeit—just as it has
taught you, remain in him.

—1 John 2:27

I was reading an article in the paper a few days ago about Halloween masks, and how the masks of political figures just aren't selling anymore. It goes on to explain that the costumes we choose say something about who we are or who we wish to be. So what do we look like the rest of the 364 days? Do others see us wearing a face of caring? Can others see in our behavior a costume of love and helpfulness as we move about our day? Do we reflect in our dress that we have slipped on a suit of compassion and understanding to those we meet and greet throughout our day? Let us start each day not with a costume of make-believe characteristics but of real and honest faces that reflect that we are the children of the most high God. No need to fantasize about who we are, for he has assured us that we are his. As it says in 1 John above, "His anointing is real, not counterfeit." May we show the whole world that this real and precious gift belongs to all who believe in him.

November 1. "Dance with the One That Brung Ya"

How great is the love the Father has lavished on us,
that we should be called children of God!
And that is what we are!

—1 John 3:1

I was talking with our daughter and son-in-law last weekend about getting the gate repaired on a relatively new fence that was installed at their home. Just a few years ago, the new fence and gate were installed, and now it does not work due to a couple of things: the drought has caused the posts to slip and the motor on the gate is not working properly. They had a new company give them a bid on fixing the gate, which included a new motor. Then they spoke with the company who originally put it in, and the sales rep told them that the motor was under warranty and would not cost anything to fix. This reminded me of the saying, "Dance with the one that brung ya." Quite popular in the south, it means you should dance with the one who brought you to the dance. As sayings have a way of doing, this one has evolved into meaning that we should stay the course with the talent, process, or system that got us there. How applicable this saying is to followers of Jesus Christ. He is the one who "brung" us here. He is the one who gave us life and life abundant. He is the one to whom we owe everything. He asked us to the party, he freely paid our way, he has stayed the course with us the whole night long, and he will take us home in due time, safe and sound. Now can we think of absolutely any reason not to give him our total love, undivided attention, and every dance that we have? He is the perfect partner, and we are blessed to be called his—tonight and forevermore!

November 2. The Gatekeeper

> I tell you the truth, I am the gate for the sheep. All who
> ever came before me were thieves and robbers, but the
> sheep did not listen to them. I am the gate; whoever
> enters through me will be saved. He will come in and go
> out, and find pasture ... I have come that they might have
> life, and have it to the full.
>
> —Genesis 1:26

I kept our new grandson last week for a while so that his mom could get some things done. She brought him over to our house, and he was in his car seat carrier. He sat in it on the floor for a while, sleeping peacefully. Our dog, Mojo, was fascinating to watch. He gently went over to the baby and checked him out with some sniffs. Then, satisfied that all was well, he sat down in front of his car seat to keep watch and guard him from harm. Amazing dog, and an amazing lesson for all of us to remember. Watching Mojo guard his precious one reminds us of how the Lord and Savior guards us as he is the gatekeeper of our lives. This idea of keeping the gates comes from the words above in John, knowing that our Lord and Savior is the gatekeeper of our hearts and minds. It is through his everlasting love for us that our lives are guarded by his protection, his strength, his love. We, too, are called to be the gatekeepers for those we love. In visualizing our Mojo take his responsibility so seriously, let us meet each day knowing that we, too, are seriously well guarded by the one who guards us best, Jesus. It is in his care for us that we "have life and have it to the full," protected and secured by Jesus, our Redeemer and Friend.

November 3. On the Wings of Love

> He who dwells in the shelter of the Most High will rest
> in the shadow of the Almighty. I will say of the Lord,
> "He is my refuge and my fortress, my God, in whom I
> trust." Surely he will save you from the fowler's snare and
> from the deadly pestilence. He will cover you with his
> feathers, and under his wings you will find refuge.
>
> —Psalm 91:1–4

Some of you probably have seen the photo of a mother dove with two of her children, each one hovering under one of her wings, nestled close for her protection and love. It really is the sweetest photo, and one that I always remember when I think of how we, as children of Almighty God, hover under his wings in exactly the same way as the baby birds of this mother dove. Isn't it just so precious how the Lord's love is mimicked in nature, showing us his ways through his perfect design? It is so very helpful to visualize something that brings us comfort when times get bumpy, and this picture in our mind's eye of the mother dove covering her children with her wings is one that reminds us of the unfailing love of the Lord. It will lead us to feeling the wings of our Father covering us as we seek his protection and help in difficult circumstances. God will put us on his protective wings and soar with us above the storms of life, gliding peacefully above our troubles to a place of calm and restoration. So when we find ourselves dealing with the unpleasantness of life, let this image in our minds take us on the wings of love to that place with the Lord where we will find respite from the storms of life.

November 4. No Replacement

Therefore, since we have been justified through faith,
we have peace with God through our Lord Jesus Christ,
through whom we have gained access by faith into this
grace in which we now stand.

—Romans 5:1–2

Text, text, text…oops, oops, oops…retype, retype, retype. This is how it has been going for me lately on my cell phone. I must either be in too big of a hurry to type the words correctly or I have fingers that are too big to hit the right key. But all throughout the day, I get this notice from my cell phone, "no replacement." When I wrongly type in a word (which is often!) that the cell phone cannot self-correct, it sends me this message "no replacement," meaning it cannot find the correct word to put where I have typed something that spells nothing. Funny how I often feel that my cell phone has a mind. We may not know it, but our cell phones could be running the world. Here I am, typing words that my phone cannot discern, fighting with my cell phone to get the right word typed in so crazy messages don't pop up. "No replacement," the perfect phrase for Jesus. No matter what we hear, who comes along, or who has already been, there is absolutely no replacement for Jesus. He is our Lord and Savior, Redeemer and Friend, All in All, the Great I Am. No one and nothing can replace him, no matter how great they are, how important they seem, how good they are, nor how much they have changed the world. No one ever has nor ever will be who he is, everything in every way. He has been, is, and will always be exactly what we need in this life and forever. No replacement needed!

November 5. "Be Still My Soul"

Peace I leave with you; my peace I give you.
I do not give to you as the world gives.
Do not let your hearts be troubled and do not be afraid.

—John 14:27

These are uncertain times. I don't think that anyone could deny that. There are times in the day when we all must feel a sense of unrest and uneasiness as we hear the news. Not only is there so much news concerning so many things that seem out of our control, but more and more the details keep changing about how to address them. It all becomes one big confusing mess. So I was walking yesterday, and the hymn "Be Still, My Soul" began to play on my headset. The Lord's peace immediately washed over me. As happens so often, we let the world press in on us causing us to wonder how things will get better. We let our minds search and search for the answers. Then we remember. Yes, we remember. The Lord is on our side. A peace and calm wash over us like the gentle tides of the ocean, gently sweeping upon the seashore. He gives us his peace, and our souls become still once again. The opening lines of this hymn written in 1752 by Amalia Dorothea Von Schlegel say, "Be still, my soul; the Lord is on thy side. / Bear patiently the cross of grief or pain; / Leave to thy God to order and provide; / In every change he faithful will remain." Just as the message written here brought a soothing balm to the people of that time, so it is for us. What more do we need to know than the words written so beautifully in this hymn: "Leave to thy God to order and provide; / In every change he faithful will remain... Through thorny ways leads to a joyful end." Storing these words close to our hearts brings a peace that nothing else can, and our souls are still and comforted once again.

November 6. Detours of Life

God, who has called you into fellowship with
his Son Jesus Christ our Lord, is faithful.

—1 Corinthians 1:9

Right here where we live there is relentless construction. It is
almost as if someone said that redoing your home or building a
new one will be free if you would like. It is really unbelievable.
I don't care what residential street we try to travel, trucks and
cars are piled up along both sides, making passing difficult at
best. Now this is a tiny little aggravation in the whole scheme
of things. But it does bring to mind the bigger detours of life
that we have all faced. We are cruising along our road of living,
clear sailing with no trucks or cars in sight. Life is good. Life is
comfy. We can get wherever we want with ease and joy. Then all
of a sudden, we come to one of life's detours, one of those times
when we have no choice but to go another way for a while. This
is most likely not the way we would want to go. Yet here it is, a
time when we have no other option than to redirect our lives to
go a different path to get where we were headed in the first place.
Just like the detours in our neighborhood at the moment, we can
choose two options: we can grumble and become unhappy and
balk against being redirected, or we can know with all certainty
that the Lord has gone before us to make this detour covered
with his comfort and his grace. As believers, we know that he
is traveling with us and will put our lives back on track in his
perfect timing. How much better for us to take this time in our
lives to trust in the Lord and feel his protective mercy, drawing
us closer to him than possibly when we started. This is where the
joy is found, knowing that the promises of God are true and that
he is faithful, always faithful, to show us the way home.

November 7. Around the Clock

Praise be to the God and Father of our Lord Jesus Christ,
the Father of compassion and the God of all comfort...

—2 Corinthians 1:3

I was recently invited to an around-the-clock shower for a new bride. This is a party where the guests are given a time of day on the invitation, and they are asked to bring a gift for the new couple that would be used at that time of day. I have gotten some challenging times in the past such as 11:00 p.m. Yet that really made it fun to think of a gift for that particular time of day. This party theme got me to thinking, *Let's all write down a praise to the Lord for each hour of the day that we are awake, maybe twelve of them, and keep them with us throughout one day, just one day to lift a different praise hourly to the Lord. This simple act will not only please our Father, but also give us a few precious minutes in each hour of this one day to be in close companionship with the Lord.* So here's the challenge. It will take a moment or two of our time, yet the rewards will be meaningful. Write down on a card that you take with you twelve praises or more that can be lifted up one by one, on each hour of the day, to celebrate and thank God for his mercy and grace. He longs to hear our voices as we pray to him, and the best guess is that not only will we be returning joy to the one who gives it to us, but our joy will increase tenfold by remembering and praising God for what he has done and will always provide for us.

November 8. Push or Pull?

And we pray this in order that you may live a life
worthy of the Lord and may please him in every way;
bearing fruit in every good work, growing in the
knowledge of God, being strengthened with all power
according to his glorious might so that you may have
great endurance and patience...

—Colossians 1:10–11

Do you remember when we were little, small enough to have a little red wagon in which either we sat and someone pulled us, or we piled our stuff into the wagon and pulled it ourselves? I cannot remember a time when I pushed the wagon, for that was much more difficult than pulling it behind me. I remember that if someone did try to push, the wheels would go crazy and veer the wagon off into the grass, causing a problem getting to my destination. Now here we are in life, all grown up and still pushing or pulling. We probably don't have a wagon piled up with our adult stuff, but we still have a wagon called life that we are either pushing or pulling to get through our days. We now know that sometimes we will find ourselves pushing, and sometimes we will find ourselves pulling. But if we can remember the lesson learned from the little wagon of our childhood, as we go through our trials, pulling will always make it easier, for Jesus's hand is on the handle of life. He is by our side, pulling right along with us to make sure that our wagon doesn't veer off course. He is the one who always has the easier way. He moves with us through our trials so that we arrive to where we are trying to go with his peace and comfort paving the way, bringing an end to whatever we are pulling behind us. His hand on ours, sharing the load and guiding the wagon, is how it is best done so "with all power according to his glorious might you may have great endurance and patience" and find joy in all things.

November 9. Stuck in the Gutter

> God is our refuge and strength, an
> ever-present help in trouble.
>
> —Deuteronomy 31:8

Yesterday while I was walking, I passed a two-story house. When I looked up, I saw a cat stuck in the gutter on the second floor, and a teenage girl was climbing out of the upstairs window, moving ever so slowly toward the cat. She got to where it was unable to move, and she reached out, gently gliding her hand along its back so as not to scare it in any way. She helped it get out of its predicament with love and trust. Standing there watching this scene, I realized how amazing she was at calming the cat down, gaining its trust so that she could help get it out of the gutter. Isn't this just like life? We are going along then all of a sudden we get stuck in one of life's gutters, not able to free ourselves. Our earth gives way, and we quake in our hearts. But our Jesus is there, our refuge and strength, ever so gently reaching out his hand to help us from this predicament. He slowly but surely helps us safely move from this place where we are unable to free ourselves. He is always able to guide us to safety through his mercy and grace. Unsticking us from life's sticky situations, Jesus is our slow and steady Savior, there to lift us up to safety no matter where we get stuck along the way.

November 10. You Can Count on It!

Now faith is being sure of what we hope
for and certain of what we do not see.

—Hebrews 11:1

Walking last week, the sky began to cloud up and became filled with various shades of gray rain clouds, the likes of which we haven't seen much of in a while. It was delightful to be walking along in milder temperatures, enjoying the overcast sky above that kept the heat out. All of a sudden I heard a noise from above, the sound of an engine. I immediately thought of our twin grandsons. Every time they hear that noise, they immediately look up to the sky and say, "Airplane!" Now this seems to be pretty prevalent among young children, and I started thinking about how they know, with all assurance, that the noise of an airplane engine would always reveal an airplane flying up in the sky. With childlike faith, they never doubt that when they look skyward, a plane will be flying by. The reason that they know this with certainty is that each time they hear that sound coming from the sky, yep, a plane is up there, flying over their heads. Have they ever looked up at the sound of that noise and seen a whale swimming overhead? Nope. Have they ever looked up at the sound of that noise and seen a lion roaring? Nope. Just as we can rest assured that there is a plane passing overhead when we hear its motors, even more so we can know without a doubt that the Lord and Savior of all the earth is always here among all of us, ready to guide and direct us in the way we should go. We don't need to hesitate for even one second in questioning whether he is here. Can we see him? No. But just as that plane was in the sky today, we can all know for sure and be positive that the Lord is with us always, here by our side.

November 11. Sweetening Our Days

> I seek you with all my heart; do not let me stray
> from your commands. I have hidden your word in
> my heart that I might not sin against you.
>
> —Psalm 119:10–11

I have been hearing for years that we all need to try to keep our systems alkaline by adding lemon or alkaline drops to our water. This process of making our systems more alkaline reminds me of what Jesus can do for our spirits. The more we add his words daily, the better we will feel. It only takes a little dose of his precious words to put us in the right frame of mind each day as we start out. Sounds pretty simple, right? The catch is that you have to actually do it for it to work, and the more we do it, the better it works. As our day begins, let us add a dose of Jesus to our mornings. We will find that the days just go more smoothly and our thoughts have a better context when Jesus is taken at the beginning of our day. We can all believe without any hesitation that adding Jesus to our mornings will make each day just so much sweeter.

November 12. Just in the Nick of Time

He hears their cry and saves them.

—Psalm 145:19

I was really writing at a furious clip yesterday, when I realized that a familiar smell was coming from downstairs. Yup, I was once again on the verge of burning something. I had put on some chicken to boil for my dog, Mojo, and I think that I had spent a little too long writing. All the water had boiled out of the pot. The chicken in the pot was starting to stick, and I knew that I got there just in the nick of time. Isn't this just the way life is so much of the time? We start out with a plan, then we get distracted by another project, and the first plan starts to go awry. This fact isn't too bad if we are talking about cooking. But when it starts to impact more serious situations, that's when we need to lean into Jesus, helping get through something that has gotten into a mess, sometimes accidentally, yet a mess nonetheless. In the exact same way that I could smell that chicken burning, we too can tell when a situation needs the help of Jesus. He will pour more water in the pot so that whatever we are cooking will not burn but turn out just right. He is always ready to make things right as long as we call on him, even if it is just in the nick of time.

November 13. Road Maps

> He was lost and now is found.
>
> —Luke 15:24

I don't do a great deal of traveling, but some years ago one of my dear friends and I took my eighty-five-year-old aunt to France. Now that was a trip! We still laugh at so many experiences that we remember on this trip. We rented a car to drive about three hours to see a famous castle in an out-of-the-way town in France. Ambitious idea for three people who did not speak a word of French. A short while into the trip, we realized that we were lost. Not necessarily lost and can't find our way back, but certainly lost as to where we were going. So being undaunted, my friend pulls over in a small town that we were driving through, rolls down the window, and in her Texas drawl asks this older, nice-looking Frenchman how we get to this castle. He smiles so pleasantly, acts as if he totally understands her, and then starts telling us how to get to our destination—in French. As he is speaking, he is using hand signals like so many of us do when we are talking. He moves one hand up as if to go over something, then down and around as if to drive around a bend, and so on. All the while he is speaking in French. My friend is listening intently. After he is through, she takes off, and a short time later, we arrive at our destination. I still can't get over the fact that she could find this place with no verbal directions that she could understand. In remembering this experience, we should always be thankful that our Father does not speak a foreign language that we cannot understand. We are thankful that we don't have to guess at what he is trying to say to give us directions for our lives. We have the perfect traveling companion with us at all times, the Holy Spirit, on whom we can call for directions any time, any day. And God has provided the perfect road map for our journey through life, the Holy Bible. Just as the prodigal son in Luke was lost and is found, so are we, once lost, yet now found. So as we go about our travels in life, let us travel with confidence that our road map drawn by our Savior is secure. Nothing makes for a better trip than that!

November 14. Into the Clearing

But you, O Sovereign Lord, deal well with me for your
name's sake; out of the goodness of your love, deliver me.

—Psalm 109:21

I was walking my dog, Mojo, last week, and all of a sudden it started to rain, not heavily, but softly, a few drops falling gently on our heads. As we took a few more steps, we walked out of the rain and into the clear—it had completely stopped raining on us. As rain-filled clouds move across the sky, sometimes there are large areas of sunshine. Isn't it interesting how it can be raining on us in one spot and yet, a few steps away, it is as dry as ever? Often, though, Mojo and I have been walking and gotten caught in a deluge, and it will still be pouring rain on us when we arrive home, rain clouds covering the skies wherever you look. This is just like life. We are walking along, and life drops a few rain drops in our lives. But quickly the Lord stops the light shower, just like the few drops we felt today. He walks us right into a clearing. Then sometimes when we are in a deluge of life's rain, it takes a while longer for us to be in the clear. This is an opportunity for us to think on these rainy days as a gift from Jesus to learn to even a greater degree how to trust in him. These days of trial call us to give him the lead in taking us to a drier place where we will arrive restored and comforted. This is only a rain delay for a time. He knows the way to lead us to where we will come to a place of peace and restoration, drying ourselves off and feeling the warmth of our Father's love on our shoulders as we step into the sunshine!

November 15. Hear This

This is the confidence that we have in approaching God:
that if we ask anything according to his will, he hears us.

—1 John 5:14

The last few months I have had some sort of weird swelling in my left ear, making it difficult for me to hear someone talking. This problem reminds me of those times that we all have experienced when we needed to hear from God. We needed to be reassured that he was listening to our cries for help. Sometimes we may feel as if he does not hear us, but nothing could be further from the truth. As it says in 1 John above, we can know with all certainty that we have open access to the Lord and that anything we ask in accordance to his will for our lives will be heard. Our heavenly Father has given us an open line of communication that he will never shut off for those who believe in him. He hears every cry, every call, even every groan that we may utter, always there to provide his grace and mercy. What a gift we have in Jesus. He knows our every need before we know it, and he will provide. This knowledge leads us to what we hear so often—trust and obey—and we are now able to do that very thing, thanks to the assurance given to us by our Father, the one who always hears us call.

November 16. Sweet Dreams!

> May your unfailing love be my comfort,
> according to your promise to your servant.
>
> —Psalm 119:76

A story came on the news about a mom whose son was serving in the Army and had just arrived in Afghanistan. She received an e-mail from him that said, "Please send me a pillow." Amazed, she wrote back, asking if in fact he did not have one. The reality is that no one serving our country is given a pillow when they are sent to serve abroad. So this mom jumped into action and sent him a pillow right away. Then she thought, *If he doesn't have a pillow, then so many others do not have them either.* Into action she went again. She began to buy and collect pillows, lots of pillows. This mom realized that not only does a pillow provide physical comfort, but it provides a sense of being at home in some way. The good news is that all of us have our own pillow, day or night, on which to rest our tired and weary heads, no matter where we are or what time it is. We have an eternal source of comfort available to us in Jesus who is always there to listen to our troubles and provide a moment of respite along the way. There are times during a busy day when we just want to lean back and place our heads on his pillow, briefly feeling his love, cushioning our journey with his always-available pillow of care. As we start out this day and meet the needs of life, let's remember to lay our heads on Jesus's pillow if need be. It only takes a brief minute or two with him to restore and reenergize us to continue on. Then as we actually lay our heads down tonight on a real pillow, let's thank the Lord that his love is unfailing, always there to comfort us—no matter the time or place—with his pillow of love. Sweet dreams, all!

November 17. Bark On!

> Consider it pure joy, my brothers, whenever you
> face trials of many kinds, because you know that
> the testing of your faith develops perseverance.
>
> —James 1:2

As I walk Mojo, my dog, every day, we walk past the same dog who lives in our neighbor's yard. This dog is up near the patio of his home, resting there. But when he sees us approach, he comes racing toward us, barking up a storm, causing a big ruckus, putting his nose right up to the fence as we pass. Mojo, however, just keeps on walking, never even giving his neighbor dog a sideways glance. All of the barking and commotion going on does not affect him in the least. He knows what is coming. He has steeled himself against this attack, not letting it bother him. So this is what Jesus does for us. He has steeled us against any attack by the enemy, any trial that we may be facing. Jesus goes before to prepare our way, and he has prepared us to stand strong in the face of adversity. So when life comes roaring up, barking at us and doing its best to get our attention and get us off track, let us lean into Jesus who keeps us calm and collected as we go forward without even a sideways glance. Jesus, our Stabilizer, our Lord.

November 18. Dancing in the Sunlight

> The Lord watches over you—the Lord is your shade
> at your right hand; the sun will not harm you by day,
> nor the moon by night.
>
> —Psalm 121:5–6

Just about this time every year, I begin to really notice the way the sunlight plays among the trees as I walk. It creates all these shadows and is so beautiful when it peeps through the foliage. What we can realize is that without the shadows the sun makes, we would not really appreciate the sunlight and how it dances in and out among the shadows. These two elements work so beautifully together to show us how God uses the times of our lives in the shadows to protect us and keep us within the safety of his presence until the sunlight reveals itself again. Without going through these shadow times, we will not understand nor appreciate our Father when his glorious sunlight breaks through after life's stormy seas. It has been his providential shadow-keeping that blesses us in these times, quieting our souls so that his work could be done. Just as we find solace in sitting in the shadows during the day when the sun is shining so brightly, we also feel his comfort and presence as we rest within his shadows to wait for the storm to pass. He will lead us back into the sunlight as he always has. The warmth and sheer joy of that moment as we step back into the sunlight is so much greater because of our restorative time among the shadows. So whether we are resting in the shadow of his perfect care or basking in his sunlight, blessings flow. Great is his faithfulness. So shall we dance with joy in the sunlight once the shadow times have passed by.

November 19. Blessings Follow Obedience

The Lord had said to Abram, "Leave your country, your
people and your father's household and go to the land
I will show you. I will make you into a great nation,
and I will bless you."

—Genesis 12:1–2

Our Bible study this fall has been studying Genesis. Last week we were discussing Abram and his call by God to leave everything that he knew to follow God to another land. One of the questions that we were to write an answer to was "What guidance or encouragement has God provided you as you followed his call into an unfamiliar or frightening situation?" I sat there a minute, thinking about my answer, then wrote down, "Blessings follow obedience." Abram honored what God called him to do, and God told him, "I will make your name great, and you will be a blessing. I will bless those who bless you...and all peoples on earth will be blessed through you" (Genesis 12:3). Now, fast forward a few days to a story on the news about a high school girl who was running in a race. The number given to her was 666. This number is talked about in Revelation, referring to the mark of the beast at the end times. This young girl refused to wear this number in the race, and the officials would not give her a different number. So she didn't race. I immediately thought, *Blessings follow obedience.* She earns our respect for following her belief and not being afraid to show her peers or anyone else who heard the story that her faith is the most important part of her life. We all know from experience that our Father has blessed us when we have given a difficult experience back to him to handle. We cannot deny that God longs to bless our obedience. This young girl witnessing about her faith in this way glorifies the Lord and lets his light shine. How many of these chances do we have each day to give God the glory? Probably more than we realize, yet given the opportunity, how precious to honor the Lord each and every chance we get. Whether the blessing comes as peace or comfort or something that we could not even expect, there's just nothing like giving God the glory in all things.

November 20. Under the Sun

When Jesus spoke again to the people, he said,
"I am the light of the world. Whoever follows me will
never walk in darkness but will have the light of life."

—John 8:12

Under the sun—I was thinking the other day about the sun, for it was shining so brightly and providing a warm feeling as I walked under it. I started thinking about people far, far away, who at this very moment in time were asleep, slumbering under a beautiful full moon. We all know that on some parts of the world the sun is shining; on other parts of the world it is night, the moon having risen in the sky. Yet this sun and this moon are the same ones that each of us experience, just at different times of the day and night. No matter where we are, it's one sun, the one and only sun, that provides light and warmth for us to live; it is one moon, and only one moon, that provides moonlight for us to live; and it is one Jesus, Lord of all, who gives us the light by which to live and live life to the fullest. He is the light of the world who delivers each of us out of the darkness. He shines down on each and every human being alive. He is the Lord of all people, and he delivers his mercy and grace all day and all night no matter where we live or what time of day it is. So as we feel the warmth of the sun's rays today or enjoy the glow of the moonlight tonight, we can trust that as sure as our sun will come up tomorrow, Jesus is shining down on us, all of us, pouring his beams of love all over our lives for us to soak in with joy!

November 21. Words of Love

> He will take great delight in you, he will quiet you
> with his love, he will rejoice over you with singing.
>
> —John 1:16

As I walk Mojo, our dog, each day, I talk to him and tell him what a precious puppy he is to us. Although he really isn't a puppy, I like to call him that because it sounds so loving as it rolls off of my tongue. Sometimes he looks up at me as I am talking and sometimes he doesn't. But he always hears my words of love as they wash over him, words of acceptance, words of comfort, words of assurance that he is loved and loved dearly. We, too, can hear these same words of love all throughout our day spoken to us by Jesus. He loves us. He loves with the greatest love there is, for he is love. He reveals his love for us in a myriad of ways, in the blessings found in nature that we see and enjoy, in the shared words between friends, in the warm hugs from others. His love is endless, covering us all the days of our lives. As we approach Thanksgiving, let us start our list of thanks with one to Jesus for loving us all the day long. No matter what each day brings, we know his love, and it feels good.

November 22. The Time-Out Chair

"Be still, and know that I am God; I will be exalted
among the nations, I will be exalted in the earth."

—Psalm 46:10

The time-out chair. This chair is not only a brilliant marketing
tool, but one that actually works, just as its name implies. It is
a small chair with the name the "Time-Out Chair" to be used
with young children when it becomes necessary for them to take
a break, as it were. Our son and daughter-in-law have twin boys
who are two and a half years old. They have a time-out chair,
and the good news is that it doesn't have to be used very often.
But just the other day, one of the twins was touching and poking
the other, gently annoying him. His mom gave him the option
of stopping this behavior or taking time in the time-out chair.
Believe it or not, he wanted to go to the time-out chair. This
time-out chair is a great option, kept in a quiet place and used
to regroup for just a few minutes. This started me thinking, *We
adults need a time-out chair.* We need a chair to which we remove
ourselves from the hustle and bustle of living, a place where we
can "Be still, and know that I am God" (Psalm 46:10). What
better time than now, as we long for some quiet time to praise
God for the birth of his son, to sit and be still, listening for our
father's voice and contemplate all the blessings that flow over us
daily, to worship Jesus. Let's all seek out a time-out chair in our
lives and actually send ourselves there once a day to spend time-
out with Jesus. Is there any better use for a chair than this, a place
to worship him without distractions, closing out the world just
for a time?

November 23. Here Comes Thanksgiving!

Come, let us sing for joy to the Lord; let us shout aloud
to the Rock of our salvation. Let us come before him
with thanksgiving and extol him with music and song.
—Psalm 95:1–2

It's on the way—Thanksgiving is tomorrow. We Americans have designated this special day as a time to gather together to give thanks for all of our blessings. Most of us think of gentle men and women, settled and comfortably living life in their new home of America, gathered around peacefully sharing their banquet of thanks with the Indians. But in actuality, these were tough times. The Pilgrims had lost forty-six of their original 102 colonists in the brutal winter after coming to America, yet they managed to continue on, partly due to the tremendous help of the native Indians. To thank God for all that they had, they joined with their newfound friends to give thanks to God. The celebration of Thanksgiving came and went until George Washington's presidency in 1789, when it returned to its original intent of praising God for his blessings and thanking him for blessings to come. To bind our hearts in love for the Lord who has provided it all makes this one of the best holidays that we share. Let us gather together to ask the Lord's blessing, focusing on his abundant grace and mercy and love.

November 24. Did You Know?

"For I know the plans I have for you," declares the Lord,
"plans to prosper you and not to harm you,
plans to give you hope and a future."

—Jeremiah 29:11

Thanksgiving—thinking on this celebration brought me to do a little research on the holiday. After our settlers reached America, a few days later they were greeted in English by an Indian named Squanto. Is this amazing or what? My immediate thought after reading this was how did he know the English language? I have never really thought about that before, just assuming that somehow the settlers and the Indians had managed to communicate through hand signals or some other sort of way. But, no, as God always does, he had prepared the way for this precious moment by setting up the following: Squanto had been kidnapped by an English sea captain and then sold into slavery before escaping to London. He returned to his homeland on an exploratory expedition. Was this an accident? Hardly! Our Father, the Father of us all and the God of our country, had the perfect plan. He always does. He knew that the Pilgrims would be arriving to our shores and would need to be able to communicate with the Indians in order to survive the harsh winters and difficult problems found here. Squanto, being able to speak English, taught them how to cultivate corn, extract sap from the trees, catch fish, and avoid poisonous snakes, among other things. I just love realizing this fact that this important Indian named Squanto spoke English. Who knows what would have transpired if the Indians had not been able to communicate with our settlers? How much easier and smoother the transition must have been to be able to learn and learn quickly from Squanto. This just confirms once again that the Lord has a plan, a mighty plan, put into place before the beginning of time. By his good grace are we blessed time and time and time again because of his all-knowing, all-caring love for us.

November 25. Seeing Through a Clear Lens

For everyone who asks receives; he who seeks finds;
and to him who knocks, the door will be opened.

—Matthew 7:8

I wear a contact lens in my left eye for reading. As I was putting it in this morning, unbeknownst to me it must have popped out. I was expecting to see everything clearly, but instead everything was blurry. I tried to read but couldn't make out the words. I quickly realized that somehow, some way, my contact had not made its way into my eye. Without this visual aid, I was stuck—stuck because it is so hard to function without clear vision. I went to my drawer, got out a new contact, and popped it in. Ah, everything was right-side up! So this is how it is with Jesus. Things can get blurry pretty quickly. All of life is out of whack. When we try to get through the day without keeping Jesus the focus of our lives, it just doesn't work, plain and simple. Things may go along for a while, seeming to make sense, but then everything starts to unwind and we lose our way. This is not a difficult fix. This fix is so easy now that we have been called to his side. All we need to do is remember to pop Jesus into our minds and our hearts first thing in the morning. Starting the day with the Lord gives us clear vision for the time ahead. Even if we get on the go so quickly that Jesus isn't the first thing we do in the morning, it's never too late to focus on Jesus as we move about our day. How lovely life is when we see it through the lens of the Lord.

November 26. Bloom Where You Are Planted

While they [Joseph and Mary] were there,
the time came for the baby to be born,
and she gave birth to her firstborn, a son.
She wrapped him in cloths and placed him in a manger,
because there was no room for them in the inn.

—Luke 2:6–7

I was reading an article just the other day that says scientists are thinking that there are many other inhabitable planets out there in the Milky Way, maybe even billions, either just waiting to be inhabited or already inhabited. It could be scary to think that others unlike us could be living on another planet and possibly come to Earth for a visit. But even if they do, we can stand on the reality that Earth is where God sent his son, Jesus, to live among us, teaching us how to live with joy, hope, and love. Earth is where the Lord was born, and he has taught us how to live life the best it can be, right here where we are. No matter where the future of science may lead us, we are blessed to be here on Earth where the Lord came, preached, and loved, teaching all of us about God's mercy and grace. It is here on our Earth that we have been grafted into the Lord's family. Even if tomorrow or in a million years we do find that there is "human life" on another planet somewhere among the billions of planets out there, there is only one birthplace where the Lord was born and walked among us, right here on our Earth. Let us cherish the gift that we have been given, Jesus, born right here among us and still among us today, changing lives for the better here on Earth. He calls us to bloom where we are planted because he came to our Earth for that very reason!

November 27. Lady Luck

> Blessed are all who take refuge in him.
>
> —Psalm 2:12

In the last two days, I have had encounters with ladybugs. The first one was when I opened my wallet to buy a drink. A little ladybug was sitting right inside. The person helping me quickly said, "Oh, you have good luck." The next day I was driving in my car and felt something on my hand. Looking down, I saw a ladybug sitting on the top side of my right hand. Now, was I really lucky? Looking up the word "luck" on the Internet, I saw a quote by Lucius Annaeus Seneca that said, "Luck is what happens when preparation meets opportunity." Being prepared, then having an opportunity come your way, would certainly provide a greater probability that your opportunity could blossom into something better than it would have without being prepared. Most of us, as believers, know that our lives aren't influenced by whether or not we are lucky. What we do know is that we are blessed. We believe in Jesus Christ, the Son of God. All throughout the Bible are references to God's blessing for those who believe in him. We don't have to hope to find a ladybug to be blessed and we don't have to hope that Lady Luck is on our side for good things to happen. All we have to know is that God will bless us, time after time, because we believe in him. His promises are better than any ladybug could ever be. Our Father, the giver of all good gifts, longs to bless us each and every day. Leave Lady Luck for the gamblers of the world and bet on the sure thing, faith in God our King.

November 28. David and Goliath

> David said to the Philistine [Goliath], "You come against
> me with sword and spear and javelin, but I come against
> you in the name of the Lord Almighty, the God of the
> armies of Israel, whom you have defied...Today I will
> give the carcasses of the Philistine army to the birds of
> the air...and the whole world will know that there is a
> God in Israel...it is not by sword or spear that the Lord
> saves; for the battle is the Lord's, and he will give all of
> you into our hands.
>
> —1 Samuel 17:45–47

The television show *60 Minutes* interviewed Canadian journalist, author, and speaker Malcolm Gladwell, who has written a book entitled *David and Goliath: Underdogs, Misfits, and the Art of Battling Giants*. Gladwell has taken the success of the underdog David over his much more powerful opponent Goliath and developed a theory that underdogs (due to their limitations, whatever they might be) are forced to be creative, thus becoming embolden to solve their problems in a resourceful, creative way. At some time we have all found ourselves in the David role, somehow in the underdog position facing a dilemma with insurmountable odds. Yet, here's the thing. This underdog position is actually an advantage, the same as it was for David who killed a giant with a slingshot and a stone. Because David couldn't outpower Goliath, he found another way to win the day. He called on his Lord to show him the way. All of us have found ourselves undersized or in a fix with seemingly no way out. Just as David claimed to the Philistines that "the battle is the Lord's," so shall we do the same. Whether we are called to fight with a slingshot or trust in God's leading, we will be embolden with his power and his strength and his plan, just as David was that memorable day that he beat a giant with a single stone.

November 29. The Balance of Power

> Now to him who is able to do immeasurably more than
> we all ask or imagine, according to his power that is at
> work in us, to him be glory in the church and in Christ
> Jesus throughout all generations, for ever and ever! Amen.
>
> —Ephesians 3:20–21

In the *Dallas Morning News* today, the front page of the sports section is about the Dallas Cowboys game last night. The introduction reads "This is how it happens. This is how the balance of power shifts and how fortunes change in today's National Football League." Now to say that I do not follow professional football is an understatement. I wouldn't begin to weigh in on this article or anything else about pro football. But this opening paragraph caught my eye, and I started thinking about these two sentences: "This is how it happens. This is how the balance of power shifts and how fortunes change." The meaning of these two statements for all of us is found in knowing and loving Jesus. It is through him and him alone that our balance of power has shifted from relying on the world and everything in it to relying on the one who made us, who breathed life into us, who knows us, and who walks through each day with us. And this is how our fortunes have changed. We no longer have to rely on human beings to fix or help us, for we have the power of Christ on which to stand. The fortunes talked about in relation to Jesus are not financial. They are the fortunes of living life following the Savior of the world who strengthens and supports us as our daily fortunes change. Each day the winds of change blow through our lives, bringing unexpected experiences. Yet the one constant that we can always count on is that our Lord and Savior is here with us, keeping our lives in balance through his ever-present love, mercy, and grace. This is our balance of power, Jesus, whose power is enough for any and all things.

November 30. A Snapshot Moment

This is how the birth of Jesus Christ came about:
His mother Mary was pledged to be married to Joseph,
but before they came together, she was found to be
with child through the Holy Spirit.

—Matthew 1:18

With the holidays ahead, the thought came to me, *How many times have we rushed through these very special days, letting the hustle and bustle of them take away our joy? How many times have we not taken a deep breath, stepped back, and realized how blessed we really are to be living as children of the Almighty Lord?* Let's take mental snapshots of the special moments that we are given by Jesus as the holidays roll around and we are right in the thick of them. Take a deep breath, lean back, and during that special moment in time when someone is laughing or when you are sharing a warm and loving moment with a loved one, take a mental snapshot of how that looks and store it away in your memory bank for the days to come. It seems that so often, by the time the holidays arrive, all that we want to do is get through them. We have worn ourselves out in preparation, and we just push through so we can begin to get those decorations down and get back to normal. This year let us focus on what really matters, the birth of the Lord, and how that has changed our lives for the best forever. All too soon our holidays will have flown by, and our routine will return. But how lovely to store a treasured moment in our memory bank, keeping it there for a time in the future when we want to remember and thank God for all he has given us. He longs for us to appreciate the moments that mean so much yet cost nothing. So here's to snapping away with our mental camera, taking snapshots in our minds, saved for a rainy day!

December 1. The Present of Your Presence

You have made known to me the path of life; you fill me
with joy in your presence, with eternal pleasures at your
right hand.

—Psalm 16:11

Everywhere we go, people are asking each other what they want for Christmas, what their children want for Christmas, or what they are giving their friends for Christmas. Lots and lots of talk about presents and what they will be. In the newspaper and on television and radio are advertisements for the perfect present—that one special thing, that one and only present that someone near and dear to you will want and cherish forever. Here is the perfect present that all of us can give our families and friends this year, and it won't cost us a thing. Just be present. That's it, just be in the moment as we celebrate the birth of our Savior, that one precious time set aside for us to worship our king. Just as we are filled with joy in the presence of the Lord, so we bring joy to those we love by simply being present. All of us, no matter who we are, will be somewhere on Christmas Day, bowing our heads in gratitude for such a gift as this, Jesus. Then let us give the gift of our presence to whomever we are sharing this special day. Put down the cell phones, turn off the television, throw away the paper, and give the gift of our full attention. The day will pass all too quickly as it is. Now it is here. Now it is time. Now we have the opportunity to make those whom we love feel as special as we think they are by just simply being present, and best guess is that this will be one of the best presents—our presence—that they will receive this year.

December 2. Sophomore Slump

> Love the Lord your God with all your heart and with all
> your soul and with all your strength.
>
> —Deuteronomy 6:5

In reading the paper last week, I came across an article on the success of Klyde Warren Park here in Dallas and the fact that the park's popularity has exceeded the city's highest expectations. It goes on to say that the challenge going forward is to extend that popularity into the second year. "Some people call it the sophomore slump. For something like this, you get a great reception the first year, but then we have to find ways to keep the people engaged," said the park's president, Tara Green. I immediately thought of us, God's children, and whether this applies in some way to how we live out our faith. Sophomore slump—this phrase actually refers to the second year of something, but I think that we can take it one step further, thinking of how life in relation to our focus on our faith often brings a sophomore slump into our lives, whether it is year two, ten, or thirty. So how can we, who love the Lord, not fall into a slump with our faith? How can we bring an eager heart into how we love the Lord right now, this very day? This is the perfect time of year to reignite our faith and become zealous for the Lord. Christmas is coming. Let us prepare our hearts and minds right now, this day, going forward, for remembering why we celebrate Christmas and what we need to focus on in the special days ahead. As we celebrate his birth and truly enjoy the holidays for what they mean to us as believers, we will skip that sophomore slump that can come from overexposure to too many Santas and Christmas carols ringing throughout each and every store we enter. Instead, we will be humming his precious Christmas hymns that bring such inner joy to our hearts and minds as we share in the glory of Christmas.

December 3. Unique in Our Own Way

If one falls down, his friend can help him up.

—Ecclesiastes 4:10

Walking and admiring all the houses in my neighborhood has become a delightful treat for me as I go by each one, noticing the differences and thinking how beautiful each one is in its own unique way. They all seem different, yet they each serve the same purpose: to provide shelter and a place for the residents to live, protected from the wind, the cold, and the elements of nature. A place where one can be restored. Some are quite stately, others warm and welcoming. In the same way as these houses, we as believers are each unique and special in our own way. Our Jesus has given each of us the tools with which to provide his shelter and protection to those we meet, the ones that he brings to us with whom we share life. Sometimes we share life with someone who needs to know his love and protection as they are walking through one of life's storms, and we are uniquely positioned to provide his word and actions for their comfort. It could be that we are in prayer for them, are a good listener for them, and can impart some words of wisdom to help them along their way. But no matter what the role is that we play, we can know with all certainty that he will give us what we need to let them know that they are loved by the Lord most high, for as he has loved us, so may we love others again and again and again, sheltering those who come to us through his mighty plan for all of us.

December 4. What's in a Name?

"I tell you the truth," Jesus answered, "before Abraham
was born, I am."

—John 8:58

The names of Jesus. As we continue the days of celebration
leading up to the Christmas season, rejoicing in the birth of our
Lord and Savior, Jesus Christ, let us think on the names of Jesus.
Let us treasure them deep in our souls so that, when life brings
along a time that we call out his name, we will remember that
he is all things to us, and we will know with all certainty that he
will be that very name that we need. In John, Jesus says, "Before
Abraham was born, I am." Using this name for himself, Jesus tells
us that he is God, he is everything, all that there is, all that we
need. He is our All in All. He is our Comforter, our Deliverer,
our Good Shepherd, our King of Kings, our Light of the World,
our Living Water. There is not any description of the Lord that
we cannot find whenever we need him to be what we need at
any moment. Yes, he is everything. Not one need does he leave
unmet. Today do you need a safe place from one of life's storms?
Call on Jesus, the Prince of Peace. Today do you need wisdom?
Call on Jesus, the Way, the Truth, and the Life. Today do you
need healing? Call on Jesus, our Great Physician. When we need
to be sure that he has a plan and that it is the perfect plan, we
can know that Jesus is the beginning and the ending and that
all things pass through his mighty and loving hands. No matter
what gift you may receive this Christmas, none can come close
to being the child of the great I Am. His name will always meet
your smallest or greatest need, whatever life brings our way.

December 5. The Alpha and the Omega

"I am the Alpha and the Omega," says the Lord God,
"who is, and who was, and who is to come, the Almighty."
—Revelation 1:8

Friends—friends are what make the world go round. There are as many types of friends as there are snowflakes on a wintry day, all completely different, and all very special. And when they pile up altogether, they make a winter wonderland of joy for us to cherish. Some are quiet, some are outgoing, some are funny, some are sweet, but all are important. This is a quote from Charles Dickens that I just love: "Friendship? Yes, please." There is one type of friend that everyone loves to be around—the large-and-in-charge friend. For it is this friend who keeps the conversation going, keeps the group moving toward fun destinations, and keeps life happening! The Lord is our most important large-and-in-charge friend, and what good news that is. To know that he is in charge when we face difficulties is such a relief. It has been said that the closer we stay to God, the larger he becomes and the smaller our problems turn out to be. We need to look at ourselves through that small end of the magnifying glass and keep God at the large end of it. Our friends are like a paper chain made of many different colored circles, all glued together to form one glorious chain of love and care. It is a precious thing to add another beautifully colored link of friendship to it as time goes by. The Lord is the beginning link and the ending link in our paper chain, for, at the end of it, we glue the last one to the first. He is the first and last, the Alpha and the Omega, and the most important link we have in our circle of life!

December 6. The Light of the World

When Jesus spoke again to the people, he said, "I am the
light of the world. Whoever follows me will never walk
in darkness, but will have the light of life."

—John 8:12

Winter is here. The days have grown much shorter, and the
daylight is gone before we know it. The darkness of night calls
us to draw in and take refuge inside where we can find light,
warmth, safety, and calm. As I walk through the neighborhoods,
the lights go on in the homes, revealing life and all that it holds.
Isn't it delightful to see all of the beautiful Christmas lights on the
houses go on as dusk settles on the city, those bright, twinkling
lights of joy? These lights remind us of the joy that our Savior
brings to us and the precious gift of his birth this time of year.
As we see all these lights, we are reminded of our Savior, Jesus
Christ, and his name being the Light of the World. Before his
birth, God's people longed for a Savior to come and bring hope,
peace, and joy through his life to theirs, lighting up the world
with the things of God that only his precious son could bring. So
God, because of his love for us, sent his only begotten son, Jesus,
to be the light of the world for us to use to find our way through
the darkness. Jesus promises in John 8:12 above that he, being
the light of the world, will always remove the darkness from our
lives, for he is the light of life. It's so true, isn't it? So many times
we have all walked a dark way, yet when we turned to Jesus for
direction, his light always shooed away that dark time by giving
us his peace, his comfort, his grace, or his mercy—whatever the
situation at the time required. Darkness is understood to be the
absence of visible light. In processing this thought, what comfort
we can know to be loved by the Light of the World, for the
presence of Jesus in our lives will never let the darkness overcome
us, no matter what the circumstance. So as we go about our way
this Christmas, enjoying the beautiful Christmas lights as we go,
let them remind us time after time that the Lord is our light of
the world and we will never walk in darkness again. Praise be
to God!

December 7. Mighty Restorer

> The Lord is my shepherd, I shall not be in want. He
> makes me lie down in green pastures, he leads me beside
> quiet waters, he restores my soul.
>
> —Psalm 23:1-3

Dallas has been under a winter ice storm, the likes of which we haven't seen in years. So many of our beautiful Texas trees have broken limbs while others are bent over, touching the ground with the weight of the ice. Yet as soon as the ice melts, many of these limbs will rebound and straighten back up, just as they were before the storm. So it is with us. The winter times of life may bend us over, and often we may feel as if we have been broken in two. But for those who love the Lord Jesus, our Restorer, we will be returned and stood back up by his mercy to know joy again. We may have had some limbs trimmed out by the icy blast of life, but we are never completely broken because our Lord and Restorer has a mighty plan for us to return again to the joy known in living. He comes in and takes whatever we are facing, trimming out the dead wood and cleaning up what has been fractured by our trial. Then he begins the process of restoration. Just as our trees will know warmth when the ice melts and our city returns to normal, we will feel the Lord's warmth as he wraps us in his love, melting away the freezing chill that has stopped us in our tracks, budding out new growth and revealing life from within. He never fails to restore those who call on his name— Jesus, Mighty Restorer. Just calling on his name brings such power with it that nothing can keep us from feeling his warmth and knowing that his plan will not be thwarted for our lives. So as we worship the birth of the Lord in the days ahead, let us thank him for coming to our earth to restore all things and make them new, even us!

December 8. Bread of Life

Then Jesus declared, "I am the bread of life. He who
comes to me will never go hungry, and he who believes in
me will never be thirsty."

—John 6:35

I was listening to the news last night, and I heard employees interviewed at a grocery store. They were asked which items customers were there to buy during this ice storm that we have been enduring in Dallas for the last few days. The overwhelming answer: bread. Yes, that's right. Bread is the one item that most people were buying, and it is the one thing the store keeps running out of due to its popularity at this frozen moment in time. Now I can totally understand this. I love bread. I don't really like sandwiches, I just like bread. So here's the thing. We could all live without eating actual bread. Yet there is a bread that we cannot live without. Or, living without this bread, our lives would not be the same. This bread, our Bread of Life, is Jesus. Plenty of people are living without him today, yet we, his children, have been given this bread of life not only for today but for every day. We will never run out of this bread, even in the most wintry times of our lives, for Jesus, our Bread of Life, has promised us that he is with us always. Each and every day, whether it be sunny, cloudy, icy, or cold, that we pull up to the table of life, we will find all this bread that we could ever need and more. Our breadbasket is always full. Full of his grace, his mercy, his guidance, his peace, his light, and his love. So if there is any time from this moment on that we need to be filled with the things of Jesus, just call on his name, the Bread of Life, and he will provide exactly what we need, even without going to the market to get it, and he never runs out of anything!

December 9. The Lion and the Lamb

> Then one of the elders said to me, "Do not weep! See,
> the Lion of the tribe of Judah, the Root of David, has
> triumphed. He is able to open the scroll and its seven
> seals. Then I saw a Lamb, looking as if it had been slain,
> standing in the center of the throne..."
>
> —Revelation 5:5-6

Through the years we have heard these two names for Jesus, and it serves us so well to think of the two together, for they say it all. He is our Lion; he is our Lamb. What a powerful image we can think on by seeing Jesus as a roaring lion, reigning over all the world just as the lion, the king of the jungle, does over his territory. Known as the conquering Lion of the tribe of Judah fulfills one biblical prophecy; the Lamb who was slain fulfills another. They both speak volumes as to his nature, revealing characteristics of both names that we need all throughout our lives. How many times have we called out his name, needing him to come in boldly and rescue us from a desperate and terrible situation that only a lion could handle? And how many times have we needed the lamb to softly enter one of our situations and gently lead us to another place of comfort, trust, and love? The name for Jesus as lion conveys kingship, and he is just that—our King of Glory. He is the King of God's people, the one to whom we will bow and pay homage to in the days ahead at his birth. Just as the lion is the king of the jungle and conquers all who oppose him, so our Lord Jesus has conquered sin and death on our behalf at the cross. As the Lamb of God, he has given us life eternal. As Jesus approaches John the Baptist, John calls out, "Behold the Lamb of God who takes away the sins of the world." The blood of a lamb saved the Israelites from death during the Passover. Jesus, our Lamb, saves us from eternal death with the covering of his blood. The Lion and the Lamb—our Lord, Jesus Christ. The time will come when we will again cry out for our Lion, our

Lamb, to again lead the way to safety where he will restore us with his grace and mercy, and all because we know the power in his name.

December 10. Our Confidant

> The fruit of righteousness will be peace; the effect of
> righteousness will be quietness and confidence forever.
>
> —Isaiah 32:17

I was walking yesterday morning, reveling in the glorious sunshine filtering through the trees and thinking about all the names for Jesus. I asked myself what name really stands out in my mind as being important to me, the name that reflects how Jesus impacts my life each and every day. The name that popped into my head is Confidant. Now I don't know about you, but the Lord Jesus is my greatest confidant, the one to whom I speak of things each and every day. Most of us may think of a confidant as someone with whom we entrust secrets. Jesus is, of course, the best person with whom to share a secret, but knowing that the word "confidant" comes from the word "confide" leads us to talk to the Lord about any and everything that goes on. It's not about secrets but about looking to the one who offers us his perfect input and guidance throughout the day. Sometimes we just chat with the Lord, and other times we ask him questions, seeking answers to things that happen and need his clarification. Confiding in someone means to trust them with our thoughts and trust in their care for us, and this is what we do with Jesus. We all love Jesus, our Confidant, in this way, for whom greater than he do we trust with our plans, our prayers, our lives, laying these down at the foot of his throne. This root word, "confide," is the main part of the word "confidence," whose synonyms are assurance, belief, certainty, faith. To know the Lord and to call on his name in this way provides confidence in all things in our lives, assurance from Jesus that we are his, belief in the reality that he is the perfect Son of God, certainty in knowing that all things pass through his holy hands, and faith in believing that through his birth and death we have been reborn, freed from sin. So as Christmas is right around the corner and we kneel to pray a prayer of thanks for this Child born to save us from our sin, let us feel the confidence that only comes from knowing Jesus as our Confidant, the one with whom we can share all things and feel his hand upon us, guiding and directing us every step of the way.

December 11. Call Him Jesus

> She [Mary] will give birth to a son, and you [Joseph]
> are to give him the name Jesus, because he will save his
> people from their sins.
>
> —Matthew 1:21

Jesus—even since I can remember as a little girl in Sunday school, I learned about a man named Jesus. I loved to sing the hymn by Anna Bartlett Warner about him that goes, "Jesus loves me, this I know, / For the Bible tells me so." I don't think that I have ever thought much about why his name is Jesus except that it is. That's what I was told, and that's all that I have ever known. But since we are thinking on Jesus and some of the precious names for him that we know and love, I thought that maybe I would look into his name and its origin. His Hebrew name is Yeshua, meaning "Yahweh [the Lord] is Salvation." Its English spelling is Joshua. This leads us to know that Joshua and Jesus are basically the same name, one being translated from Hebrew into English the other from Greek into English. All of these names—Yeshua, Joshua, Jesus—coming from different languages, essentially mean Savior and the Salvation of the Lord, graciously giving us deliverance from sin and penalty. That's who Jesus is, that's why we call him Jesus, and that's what we need to remember time and time again as we call on his name. Acts 2:21 says, "And everyone who calls on the name of the Lord will be saved." All throughout the scripture we read that living and praying in Jesus's name empowers us with his truth, empowers us with his goodness, and empowers us with his strength. As it says in Proverbs 18:10, "The name of the Lord is a strong fortress; the godly run to him and are safe." Now we can know and rest in the certain truth that there is power in the name of Jesus, for not only does he supply our every need, whether it be love, strength, comfort, or grace, he has given us the very thing that we could never provide for ourselves—alvation, now and forever! Thank you, Jesus!

December 12. Immanuel

> All this took place to fulfill what the Lord had said
> through the prophet: "The virgin will be with child
> and will give birth to a son, and they will call him
> Immanuel"—which means "God with us."
>
> —Matthew 1:22-23

So here we are, a few days from celebrating the birth of our Lord, and thinking on all the names for Jesus that we can use to call him to us. There are countless names known for the Lord, over two hundred to be sure, but to keep some of them in our hearts and minds will keep his name ready as needed, and we all know that he is needed, time and time and time again. Each of us could write down many precious names that we know for the Lord, for he has fulfilled them for us as we have gone through the days calling upon his name. Without a doubt, we will never encounter a time or place that his name will not impact the outcome of what is happening in our lives, for his name, all his names, bring power and presence when we call on them. No matter what name we use to call Jesus, he brings all of the characteristics that each name provides to the place where we need him. It doesn't really matter which name we use, he will provide. He answers to any and all of them or just simply Jesus, Lord, Immanuel. This name for the Lord, Immanuel, only appears three times in Scripture, and this name means "God with us." This name brings such majesty with it and we hear it often through December as we begin to celebrate his birth. Immanuel, God with us, born a babe and laid in a manger, sent to save us from our sins. If this was the only name that we knew for Jesus, it would be enough. All we need to remember is that he is with us, now and forevermore. What more could we ask for Christmas than that?

December 13. Let's Begin at the Beginning

In the beginning was the Word, and the Word was with
God, and the Word was God. He was with God in the
beginning.

—John 1:1-2

It's that time of year when we turn our hearts and minds toward Christmas. Decorating, presents to buy, meals to plan, and the birth of our Savior, Jesus Christ. One's thoughts immediately go to a vision of that precious baby in a manger, lying there in swaddling clothes, surrounded by all the animals that holy evening. As we think on the birth of Jesus, this was the beginning of his service and life here on earth. Most of us think of baby Jesus when we think about his beginning. But the true beginning of things in relation to our Savior is stated in John above as he writes: "In the beginning was the Word, and the Word was with God, and the Word was God." This then is the story of Christ and his beginning, if you will. Jesus, our Lord and Savior, has always been. This revelation is given by John when he calls Christ the Word. Biblical scholars believe that it is here that John is talking about our Savior, Jesus Christ, part of the Holy Triune: Father, Son, and Holy Spirit. What we can find so comforting about this revealing by John is that we can now know that Jesus was a human being, one that John knew and loved. But at the same time, Jesus was with God since the beginning. Let us be comforted to remember that Jesus was, is, and forever will be. His birth is the perfect gift from our Father, his beginning as a human whom we can trust lived as we live, knew humanness as we know it, and suffered as we suffer. Christ is fully divine yet fully human. We are given such a perfect gift as this, Jesus Christ, our Word, who was here in the beginning of time and our Savior who was born a baby, just like you and me. So now that we have begun at the beginning, let us think on those who were there when he was born, and let us treasure the story that they have to tell. The beginning continues.

December 14. And Then There Was Mary

This is how the birth of Jesus Christ came about: His
mother Mary was pledged to be married to Joseph, but
before they came together, she was found to be with child
through the Holy Spirit.

—Matthew 1:18

Twelve years old. This is the age that most biblical scholars believe
Mary to be when she was greeted by the angel of the Lord and
told that she would be with child through the work of the Holy
Spirit. Truly just a child herself by today's standards, not only was
Mary visited by the angel of the Lord, but he brought the most
unexpected message to her. To hear this news that she, a virgin,
would soon be carrying the child of God was big. But more than
that, she was betrothed to Joseph and now had to share this news
with him. That was most likely some conversation! Fortunately
for Mary, an angel of the Lord intervened on her behalf and
spoke to Joseph, as God always goes before us to exact his perfect
will. I often wonder at Christmastime what it must have felt like
to be Mary. Mary, the mother of our Lord. Mary, the mother of
our Savior. Mary, the mother of the one and only perfect human
being ever to live, Jesus Christ. I mean, wouldn't you love to sit
and hear how she truly felt when she heard the news that she
would be the mother of the Jesus? The mother of the Savior of
the universe. The mother of the one to work miracle after miracle
after miracle. The mother of the one who loved as no one else
could ever love. She was to be the mother of our Lord who
would save the entire world from its sins. Mary's response when
she heard the Lord's plan from the angel was, "I am the Lord's
servant. May it be to me as you have said" (Luke 1:38). Oh that
we could all respond as Mary to the Lord's call in our lives when
he gets us out of our comfort zone. Was Mary scared? Maybe.
Was she curious? Maybe. Faithful? Certainly. So in knowing this
precious story of Mary, let us have just a touch of the faith that

she had when she learned of the news that she would be the mother of Jesus Christ, Son of God and Son of Man. God saw something in Mary that he treasured—her faith. As we look upon the Christ Child in the manger this Christmas, keep the story of Mary close to your heart. When life might scare us, cause us to question, or create a curiosity that we really don't understand, let us love with Mary's deep, abiding faith. Let us love with Mary's motherly fierceness. Let us love as Mary loved, standing on the promises of God.

December 15. And Then There Were Angels

In the sixth month, God sent the angel Gabriel to
Nazareth, a town in Galilee, to a virgin pledged to be
married to a man named Joseph, a descendant of David.
The virgin's name was Mary. The angel went to her and
said, "Greetings, you who are highly favored! The Lord is
with you."

—Luke 1:26-28

But after he [Joseph] had considered this [Mary's being
with child], an angel of the Lord appeared to him in a
dream and said, "Joseph, son of David, do not be afraid to
take Mary home as your wife, because what is conceived
in her is from the Holy Spirit. She will give birth to a
son, and you are to give him the name Jesus, because he
will save his people from their sins.

— Matthew 1:20-21

Angels among us. I guess that I have heard of angels all my life,
ever since I can remember. Angels are generally characterized as
creatures of good, spirits of love, and messengers of our holy God.
In the two verses above, one from Luke and one from Matthew,
we can read how very important the messages from the angels
are, for without these two impactful visits from angels, one to
Mary and one to Joseph, one can only imagine what they would
have thought or would have done with this situation. The books
written about angels are too many to count, and the depiction of
angels is everywhere, particularly at this Christmas season. To us
humans, angels play a very significant role in our understanding
of God's word. In reading his word of the foretelling of Christ's
birth, it is reaffirmed for all of us the significance of angels to our
salvation and to God. He sent his messengers to prepare Mary
and Joseph's hearts to accept this gift of the Holy Child that he
had given them, and what a gift he was and is! Many of us think

that we have somehow been touched by an angel when some unknown stranger appears to help out in a stressful situation or when we are befriended by a person who has no reason to draw near to us yet brings much-needed help at a difficult time. We can read time and time again accounts of someone being cared for by a total stranger during an accident, bringing the touch of an angel, and then they disappear, never to be seen again. To many people, angels represent kindness, direction, and love. As they are revealed in the Bible to be God's messengers, they hold extreme importance to the Lord, for who would use those less than the most trusted ones to deliver messages as crucial as those the angels delivered to Mary and Joseph? As it says in Hebrews 13:1 -2, "Keep on loving each other as brothers. Do not forget to entertain strangers, for by doing some people have entertained angels without knowing it." We will all be celebrating and entertaining in the upcoming weeks, and as we do, let us remember that there are angels among us. May they see God's goodness in us, reflecting his grace and mercy delivered to us in one small child, Jesus.

December 16. And Then There Was Joseph

> When Joseph woke up [from a dream], he did what the
> angel of the Lord had commanded him and took Mary
> home as his wife. But he had no union with her until she
> gave birth to a son. And he gave him the name Jesus.
>
> —Matthew 1:24-25

Joseph—the earthly father of our Lord, Jesus Christ—was a carpenter by trade who was betrothed to Mary and taking her for his wife. Joseph did not know yet that the Lord had already singled him out to be his only son's earthly father. In thinking on Joseph and wrapping my mind around who he was, so many attributes come to mind. Here was a man who had plans to marry a beautiful young woman named Mary. But before he could, he finds out that she will conceive a child by the Holy Spirit and will be the mother of our Savior, God's only son our Lord. That is a message that might stop some men in their tracks. But not our Joseph. God knew his heart, and he knew what kind of man Joseph was. God entrusted his very own son to this man, this earthly man, to raise and care for and love Jesus as his own. This is a mighty task to be sure. But God knew for certain that Joseph was the man for the job, and he was. Joseph willingly obeyed God in spite of the public humiliation that he would face once everyone found out that Mary was with a child that she did not conceive by Joseph. Joseph had the noble qualities necessary to be Jesus's father here on earth, those of obedience to God, integrity to do what was right, self-control of his emotions, and a love for his wife that would not allow him to publicly disgrace her before he knew the truth about the situation. Gentle in spirit, kindhearted, and willing to listen to God's leading, Joseph revealed a godly character that lifted him above all others. Just like Mary, the strongest characteristic that I find in Joseph is his trust in the Lord. Joseph listened to the angels, trusted in the words from God that the angels brought, and followed his Lord's directions. Was he scared? Maybe. Curious? Maybe. Faithful? Certainly. Was this union of Mary and Joseph a match made in heaven? Absolutely. Praise be to God for entrusting his one and only son, our Savior, to two earthly human beings so faithful that we could know him not only as our Savior but the one who walked among us, knows us, and loves us just the same. When life steps in and we need self-control, a patient spirit, or love beyond our usual capacity, let us follow the lead of Joseph. May we be gentle in spirit, kindhearted in our treatment of others, and trusting in God's provision. Let us be people like Joseph, who, when we are called by God, reflect his selfless love, as we celebrate at this Christmas season.

December 17. And Then There Were Shepherds

And there were shepherds living out in the fields nearby, keeping watch over their flocks at night. An angel of the Lord appeared to them, and the glory of the Lord shone around them, and they were terrified. But the angel said to them, "Do not be afraid. I bring you good news of great joy that will be for all people. Today in the town of David a Savior has been born to you; he is Christ the Lord."...When the angels had left them and gone into heaven, the shepherds said to one another, "Let's go to Bethlehem and see this thing that has happened, which the Lord has told us about"...The shepherds returned, glorifying and praising God for all the things they had heard and seen, which were just as they had been told.

—Luke 2:8-11, 15, 20

How wonderful of the Lord to use shepherds to seek out his Son, using them to reveal Jesus's mighty and glorious birth to the people! When I think of a shepherd, I think of someone who is selfless, caring mightily for those things that have been placed in his care. The shepherds in the fields that night that the angels revealed the coming birth of their Savior were watching over their flocks, guarding their sheep from predators and harm. This relationship helps to enhance the connection to Jesus, our Good Shepherd, the one true Shepherd of all people, who guards us, his sheep, from predators and harm. These shepherds were terrified, and who wouldn't be? Here they are, minding their own business, guarding their animals, when a bright light and a magnitude of angels appear in the night sky. One angel begins to speak, terrifying enough. The shepherds listen closely and follow the directions without questioning, "Should we go? It seems kind of far. Who will watch over our flocks? We will really be tired when we return." No, these were men of God. These were men of faith. These were men who trusted in the Lord and followed his command. Were they scared? Maybe. Were they curious? Maybe? Were they faithful? Certainly. So they took out in search of a baby, not sure of the end result but trusting in the call of the Lord. Then they did as the Lord had asked through the angels. They returned and boldly spread the word concerning what had been told to them about this child, glorifying and praising God for all the things that they had heard and seen, just as they had been told. We can rest assured that this story was bold, mighty, and changed the hearts and lives of those who heard it. We can be certain that these were men after God's heart, not questioning but trusting. The revelation from the shepherds on their return told of the coming Good Shepherd born a babe in a manger who will never leave us alone and will always go the distance to find even just one of us who has strayed. For as it says in Luke 15:4, "Suppose one of you has a hundred sheep and loses one of them. Does he not leave the ninety-nine and go after the lost sheep until he finds it?" The baby they found on their trip lying in a manger is that Shepherd, our Shepherd, who loves us beyond measure. Let us think on these things when we are scared or curious. Let us trust in our Good Shepherd. May the Lord see in us what he saw in those shepherds that night and trust us to do the same as they, boldly glorifying and praising God for all that we have seen and heard as he guides us through our days.

December 18. And Then There Were Wise Men

> After Jesus was born in Bethlehem in Judea, during the
> time of King Herod, Magi [wise men] from the east
> came to Jerusalem and asked, "Where is the one who has
> been born king of the Jews? We saw his star in the east
> and have come to worship him."
>
> —Matthew 2:1-2

Wise men—when I hear the story of the wise men, I have a visual of three kings dressed in royal garb, kneeling at the foot of the newborn baby Jesus with gifts in hand. In reading the actual words in the Bible and following up with commentary, it seems that much of what we know of these wise men is from tradition, not actual words written there. What is factual, however, is that these wise men, unknown in number, saw the star of Bethlehem and went to find this babe who was born King of the Jews. Did they greet him in Bethlehem or later after his parents had returned to Jerusalem? This is not stated specifically. Were there three wise men? Not sure. But we do know that three gifts were brought to our King. These men were wise, for they wanted to find this king, their king, in earnest, and they traveled long distances to do so. We can learn so much from so little actually written about these men. What makes them so wise? They were willing to travel as far as necessary to find their King, and he was no ordinary King. He was much different, actually, a babe wrapped and placed in a manger. We should be this willing to travel as far as it takes to find Jesus, our King. These wise men realized the trickery of King Herod who wanted to use them to destroy our Savior. So should we watch out for the trickery of Satan to use us to destroy Jesus in our own lives. They longed to pay him homage. They did so by bowing down to him as a sign of great respect, revealing that Jesus is King. In the same way, we should honor him in all that we do, bowing down in gratitude and service to our King of Kings. When they found the baby Jesus, they were overwhelmed with joy. Let our joy in finding our Savior again and again all through Christmas be outwardly known to all we see. If these wise men had returned the way that they had come, letting Herod know of Jesus and his whereabouts, the world's story, our story, would be much different. Wise men with wise ways! When they found Jesus, were they scared? Maybe. Were they curious? Maybe. Were they faithful? Certainly. They knew that they could not reveal where Jesus was to Herod. As we come closer to the day that we celebrate our Savior's birth, let us reflect the wisdom shown by these wise, wise men who seek him in earnest, bowing down before him to honor him, revealing a joy that can only be known to those he calls by name. Let us remember not to return from where we have come; then, we too will be called wise by the one who knows us best, Jesus!

December 19. And Then There Was The Gift

Today in the town of David a Savior has been born to
you; he is Christ the Lord. This will be a sign to you: You
will find a baby wrapped in cloths and lying in a manger.

—Luke 2:11-12

The Gift—our baby Jesus, the one perfect Gift among all gifts, was born in a stable. It is here that he was laid, wrapped in swaddling cloth, on hay in a manger with animals gathering round. Most people then, and some now, expected Jesus to be born into wealth and power, for he was to be our king, right? Didn't kings own a lot of stuff, rule over their people, and go charging around on a black steed with sword in hand and a crown on their heads? How then could this baby Child, lying in a manger on hay meant to feed the cows, be our Savior, the Holy One, the one whom God had sent to save us from our sins? I just love the fact that God sent Jesus to the world as a baby, born to earthly parents of little means. He had to be put in a stable at his birth because there was no room in the inn. In this way, Jesus is exactly whom he is meant to be, the God of all people, the Savior for each and every one of us. How much better that anyone and everyone can know that it is not about what he owned on this earth, where he was born, nor with what riches that calls us to follow him. He came to deliver a simple but life-changing message: "Believe in me, and you will receive deliverance from sin and death." Because of how he came, no one needed to be distracted by finery, power, or might. For certain he is powerful, but not in the way the world thinks of power. For certain he is mighty, but not as the world thinks of mighty men. Although many of the people of that day were looking for someone to deliver them from Roman rule and lives that were hard, God, our heavenly Father, sent the best gift of all, a Baby who would become man, dwell among men, and offer everlasting life to those who know him as Lord. How wise of God to send a Babe wrapped in torn rags so that we must accept him on faith and God's promise, just as he was. Things that require a deeper commitment, taken on faith and faith alone, mean so much more, and Jesus is just that gift. As we slow things down a bit and focus on what we are celebrating and why, let us rest our minds on Jesus, the Prince of Peace. We all long for peace this time of year as the days get hectic with so much to do. This perfect Gift of the Christ Child brings peace of mind to all who love him. We will give out and receive gifts in the coming weeks, but none can compare to the perfect Gift of this baby known as our Savior. To God be the glory and thanks, and if given the chance in the days ahead, share this gift of his love to any who are seeking their Savior this Christmas season. It's a gift that they will never forget.

December 20. The Christmas Wreath

> But from everlasting to everlasting the
> Lord's love is with those who fear him.
>
> —Psalm 103:17

The decorations are out, filling the stores, homes, and yards with the adornments of Christmas everywhere we look. Most of these decorations have a meaning that relates to the birth of our Savior: Christmas trees, wreaths, stockings, stars, lights, nativity scenes—the list goes on and on. Let's look a little deeper at these beautiful representations of the Lord and his coming birth so that we not only see the glitz and glitter, but we see our Holy Child, the Son of God and his birth, the perfect gift from our father. The Christmas wreath is found almost any time Christmas decorations are present, for it represents the unending circle of God's love with no beginning and no ending. He has loved us from before time began and will love us eternally, just as the Christmas wreath suggests. It is usually made of evergreens like holly or pine branches. Since these plants never die in winter, their use signifies our father's gift of eternal life and his love for us that never dies, assuring us that we will live forever in heaven with him. Let us be reminded by the Christmas wreath that we have God's never-ending love in all the seasons of our lives, even the dry seasons, and he will always provide for us, no matter what season we are in. As we look upon the Christmas wreath this year, treasure all the blessings that the birth of our Savior brought to us: freedom from sin and death, eternal life, fellowship with the one who made us, love and life fully provided by Jesus, ever present, ever loving, eternally ours, forever and ever, everlasting to everlasting!

December 21. The Dove of Peace

And they will live securely, for then his greatness will
reach to the ends of the earth. And he will be their peace.

—Micah 5:4–5

Quite often we will see doves used all throughout the Christmas season, beautiful, white doves heralding the arrival of Christmas. The dove is considered to be the symbol of peace, and peace is exactly what Christmas brings to all of us in the world. Jesus, our Savior, the babe born on Christmas Day, was born to bring that peace between God and mankind. Most of us remember the story of Noah, and how after being confined in the ark for many days, the dove is sent out to see if the earth was still covered in water. If the dove returned with a fresh branch in its beak, then Noah would know that the flood waters had receded and that it was time for him and his family to disembark from the ark. The dove revealed to Noah that it was time to go forth in peace to have a new beginning on the earth. The dove is also used by our father in the New Testament when Jesus is baptized by John the Baptist. "As Jesus was coming up out of the water, he saw heaven being torn open and the Spirit descending on him like a dove. And a voice came from heaven: 'You are my Son, whom I love; with you I am well pleased'" (Mark 1:10–11). Here the Lord uses the dove as his representation of the Holy Spirit that he sends to live within us and bring us peace. So we can see that the dove has held a very important place with God in the Bible and represents the peace that the birth of Jesus provides us. There are days that, well, don't seem that peaceful. There are Christmases that, well, don't seem that peace-filled. There are times all throughout our lives when it is hard to find peace, the peace that we long to know. But because of the birth of Jesus, we can always know this peace, this inner calm, this communion with God, because "Today in the town of David a Savior has been born to you; he is Christ the Lord" (Luke 2:11). So as night closes around us, may we, like the dove of peace, be surrounded by the ever-present love of our Lord, Jesus, and know his peace, no matter what unfolds in the days ahead. This very reason is why Jesus was born on Christmas Day—to give us a "peace of God, which transcends all understanding" (Philippians 4:7). May his perfect peace, just like a dove lighting on our shoulders, rest in your hearts and minds today and forevermore!

December 22. The Forever Gift

Thanks be to God for his indescribable gift!

—2 Corinthians 9:15

The word "gift" is defined as "that which is voluntarily bestowed without expectation of return or compensation." At Christmastime, when we hear the word "gift," most of us think of a brightly wrapped box covered with red and green paper and tied up with a beautiful bow. Everywhere we go, we see boxes already wrapped with a gift inside, waiting for someone to buy them. But those of us who love the Lord know that as wonderful as a particular gift might be, the real gifts that mean something are the forever gifts that cannot be purchased. These are gifts that come from a heart that serves others, loves the Lord, and can be given all throughout the year. These gifts are gifts of caring for someone who needs help, being courteous as we move about our day, stopping to let someone in as we drive, opening the door for someone, making a quick call to check on someone just to see how they are doing, stopping by for a short visit with someone who cannot get out by themselves—serving others in a myriad of ways. Why do we do these things? What makes us want to be this type of *gift giver*? It's because we love Jesus. He taught us to love and serve others, putting them before self. In this season of Advent, we all know that the greatest gift ever given was the gift of God's Son, Jesus, brought to our world as a man to live among us and teach us how to live. God, the first gift giver, selflessly gave himself to us in the person of his Son, and all true gift giving is our response of pure and meaningful thanks for this priceless gift. The gift of the Christ Child will once again reignite our hearts and minds to not only treasure this perfect and holy gift that brought salvation to our world, but also to go forth and spread his love to everyone we meet, giving the gifts that really matter, not just at Christmas but all through the year, forever gifts of the heart!

December 23. Are You Ready?

> No eye has seen, no ear has heard, no mind has conceived
> what God has prepared for those who love Him.
>
> —1 Corinthians 2:9

Christmas is right around the corner. Everywhere we go people are asking, "Are you ready?" Asking whether we are ready with all of the preparations for Christmas Day. People are scurrying around still buying presents, rushing home to wrap, trying to get their Christmas cards in the mail, stopping by the grocery store to buy food for Christmas Day. Ready, ready, ready? Well, ready or not, here it comes—the celebration once again of the birth of our Savior, Jesus Christ. It is during this important time of the year that we are called to stop the preparation and be still, letting our hearts and minds rest on what a gift that we have been given. Because of his birth, we are ready, always ready, for anything that may come our way. Jesus brings to us this day the gift of readiness, for he has gone before us to prepare the way, just as Mary and Joseph went to Bethlehem on that special night to get ready for his birth that has brought to us the certainty of always being ready in life. Our Savior has not only promised us eternal life, but he has promised to be with us all along the way, keeping us perpetually ready through his merciful love. In 1 Corinthians above, we are told that we cannot even begin to conceive what the Lord has prepared for us, here on earth and eternally in heaven. So let us celebrate his birth with hearts full of gratitude and joy, knowing that he has prepared the way for us. He covers our path with his grace and mercy, making it ready through the promise that he is always ready and waiting to open up each new day with his precious love.

December 24. Home for the Holidays

The Word became flesh and made his dwelling among us.

—John 1:14

So many people are traveling during these last few days before Christmas, going here and there, hither and yon. Many of us leave our homes to visit those we love at this precious time of year. Some of us just hop in our cars and drive across town to spend time with loved ones. Some stay in our own homes and people we love come over to celebrate the birth of the Lord. Then some of us are with one or two others, spending a lovely quiet time. Let's all take part of our day, if even for a moment or two, and focus deeply on what Christmas truly means. Let us reflect on what the birth of this Child signifies to us, not just on Christmas, but on every single day of our lives. With all the hustle and bustle of the season, often we can get lost in the busyness and excitement. Here is a thought to carry with us this Christmas Day, coming with the morning light. Although so much is happening and it is easy to get caught up in all that is going on, we need to remember that Jesus, born this day in a manger, is here at home with us. We don't have to fly away to find him, we don't have to get in a car to seek him out, we don't even have to go next door and ring the bell in hope of finding Jesus. Look inside ourselves, for he is there, the perfect gift given this day to us by our Father. How can a Father love us so? Because that is who he is. He is love. So he gave us his only begotten Son with whom to share each and every day, whether it be a special day or a normal one. As we go out and about this Christmas Eve or welcome others into our homes to share in the pure joy that tomorrow, Christmas Day, brings, let us not forget that Jesus is home for the holidays, right here, living each and every moment with us, today, tomorrow, and forevermore!

December 25. We Already Do!

Today in the town of David a Savior has been
born to you; he is Christ the Lord.

—Luke 2:11

Oh me oh my! So many ideas have been suggested for gifts to give for Christmas. Every magazine, news story, and friend that we meet has had great and exciting suggestions for what to buy for those on our lists. The electronics selections alone are enough to boggle one's mind, much less all the other new and creative items that have been for sale this year across the globe. In one of my magazines for December is a page of quotes from celebrities weighing in on what they think is one piece of advice to take to heart. I once heard someone say that the secret of having it all is believing that you already do. For us who love Jesus, nothing could be truer than this. We do have it all. Yes, we may have gotten some pretty packages from family and friends, and some will be filled with things that we think we want. But the one gift that we will get, born on this Christmas Day, is the only gift that truly matters, the gift of the Christ Child, Jesus. Because our Father graciously sent his son to us, a special delivery for us born this day in the town of David, we do have it all. Jesus Christ not only comes to save us from our sins, but he comes to give us everything that we will ever need. What is delivered this Christmas Day in the birth of a small child is peace, comfort, joy, strength, guidance, mercy, grace—everything and anything that we may need each day—and on top of this most precious gift is the bow of salvation. So as we spend time with family and friends and open gifts, let us think on this—the one gift, the Christ Child, given to us that tops it all. Let us remember this Christmas Day and every day that follows that we do already have it all in Jesus Christ, because we believe.

December 26. Back to Back

> You will not have to fight this battle. Take up your
> positions; stand firm and see the deliverance the Lord
> will give you, O Judah and Jerusalem. Do not be afraid;
> do not be discouraged. Go out to face them tomorrow,
> and the Lord will be with you.
>
> —2 Chronicles 20:17

Walking in the mall early last week, I saw many employees waiting for businesses to open so they could go to work for the day. They were all sitting on hard benches, patiently passing the time. The greatest idea that I saw as I walked past a group was a couple sitting back to back, using each other for support. How creative and smart to use each other as a backrest for support and comfort. It immediately reminded me of Jesus, our Savior, who always has our backs to support us and provide comfort as we meet our trials. Just like this couple who relied on each other to make the wait easier and less difficult, we have our Savior, Jesus Christ, with us always at our backs as we move through a difficult time. He will always be with us to provide whatever support that we may need. So when we face another uncomfortable and hard place in life, we can rely on Jesus to give exactly what we need to make things easier. Back to back—Jesus with us!

December 27. It's up to You

> So do not fear, for I am with you; do not be dismayed,
> for I am your God. I will strengthen you and help you;
>   I will uphold you with my righteous right hand.
>
> —Isaiah 41:10

A well-known pain reliever has an ad that says, "We give you your day back. What you do with it is up to you." This is a very clever way to get someone to purchase their products, thinking that their use will return people to pain-free days and allow them to live life feeling good. This same thought applies to our days as believers in Jesus Christ. He gives us each and every day to live standing on his promises to love us, to comfort us, to strengthen us, and to be with us in all things. Then what we do with our days is ours to decide. These words from the Lord assure us that "goodness and love will follow me all the days of my life" (Psalm 23:6), and remembering his words just makes us feel good. What glory is found in knowing that no matter how we structure our days, we are moving through them with the power of Jesus upholding us. It's up to you, it's up to me, it's up to all of us to do with our days as we see fit. Let us remember and cherish the promise that we never walk alone, for Jesus is with us always.

December 28. Just Not the Same

To him who is able to keep you from falling and to
present you before his glorious presence without fault
and with great joy—to the only God our Savior be glory,
majesty, power, and authority, through Jesus Christ our
Lord, before all ages, now and forever more! Amen.

—Jude 1:24–25

We have just returned from a short trip with our son and his family. When we leave town, we board our precious dog, Mojo. In order for him to stay at this particular facility, I need to take him at certain times, and this time that meant leaving him there the day before we left. It is always so odd for me to come home during the day without Mojo there. Walking that afternoon without my Mojo was just not the same. And life is just not the same without Jesus. I started thinking about Mojo's being gone, and it immediately reminded me of what would we do if we didn't have Jesus in our lives to call on and walk through our days with us. None of us can imagine life without Jesus. So praise be to God that we do not ever have to face a day without Jesus. He is never gone, not even for a minute. He is ours, our Savior, now and forever more.

December 29. The "New Normal"

Jesus Christ is the same yesterday and today and forever.

—Hebrews 13:8

Every few days I hear about a friend, about parents of friends, or about the children of friends who are moving into a new phase of life, and they refer to this as the *new normal*. This phrase is the current one used for those times in life when things have to change, whatever the reason. We then begin life in a new state of affairs, thus this becomes our normal type of living going forward—our new normal. So many times people don't want a new normal. They were perfectly happy with the old normal, yet circumstances beyond their control have made it necessary to move into that new normal place of living. But one fact remains: No matter how many new normals that life presents to us, Jesus is there. He is not new; he is the same yesterday, today, and tomorrow. He will be exactly who he was when we walked into that new normal, ready to ease us into our new way of living. We can put our burdens down because he is there, longing to lighten the load, assuring us that his mercies are new every morning. He will never forsake us, no matter how many twists and turns our road of life may take. Our new normal will be easier and more doable with Jesus by our side, loving us through each day. Praise God that whether our lives continue on the same or we face a new normal, Jesus moves with us into the new year. Jesus lives!

December 30. Motto for the New Year

Show me your ways, O Lord, teach me your paths;
guide me in your truth and teach me, for you are
God my Savior, and my hope is in you all day long.
—Psalm 25:4

In looking through ideas scribbled down this morning, I found this motto written on a scrap of paper: "When nothing goes right, go left." Now this is such a simple idea, but I think that it leads us to a thought that often we may miss. Sometimes when things are not going right, we continue to butt our heads against the situation, not realizing that we can go in another direction. The New Year is upon us, and some of us may be making New Year's resolutions. This idea is one that will serve us well, for certainly everything will not go right in the coming year. Here is the good news for us as we face the days ahead. Our Savior, Jesus Christ, always leads us in the right direction if we just remember to give him the lead. He knows how to direct our ways so that we can make something right out of something gone awry. Whether he leads us up or down or to the left or right, if we turn to him for direction, we will always be going in the right direction, no matter which way we are truly going. Let us look with peace and calm assurance to the days ahead, knowing that all our days are directed by Jesus, who never leads us in the wrong direction but shows us how to make each day the priceless gift that it is.

December 31. Reflections

> Therefore we do not lose heart.
> though outwardly we are wasting away,
> yet inwardly we are being renewed day by day.
>
> —2 Corinthians 4:16

The celebrating of Christmas is over, and we are moving toward a New Year. The world and everything in it doesn't look particularly new. We see that God's world has hunkered down for the winter, drawing in for a time to restore and replenish itself for the upcoming spring. Even though the world around us doesn't seem new, we can rest assured that it is preparing for that time soon to come when new plants begin to bloom, animals everywhere will have new young, and the weather turns from gray to blue. The time of renewal that our world goes through during the winter months will bring a freshness about it that will be evident with the first days of spring. As we step into the New Year, however, we do not have to wait for spring to have the opportunity to find a newness in our lives. It is always here, brought to us by Jesus. His promise is that his mercies are new every morning, and inwardly we are being renewed day by day. So as we turn one year into the next, we are encouraged and sustained by the promise supplied daily by our Lord and Savior. It is this eternal flame that burns within us, his flame of hope, renewing us daily and continually reminding us of the promise of life eternal with Jesus. It's a New Year. It's a renewed me and you. Praise the Lord!

Janet Evans is married and lives in Dallas, Texas. She has four married children and eight precious grandchildren. Having survived pancreatic cancer at the age of fifty-two, she began to know God in a mighty way as he walked her through this journey. Her daily writing is a result of that journey. She continues to write, seeing God reveal himself as each day unfolds. Her hope is that those who read these daily reflections are encouraged and equipped to see our Lord as they go about each day, for he is always with us. We only need to open our hearts and minds to his presence found in all things. May he be glorified in all that we do. Thanks be to God for his infinite mercy and grace!

CPSIA information can be obtained
at www.ICGtesting.com
Printed in the USA
FSOW03n1325080916
24714FS